Palgrave Hate Studies

Series Editors
Neil Chakraborti
Department of Criminology
University of Leicester
Leicester, UK

Barbara Perry
Faculty of Social Science and Humanities
University of Ontario Institute of Technology
Oshawa, ON, Canada

This series builds on recent developments in the broad and interdisciplinary field of hate studies. Palgrave Hate Studies aims to bring together in one series the very best scholars who are conducting hate studies research around the world. Reflecting the range and depth of research and scholarship in this burgeoning area, the series welcomes contributions from established hate studies researchers who have helped to shape the field, as well as new scholars who are building on this tradition and breaking new ground within and outside the existing canon of hate studies research.

Editorial Advisory Board
Tore Bjorgo (Norwegian Institute of International Affairs)
Jon Garland (University of Surrey)
Nathan Hall (University of Portsmouth)
Gail Mason (University of Sydney)
Jack McDevitt (Northeastern University)
Scott Poynting (The University of Auckland)
Mark Walters (University of Sussex)

More information about this series at
http://www.palgrave.com/gp/series/14695

Barbara Perry · Ryan Scrivens

Right-Wing Extremism in Canada

palgrave
macmillan

Barbara Perry
Faculty of Social Science and Humanities
University of Ontario Institute of
Technology
Oshawa, ON, Canada

Ryan Scrivens
School of Criminal Justice
Michigan State University
East Lansing, MI, USA

Palgrave Hate Studies
ISBN 978-3-030-25168-0   ISBN 978-3-030-25169-7   (eBook)
https://doi.org/10.1007/978-3-030-25169-7

This Palgrave Macmillan imprint is published by the registered company Springer Nature Switzerland AG
The registered company address is: Gewerbestrasse 11, 6330 Cham, Switzerland

For all of those who challenge hatred.

Acknowledgements

This work would not have been possible without the time and insights provided by all of those people who shared their expertise with us—law enforcement and intelligence officers, community organizers and activists, and former and active members of the right-wing extremist movement. The research was funded by Public Safety Canada's Kanishka Project, #680090-1A-KPCP R2.

Contents

1

Thinking About Right-Wing Extremism in Canada

In April of 2009, the US Department of Homeland Security released an assessment of right-wing extremism (RWE) aptly entitled "Rightwing Extremism: Current Economic and Political Climate Fueling Resurgence in Radicalization and Recruitment". Within months, it had been purged from virtually every intelligence and law enforcement database, a victim of conservative backlash and the related resistance to admit to the presence of extreme-right-wing activism (U.S. Department of Homeland Security 2009). A similar reticence pervades the Canadian extremism debates. In fact, at the opening conference for Public Safety's Kanishka Project in 2012, several keynote speakers also denied the presence of any threat from "the right".

That terrorism associated with RWEs is largely absent from the public agenda in Canada is evident from even a cursory review of the *Integrated Terrorism Assessment Centre (ITAC)* website, for example. The list of "Terrorist Incidents", while international in scope, includes only one right-wing terrorist incident: Anders Breivik's horrific attacks in Norway in 2011. Until 2019, the list of "Terrorist Entities" did not include any reference to RWE or white supremacist organizations. In that year, *Blood & Honour* and the affiliated *Combat 18* were added. Additionally, none

© The Author(s) 2019
B. Perry and R. Scrivens, *Right-Wing Extremism in Canada*,
Palgrave Hate Studies, https://doi.org/10.1007/978-3-030-25169-7_1

of the publications included on the *ITAC* site mention these extremist elements. In contrast, that the extreme right continues to represent a viable and active presence is clear from recent events in Alberta, British Columbia and Quebec, for example, where multiple RWE attacks, demonstrations and prosecutions have been recorded (e.g. *Blood & Honour*, *White Nationalist Front* and *PEGIDA*) in recent years. The *B'Nai Brith*'s audits of antisemitic activity document white supremacist activity yearly. Moreover, looking to our south, indications from such bodies as the *Southern Poverty Law Center (SPLC)* are that right-wing terrorism and related activities are far more common than those associated with Islamic fundamentalism. Indeed, based on their analysis of the distribution of terrorist activities recorded in the *Global Terrorism Database (GTD)*, Webb and Cutter (2009: 448) conclude that

> While many researchers and government officials focus on the transnational threat to the U.S., such as the perpetrators of 9/11, we argue that the historic pattern of terrorist activity in the U.S. is more locally-focused, home grown, and derived from political and social activism by U.S. citizens against other U.S. citizens.

Among this home-grown threat is RWE.

The attacks of 11 September 2001 shifted terrorism from the periphery to the centre of the public consciousness. What had heretofore been restricted to "fringe" groups, or something that happened "over there", suddenly appeared to be something much larger, much more threatening and much closer to home. However, one significant consequence of the 9/11 terrorist attacks is that they drew attention away from the more typical white domestic terrorist—such as Timothy McVeigh and members of RWE groups. Now the terrorist is defined by his brown skin and his Muslim religion (Chermak et al. 2010; Jaggar 2005; U.S. Department of Homeland Security 2009). Yet it behoves us, in the interests of domestic security, to continue to pay attention to the more traditional form of "home grown" RWE. RWEs continue to represent a distinctive threat to the well-being of Canada's diverse communities. This book aims to paint a picture of the contemporary RWE movement in Canada, providing an analysis of membership, distribution and activities during the time in which we conducted our fieldwork. In the remainder of this introductory chapter, we define what we mean by RWE and offer an overview of our theoretical and methodological approaches. This is followed by a historical overview of the RWE movement in Canada, and a summary of our observations of the make-up and distribution of the movement during the time of our fieldwork in Chapter 2. In Chapters 3 and 4 respectively, we unpack some of the key endogenous and exogenous factors that both inhibit and facilitate the development of and propensity for violence associated with Canada's RWE movement. We end with a discussion of strategies to defuse RWE in Canada, and an epilogue accounting for "post-Trump" patterns of extreme-right activism in Canada. It is important to stress from the outset that the RWE movement is fluid and ever-changing. The bulk of our analysis derives from fieldwork conducted between 2012 and 2015. A great deal has changed about the movement since then, as reflected here in our epilogue. Nonetheless, many of the core characteristics of both the nature and environment of RWE in Canada remain the same and remain critical to our understanding of the sustainability—or lack thereof—associated with the movement.

Defining Right-Wing Extremism in Canada

In spite of the fact that RWE has not been the focus of much policy or academic work in Canada, there are myriad strands of substantive analyses of RWE within the broader literature. Among them: the links between terrorism and hate crime (Deloughery et al. 2012; Mills et al. 2015) and the related notion of "cumulative extremism" (Bartlett and Birdwell 2013; Busher and Macklin 2015); RWE ideologies (Oaten 2014; Pollard 2016; Schafer et al. 2014); classes of violence associated with RWE (Bérubé and Campana 2015; Mulholland 2013; Petrou and Kandylis 2016); and comparative/international analyses (Mammone et al. 2012). By way of introduction, however, we restrict our comments to three central foci: definitions; RWEs' use of media/social media; lone actors; and the contexts of the rise of RWE.

One of the first points of contention in discussions around far-right extremism revolves around defining RWE. The challenge is a reflection of the heterogeneity of the groups in question. Nonetheless, there is no shortage of efforts to define what is meant by "right wing" extremism. A US team of scholars, for example, has adopted a broadly descriptive conceptualization of the term:

> We define the American far-right as individuals or groups that subscribe to aspects of the following ideals: They are fiercely nationalistic (as opposed to universal and international in orientation), anti-global, suspicious of centralized federal authority, and reverent of individual liberty (especially their right to own guns, be free of taxes), and they believe in conspiracy theories that involve a grave threat to national sovereignty and/or personal liberty, that one's personal and/or national "way of life" is under attack and is either already lost or that the threat is imminent (sometimes such beliefs are amorphous and vague, but for some the threat is from a specific ethnic, racial, or religious group), and in the need to be prepared for an attack by participating in paramilitary preparations and training, and survivalism. (Adamczyk et al. 2014: 327)

This is perhaps an apt characterization of the RWE movement in the United States, but may not be as useful in the Canadian context. There is much less emphasis here, for example, on gun rights, or survivalism. Other observers have identified key pillars of RWE that likely have more resonance here. Jamin (2013) suggests that the core tenets are

a. The valorizing of inequality and hierarchy, especially along racial/ethnic lines.
b. Ethnic nationalism linked to a mono-racial community.
c. Radical means to achieve aims and defend the "imagined" community.

Perliger's (2012) list adds some elements:

1. Nationalism
2. Xenophobia, racism, exclusionism
3. Traditional values
4. Anti-democratic

Finally, Lauder's (2002) enumeration of core themes includes:

1. Race/ethnicity as the foundation of social solidarity/nationalism
2. Xenophobia, racism, especially antisemitism
3. Illegitimacy of established regime of power

With these frameworks in mind, we suggest that RWE in Canada is a loose movement, characterized by a racially, ethnically and sexually defined nationalism. This nationalism is often framed in terms of white power and is grounded in xenophobic and exclusionary understandings of the perceived threats posed by such groups as non-whites, Jews, immigrants, homosexuals and feminists. As a pawn of the Jews, the state is perceived to be an illegitimate power serving the interests of all but the white man. To this end, extremists are willing to assume both an offensive and defensive stance in the interests of "preserving" their heritage and their "homeland". Different RWE groups might well emphasize one of these tenets over others, or integrate additional concerns. Thus, their rhetoric and practice may be similarly diverse.

Historically, hate groups recruited members or spread their message of intolerance through word of mouth, or through traditional media. However, by the early twenty-first century, engagement was largely transferred to the digital world. Indeed, the hate movement has been blessed with a valuable gift in the form of the Internet. Since the birth of the Internet in the 1990s, radical right-wing groups have used it as an alternative form of media, both to publicize messages of hate, and recruit and connect with like-minded others within and beyond domestic borders (Anahita 2006; Chau and Xu 2007; Wojcieszak 2010).

Scholars have devoted considerable attention in recent years to the white power movement's growing presence on the Web. Analyses of how RWE use the Internet to recruit and sustain members have generally focused on the content featured on websites (e.g. Borgeson and Valeri 2005; Bostdorff 2004; Perry and Olsson 2009) and web-forums (e.g. Anahita 2006; Bowman-Grieve 2009; Wojcieszak 2010). We have also seen a handful of studies on how members of the extreme right use social media outlets, such as *Twitter* (Berger and Strathearn 2013;

Graham 2016), blogs (e.g. Chau and Xu 2007) and online newsgroups (e.g. Campbell 2006).

An emerging strength of this focus on online hate is the recognition that digital media allow for dialogue and the *exchange* of ideas. Websites are not restricted to the provision of "information" and literature; on the contrary, they enable participatory interaction and a shared construction of identity. The "virtual public sphere" that characterizes the Internet invites active participation whereby collectives "attempt to interpret and understand crises, injustice, and adversities, and to envision alternatives and map strategies" (Langman 2005: 54). Importantly, the Internet also allows this shared project to cross the global rather than simply the local or national landscape. There have been some attempts to assess this trend at the global level (Caiani and Kröll 2014; Grumke 2013).

Ready accessibility to extreme right social media has also meant that those without formal affiliation with a hate group can also draw on their discourse. Consequently, there is growing interest in the notion of the "lone wolf" or "lone actor". Hoffman (2003) observes that there is an apparent increase in the tendency for individuals loosely or in fact not at all connected with formal organized groups to engage in extremist violence. Similarly, the Toronto Star (2015) reported on internal Canadian Security and Intelligence Service (CSIS) documents that suggested that RWE lone actors represented a more pressing threat than did Islamists in Canada. However, we are only just beginning to come to terms with the nature and potential of these extremists. There is considerable debate as to how closely these actors are allied with organized groups (Gruenewald et al. 2013). Moreover, the breadth of the notion of "lone" actor is debatable (see Gill 2015), as some would argue that the trio suspected of a Halifax mall shooting plot in Canada in 2015, for example, might loosely be described as a small "pack" of lone wolves (Hoffman 2003).

Mares and Stojar (2016) offer a comprehensive assessment of far-right lone actors globally, concluding that there is likely no profile that fits all such actors. Inspired by, sometimes loosely affiliated with organized hate groups, most of the actors identified seemed dissatisfied by the lack of action and impact of formal parts of the "movement", and thus enact "propaganda by the deed" in an effort to make a loud and clear statement. In the American context, Timothy McVeigh's 1995 Oklahoma City bombing was long held to represent the epitome of lone actor right-wing terrorism (Bates 2012; Simon 2013; Simi 2010). In more recent years, Anders Breivik has become the "poster child" for RWE lone actors and has garnered considerable scholarly attention (e.g. Borchgrevink 2013; Hemmingby and Bjørgo 2015). Breivik's case has been used to highlight the challenges in predicting and defending against lone actor terrorism (Appleton 2014; Bakker and De Graaf 2011; Pantucci 2011), as well as the intensity of the risk posed by right-wing lone actors relative to other ideological classes (Appleton 2014; Gruenewald et al. 2013).

Theorizing Right-Wing Extremism in Canada

In Canada, we have little contemporary social science scholarship on RWE organizations and there have been few attempts to methodically and systematically analyse their ideologies and activities. The latest such effort was Kinsella's "Web of Hate", last updated in 2001; however, it was largely a journalist description of the movement rather than an academic analysis. There can be little doubt, then, that a theoretically informed contemporary assessment is needed.

What has been especially disappointing about the RWE scholarship is the trend whereby—as in the broader field of hate crime—it has tended to be largely atheoretical, especially in the United States where the tyranny of positivism prevails. Data are drawn from "official" statistics and subjected to regression analyses with little to no framework to guide the selection of variables; descriptive accounts of RWE websites are offered; white power music is assessed with no reference to the conceptual tools that shape those assessments. These approaches may provide some awareness of RWE sentiment and activity, but they do not take us very far in terms of a deeper understanding of how or why the identified patterns emerge.

Nonetheless, there have been some useful attempts to apply theory to RWE. Strain theory has proven popular among criminologists (Blazak

2001; Wooden and Blazak 1995). Those drawn to hate groups, it is argued, are responding to, on the one hand, their perceived loss of access to economic opportunity, and on the other, their belief that minority groups (racialized communities, lesbian, gay, bisexual, transexual and queer (LGBTQ) communities and women, especially) are by contrast undeservedly privileged across all sectors of society. Consequently, they retreat into an alternative cultural milieu. Mark Hamm (1993, 2007) integrates traditional criminological theories to account for skinheads specifically, and terrorism more broadly. In his seminal work on American skinheads, Hamm (1993) collapses strain/anomie, neo-Marxist and differential association theories to unpack how disenfranchised youth might be socialized into a rebellious subculture. More recently, he has argued that social learning theory can account for the ways in which terrorists—including members of RWE groups—learn how to exploit opportunities for engaging in criminal activities via awareness of the routine activities of security and intelligence personnel (Hamm 2007). So, too, have Parkin and Freilich (2015) tested routine activities theory in the context of RWE, observing that both opportunity and proximity, for example, play a role in fostering violence by adherents.

Another theoretical thread that has emerged of late is grounded in identity-based theories and social movement theory. The former class of scholarship grounds analyses in the precept that engagement in RWE activism is a means by which to "do difference" and especially to construct particular kinds of identities. For some, this involves considering the ways in which RWE adherents are engaged in constructing forms of hegemonic whiteness (Hughey 2010; Simi et al. 2016), or hegemonic masculinities (Ferber 2016; Treadwell and Garland 2011), or both (Perry and Scrivens 2016). Whichever the case, RWE groups are seen as locales in which white men are able to carve out places in which to exercise and in fact enhance—often through violence—power and privilege. As an offshoot, scholars like Kathleen Blee (2002) use a similar racialized and gendered lens to understand the role of women in such movements. In essence, scholarship in this vein stresses how, as Hughey (2010: 1289) explained it, "racist, reactionary and essentialist ideologies are used to demarcate interracial boundaries, and (2) performances of white racial identity that fail to meet those ideals are marginalized and stigmatized".

Identity perspectives are closely linked to, if not explicitly derived from social movement approaches. Of particular interest here are analyses that consider how RWE adherents are actively constructing not just individual but collective identities (Bowman-Grieve 2009; Futrell and Simi 2004; Oaten 2014; Perry and Scrivens 2016). The collective identity at issue here—the universal white man—is one such illustration of what Adams and Roscignio (2005: 76) describe as a "process that allows a disparate group of individuals to voice grievances and pursue a collective goal under the guise of a 'unified empirical actor'". Efforts to frame RWE groups within the social movement literature are rapidly emerging. Interestingly, scholars working in this area recognize the tendency to focus on progressive political movements, rather than on reactionary and regressive actors like RWEs (see, e.g., Langman 2005). Nonetheless, the theoretical frame allows the space to acknowledge oppositional groups (Adams and Roscignio 2005; Tanner and Campana 2014). Writing of the racist Quebec skinhead community that was the focus of their study, Tanner and Campana (2014: 35) concluded that they could, in fact, be identified as such an oppositional movement, by virtue of the fact that they "consciously and strategically adopt a marginalized position within society, following and defending alternative rules and norms".

The current project that is unpacked in this book draws on some of the above-mentioned theoretical insights, but also more explicitly leverages a framework derived from the work of sociologist Donald Black (2004). Black (2004) has articulated an account of terrorism as a form of social control in response to deviant behaviour. From this perspective, it is "a form of justice pursued by organized civilians who covertly inflict mass violence on other civilians" (Black 2004: 12). Immediately, this resonates with the motives and intents of organized hate groups, who aim to constrain and punish those who dare to step outside the boundaries of what is deemed their "appropriate" place, defined according to their location on any number of relational hierarchies—race, gender, religion or sexual orientation for instance (Perry 2001). Black's utility does not end there, however. Following from his core definition of terrorism, Black identifies a series of characteristics that can prove valuable in analysing and describing terrorist groups, including hate groups. Heuristically, the seven derivative elements, identified and described below, provide a useful tool by which to systematically analyse RWE in general and RWE in Canada in particular. The framework allows identification of the nature of violence associated with diverse hate groups (i.e. severity, frequency, visibility), as well as key factors that are likely to contribute to the tendency to engage in violence (e.g. perceived threat/grievance, and organizational capacity of the group).

Black (2004) characterizes the methods of terrorism as recurrent, and typically as highly violent. As Mark Hamm (2007) stresses, it is important to remember that terrorism involves at root criminal events: murder, bombing, hostage taking, etc. In his recent book, "Terrorism as Crime", Hamm (2007) unpacks his relatively simple thesis—that terrorism is "ordinary" criminal behaviour, carried out for "extraordinary" purposes. Nonetheless, in its most lethal form, terrorism constitutes mass violence—multiple victims, even into the thousands. Regardless of the nature of their criminal activities, terrorist organizations typically carry out their strategies covertly, whereby they operate underground. Clearly, this is the case for organizations like *al-Qaeda*, or the *Irish Republican Army (IRA)*. So, too, does this describe the activities of right-wing hate groups. For example, beginning in the 1980s, Louis Beam, a long-time Klansman and virulent racist in the United States, was the architect of the militia movement's strategy of "leaderless resistance", which was an attempt to enhance the invisibility of white supremacist and anti-state activists (Dobratz and Waldner 2012). Beam learned from his experiences with the Klan the danger of traditional lines of leadership and communication, wherein the chain of command could be easily uncovered. "Leaderless resistance", in contrast, advocates phantom cells and individual action—from like-minded individuals—as a means of defeating state tyranny. This is not to say that such groups are wholly invisible. All too often they crawl out of their dark corners to engage in visible forms of violence, or in very public demonstrations.

The intent of terrorists, regardless of their focus, is to manage or respond to a "grievance with aggression" meant to intimidate and instil fear (Black 2004). Violence is thus perpetrated with the aim of terrorizing their targets—individual and collective—into submission. Moreover, this intimidation is not only—or even primarily—targeted at just the immediate victim. Rather, the goal is to terrorize secondary victims, or more broadly, a nation's people and/or their governing body. Looking at the "work" of terrorists like *White Aryan Resistance (WAR)*, as an example, the grievance might be what they perceive as lax immigration law or loss of white male privilege. Regardless, such groups are typically reacting against what they perceive to be threatening behaviour on the part of their victims (i.e. collective liability). Moreover, terrorists are often animated by structurally grounded grievances, derived from an interpretation of a social order as itself illegitimate. Both Christian extremists and those inspired by radical forms of Islam, for example, are waging a battle to "maintain or restore a social order based on the fundamentals of faith, family and community against a rootless world order of abstract markets, mass politics and a debased sacrilegious 'tolerance'" (Rosenfeld 2004: 26).

Typically, terrorists sport membership in identifiable bodies with the "capacity to organize: recruitment, fund-raising, leadership, internal communication, and decision-making" (Oberschall 2004: 28). This accurately describes such "traditional" terrorist groups as *al-Qaeda* and the *IRA*, noted above. These generally have a formalized structure and chain of command, as well as access to material and financial resources that facilitate their operation. So, too, by definition, do organized RWE groups. The *Ku Klux Klan (KKK)* is a classic example, having as it does a rigidly structured hierarchy, and depending on the specific clavern, access to substantial financial support. However, there is some evidence that this is becoming less the case as hate groups move towards leaderless cells, or in fact, simply collapse into loosely connected individuals and groups due to their lack of ability to garner resources (Freilich et al. 2014; Lauder 2002).

While Black's (2004) model is valuable for assessing factors among group members that might account for their viability and activity, it does not consider the environment that simultaneously shapes them. Hate does not emerge in a vacuum. Rather, it is embedded within a broader culture that often bestows "permission to hate". This may be evident in, for example, the activity and inactivity of the state and political actors. When anti-immigrant rhetoric prevails, this sends a message that xenophobia is acceptable. So too does a lack of police response enable hate groups to act with impunity. Moreover, regions that have a history of being "unwelcome" places for racial or ethnic minorities, for example, are also likely to breed contemporary extremists. In such cases, the line between "mainstream" and "extreme" may be very fine.

Scholars have written often about the fact that hate can only grow in an enabling environment (e.g. Burnett 2017; Perry 2001; Poynting 2006). We need only observe recent developments in the United States, and Europe to discern the importance of context for the emergence and strength of a viable RWE movement (e.g. Huber 2016; Inglehart and Norris 2016; Komaromi and Singh 2016; Wigerfelt and Wigerfelt 2014). In those parts of the world, populist right-wing groups have exploited a dismal economic situation and rapidly shifting demographics to foment hostility towards Others increasingly in their midst: immigrants, people of colour and Muslims in particular. To assume that the sentiments that inspire those groups are anomalous ignores the fact that they are embedded in a broader cultural ethos that bestows "permission to hate" (Bowling 1993; Young 1990).

To the extent that hate groups define their collective identity as the norm, they necessarily engage in a politics of difference which seeks to negate, exclude and repress those groups that are outside the norm (e.g. non-whites, non-Christians, non-heterosexual, even non-male). They do so by invoking ideological claims to superiority and power that represent the ongoing struggle on the part of supremacists for the right to define the limits and boundaries of inclusion. But those "boundaries of inclusion" are informed by the broader cultural and political arrangements which "allocate rights, privilege and prestige according to biological or social characteristics" (Sheffield 1995: 438). RWE adherents attempt to reaffirm their dominant identity, their access to resources and privilege, while at the same time limiting the opportunities of others to express their own needs. The performance of hate activism, then, confirms the "natural" relations of superiority/inferiority.

Right-wing activism is also, however, grounded in notions of space and place. Hate groups are situationally located; they have a spatial element that is often overlooked, although just as often implied by the language of "borders", "boundaries", "transgressions" or "territory". RWE groups are concerned with policing the appropriate "spaces for races" (Perry and Blazak 2010). Rhetorical and physical assaults are often invoked when victims are perceived to threaten the racialized boundaries which are meant to separate "us" from "them". And all of this occurs within the institutional context of what is known to be the appropriate place of victim and victimizer. There is—as many black or Asian or Native or Hispanic people know—danger in non-conformity and in challenging borders. Far-right violence and vilification becomes justifiable as a punishment for transgressions of institutionalized codes of conduct, for crossing the boundaries of race. Reactionary violence to such border crossings ensures that white people and people of colour, Christians and non-Christians, native-born and immigrants will inhabit their appropriate places in physical and cultural terms. The boundaries are preserved.

The sort of sociological and cultural analysis of hate groups suggested herein allows us to recognize that they reside in a structural complex of relations of power. As noted earlier, hate does not emerge or operate in a vacuum. Rather, it is embedded in broader patterns of subjugation and oppression. It is conditioned by structural and cultural practices that leave its subjects vulnerable to victimization. It is more than the outcome of the conscious acts of bigoted individuals. It is systematic. It represents a network of norms, assumptions, behaviours and policies which are structurally connected in such a way as to reproduce the racialized and gendered hierarchies which characterize the society in question. Our exploration of the contexts in which RWE groups ebb and flow in Canada suggests three core structural patterns that seem to enable the growth and sustainability of such groups here: the historical normativity of racism, political climates of intolerance and weak law enforcement frameworks. This is very much in line with Heitmeyer's (2005) identification of core enabling factors: resonance with broader sentiments; the complicity of the "political elite"; and the lack of sanctions, as reflected in police engagement. We take this up in more detail in Chapter 4, where we explore the contexts in which RWE groups have flourished—or not—in Canada.

The purpose of our study was to uncover those factors that shape the development of Canadian right-wing hate groups, and that make them more or less likely to plan, engage in or incite violence towards targeted objects and communities. Thus, drawing on Black (2004) paired with our own conceptualization of permission to hate, we sought to identify:

1. Which groups are amenable to violent activity;
2. The nature of such activities (e.g. recurrent, covert/overt, severity of violence);
3. Endogenous variables most closely associated with group development, sustainability and violence; and
4. Exogenous variables most closely associated with group development, sustainability and violence.

Project Methodologies

The often-scattered nature of data on Canadian RWE groups mandated a multifaceted approach that went beyond interviews with key informants. Information is fragmentary and often depends on local resources and capacities for data gathering. Those directly concerned with the policing of extremist activity tend, necessarily, to have a narrow lens that allows them to see the immediate context of their work. They typically have neither the time nor the resources to see how events and activities in their own communities may dovetail with activities elsewhere. Moreover, there are considerable challenges to studying RWE activists. Not least of these is access. The suggestion is that members of hate groups are largely clandestine, often paranoid, and for these reasons unwilling to expose themselves even to academic scrutiny (Blee and Creasap 2010; Gruenewald et al. 2009). Yet several long-term ethnographies have illustrated that building rapport and thus trust is possible (e.g. Hamm 1993; Simi and Futrell 2015). However, the ability to build the needed relationships may well be constrained by the identity(ies) of the researcher. Simi and Futrell (2015), for example, report that Simi was allowed access to their *Aryan Nations* group in the United States only on the condition that he was white. Even when groups invite academics into their midst, direct communication with extreme-right adherents may also pose some risk to researchers (see Blee and Creasap 2010).

These challenges have not stymied all qualitative research. Hamm's (1993) "American Skinheads" was an early example of the depth of insight that could be gleaned from talking to adherents—in that case, yielding 36 extended interviews. Treadwell and Garland's (2011) ethnography of *English Defence League (EDL)* adherents is another interesting case. Their very informal observations and interviews occurred "where they lived", that is, at demonstrations, and in local pubs, workplaces, homes, neighbourhoods. Perhaps because they were approached on their own turf, study participants seemed to be very forthcoming about their worldviews and their propensity for violence. A final example is Simi and Futrell's (2015) study of white power groups in the United States, which spanned the years 1996–2014, consisting of interviews, participant observation and content analysis of relevant websites. Like Treadwell and Garland (2011), they engaged with activists in their homes, favourite local hang-outs, white power events, even Bible studies.

Few such studies have been conducted in Canada. Thus, we have a limited national perspective on the threat posed by RWE in Canada. The sources of intelligence and data for this project are largely localized and time specific. For an academic, in contrast, any incident "has *meaning* only in relation to its earlier history and its political and cultural context" (Ezekiel and Post 1991: 121). The intent, then, was to engage multiple methodologies that allow us to see the "bigger picture" of the RWE movement in Canada. Consequently, the project involved a combination of archival research and primary research. The following means of data gathering were utilized.

1. *Website analysis*: This takes us directly to the rhetoric of the hate groups themselves. In line with previous work conducted by Perry (2000; see also Perry and Olsson 2009), we identified and analysed the websites established by Canadian hate groups (e.g. *Blood & Honour, White Nationalist Front*), as well as those that contain Canadian content, but might be on domains outside of Canada (e.g. Stormfront.org). The online environment has allowed unprecedented

opportunities for recruitment and for the enhancement of existing collectives, and the creation of new online-shared identities. It is thus a location that is rife with insights into the ideologies, belief systems, and strategic planning of the groups. The analysis pays attention to the "grievances" identified, where blame is ascribed, potential "solutions" to problems identified, links to other sites and organizations, etc.

2. *Media scan*: Like court records, media venues can be valuable sources of information on community impacts of extremist activities through reporting on reactions to the initial offence and subsequent legal proceedings. They often include detailed descriptions of the alleged events, and sometimes provide background details as well.

3. *Interviews with law enforcement and intelligence communities*: We interviewed more than 40 personnel associated with the Alberta Hate Crime Committee, the British Columbia (BC) Hate Crime Team, Canadian Security Intelligence Service (CSIS), the Ontario Provincial Police (OPP) Extremism and Hate Crime section and police officers from communities in which there has been white supremacist activity. These interviews uncovered additional data on activities, membership and ideologies associated with the groups.

4. *Interviews with community activists*: There are a number of national, regional and local community organizations in Canada—like *B'Nai Brith* and *Anti-Racist Canada*—that have set themselves the task of monitoring RWE activity in this country. Their publications along with interviews provided additional information about the distribution, membership, activities, ideologies and threats associated with relevant groups. They also added to knowledge and awareness of anti-hate initiatives by which extremists are challenged. In all, we interviewed more than 30 individuals from such groups.

5. *Interviews with hate group activists*: We were able to conduct three interviews with former/current members of hate groups. We also had access to a number of similar interviews conducted some years ago by Dr. Abbee Corb. These interviews provided the most direct access to the motivations for engaging in right-wing extremist activities.

References

Adamczyk, A., Gruenewald, J., Chermak, S., & Freilich, J. (2014). The Relationship Between Hate Groups and Far-Right Ideological Violence. *Journal of Contemporary Criminal Justice, 30*(3), 310–332.

Adams, J., & Roscigno, V. (2005). White Supremacists, Oppositional Culture and the World Wide Web. *Social Forces, 84*(2), 759–778.

Anahita, S. (2006). Blogging the Borders: Virtual Skinheads, Hypermasculinity, and Heteronormativity. *Journal of Political and Military Sociology, 32*(1), 143–164.

Appleton, C. (2014). Lone Wolf Terrorism in Norway. *The International Journal of Human Rights, 18*(2), 127–142.

Bakker, E., & De Graaf, B. (2011). Preventing Lone Wolf Terrorism: Some CT Approaches Addressed. *Perspectives on Terrorism, 5*(5–6), 43–50.

Bartlett, J., & Birdwell, J. (2013). *Cumulative Radicalisation Between the Far-Right and Islamist Groups in the UK: A Review of Evidence*. London: Demos.

Bates, R. (2012). Dancing with Wolves: Today's Lone Wolf Terrorists. *Journal of Public and Professional Sociology, 4*(1), 1–14.

Berger, J. M., & Strathearn, B. (2013). *Who Matters Online: Measuring Influence, Evaluating Content and Countering Violent Extremism in Online Social Networks*. London: The International Centre for the Study of Radicalisation and Political Violence.

Bérubé, M., & Campana, A. (2015). Les violences motivées par la haine. Idéologies et modes d'action des extrémistes de droite au Canada. *Criminologie, 48*(1), 215–234.

Black, D. (2004). Terrorism as Social Control. In M. Deflem (Ed.), *Terrorism and Counter-Terrorism: Criminological Perspectives* (pp. 9–18). Boston: Elsevier.

Blazak, R. (2001). White Boys to Terrorist Men: Target Recruitment of Nazi Skinheads. *American Behavioral Scientist, 44*(6), 982–1000.

Blee, K. M. (2002). *Inside Organized Racism: Women in the Hate Movement*. Berkeley: University of California Press.

Blee, K. M., & Creasap, K. A. (2010). Conservative and Right-Wing Movements. *Annual Review of Sociology, 36*, 269–286.

Borchgrevink, A. (2013). *A Norwegian Tragedy: Anders Behring Breivik and the Massacre on Utøya* (G. Puzey, Trans.). Malden, MA: Polity.

Borgeson, K., & Valeri, R. (2005). Identifying the Face of Hate. *Journal of Applied Sociology, 22*(1), 91–104.

Bostdorff, D. M. (2004). The Internet Rhetoric of the Ku Klux Klan: A Case Study in Web Site Community Building Run Amok. *Communication Studies, 55*(2), 340–361.

Bowling, B. (1993). Racial Harassment and the Process of Victimization. *British Journal of Criminology, 33,* 231–250.

Bowman-Grieve, L. (2009). Exploring "Stormfront": A Virtual Community of the Radical Right. *Studies in Conflict and Terrorism, 32*(11), 989–1007.

Burnett, J. (2017). Racial Violence and the Brexit State. *Race and Class, 58,* 85–97.

Busher, J., & Macklin, G. (2015). Interpreting "Cumulative Extremism": Six Proposals for Enhancing Conceptual Clarity. *Terrorism and Political Violence, 27*(5), 884–905.

Caiani, M., & Kröll, P. (2014). The Transnationalization of the Extreme Right and the Use of the Internet. *International Journal of Comparative and Applied Criminal Justice, 39*(4), 331–351.

Campbell, A. (2006). The Search for Authenticity: An Exploration of an Online Skinhead Newsgroup. *New Media Society, 8*(2), 269–294.

Chau, M., & Xu, J. (2007). Mining Communities and Their Relationships in Blogs: A Study of Online Hate Groups. *International Journal of Human Computer Studies, 65*(1), 57–70.

Chermak, S., Freilich, J., & Simone, J. (2010). Surveying American State Police Agencies About Lone Wolves, Far-Right Criminality, and Far-Right and Islamic Jihadist Criminal Collaboration. *Studies in Conflict and Terrorism, 33,* 1019–1041.

Deloughery, K., King, R., & Asal, V. (2012). Close Cousins of Distant Relatives? The Relationship Between Terrorism and Hate Crime. *Crime and Delinquency, 58*(5), 663–688.

Dobratz, B., & Waldner, L. (2012). Repertoires of Contention: White Separatist Views on the Use of Violence and Leaderless Resistance. *Mobilization: An International Quarterly, 17*(1), 49–66.

Ezekiel, R., & Post, J. (1991). Worlds in Collision, Worlds in Collusion: The Uneasy Relationship Between the Policy Community and the Academic Community. In C. McCauley (Ed.), *Terrorism Research and Public Policy* (pp. 117–125). Portland, OR: Frank Cass.

Ferber, A. L. (2016). White Supremacy and Gender. *The Wiley Blackwell Encyclopedia of Gender and Sexuality Studies,* 1–4.

Freilich, J., Chermak, S., & Belli, R. (2014). Introducing the United States Extremist Crime Database (ECDB). *Terrorism and Political Violence, 26,* 372–384.

Futrell, R., & Simi, P. (2004). Free Spaces, Collective Identity, and the Persistence of U.S. White Power Activism. *Social Problems, 51*(1), 16–42.

Gill, P. (2015). *Lone-Actor Terrorists: A Behavioural Analysis*. London: Routledge.

Graham, R. (2016). Inter-Ideological Mingling: White Extremist Ideology Entering the Mainstream on Twitter. *Sociological Spectrum, 36*(1), 24–36.

Gruenewald, J., Chermak, S., & Freilich, J. (2013). Far-Right Lone Wolf Homicides in the United States. *Studies in Conflict and Terrorism, 36*(12), 1005–1024.

Gruenewald, J., Freilich, J., & Chermak, S. (2009). An Overview of the Domestic Far-Right and Its Criminal Activities. In B. Perry & R. Blazak (Eds.), *Hate Crime: Issues and Perspectives, Vol. 4 Offenders* (pp. 1–22). New York: Praeger.

Grumke, T. (2013). Globalized Anti-globalists: The Ideological Basis of the Internationalization of Right-Wing Extremism. In S. Von Mering & T. W. McCarty (Eds.), *Right-Wing Radicalism Today: Perspectives from Europe and the US* (pp. 13–22). London: Routledge.

Hamm, M. (1993). *American Skinheads: The Criminology and Control of Hate Crime*. Westport, CT: Praeger.

Hamm, M. (2007). *Terrorism as Crime*. New York: New York University Press.

Heitmeyer, W. (2005). Right-Wing Terrorism. In T. Bjorgo (Ed.), *Root Causes of Terrorism: Myths, Reality and Ways Forward* (pp. 141–153). London: Routledge.

Hemmingby, C., & Bjørgo, T. (2015). *The Dynamics of a Terrorist Targeting Process: Anders B. Breivik and the 22 July Attacks in Norway*. New York: Springer.

Hoffman, B. (2003). *Al Qaeda, Trends in Terrorism, and Future Potentialities: An Assessment*. Santa Monica: RAND Corporation.

Huber, L. P. (2016). Make America Great Again: Donald Trump, Racist Nativism and the Virulent Adherence to White Supremacy Amid US Demographic Change. *Charleston Law Review, 10,* 215.

Hughey, M. W. (2010). The (Dis)Similarities of White Racial Identities: The Conceptual Framework of 'Hegemonic Whiteness'. *Ethnic and Racial Studies, 33*(8), 1289–1309.

Inglehart, R., & Norris, P. (2016). *Trump, Brexit, and the Rise of Populism: Economic Have-Nots and Cultural Backlash* (Harvard Kennedy School Faculty Working Paper Series. RWP16-026).

Jaggar, A. (2005). What Is Terrorism, Why Is It Wrong, and Could It Ever Be Morally Permissible? *Journal of Social Psychology, 36*(2), 202–217.

Jamin, J. (2013). Two Different Realities: Notes on Populism and the Extreme Right. In A. Mammone, E. Godin, & B. Jenkins (Eds.), *Varieties of RWE in Europe* (pp. 38–52). Abingdon: Routledge.

Komaromi, P., & Singh, K. (2016). *Post-referendum Racism and Xenophobia: The Role of Social Media Activism in Challenging the Normalisation of Xeno-Racist Narratives.* London: Institute of Race Relations.

Langman, L. (2005). From Virtual Public Spheres to Global Justice: A Critical Theory of Internetworked Social Movements. *Sociological Theory, 23*(1), 42–74.

Lauder, M. A. (2002). *The Far Rightwing Movement in Southwest Ontario: An Exploration of Issues, Themes, and Variations.* The Guelph and District Multicultural Centre.

Mammone, A., Godin, E., & Jenkins, B. (Eds.). (2012). *Mapping the Extreme Right in Contemporary Europe: From Local to Transnational* (1st ed.). New York: Routledge.

Mares, M., & Stojar, R. (2016). Extreme Right Perpetrators. In M. Fredholm (Ed.), *Understanding Lone Actor Terrorism: Past Experience, Future Outlook, and Response Strategies* (pp. 66–86). London: Routledge.

Mills, C. E., Freilich, J. D., & Chermak, S. M. (2015). Extreme Hatred: Revisiting the Hate Crime and Terrorism Relationship to Determine Whether They Are "Close Cousins" or "Distant Relatives". *Crime & Delinquency, 63*(10), 1191–1223.

Mulholland, S. (2013). White Supremacist Groups and Hate Crime. *Public Choice, 157*(1–2), 91–113.

Oaten, A. (2014). The Cult of the Victim: An Analysis of the Collective Identity of the English Defence League. *Patterns of Prejudice, 48*(4), 331–349.

Oberschall, A. (2004). Explaining Terrorism: The Contribution of Collective Action Theory. *Sociological Theory, 22*(1), 26–37.

Pantucci, R. (2011). What Have We Learned About Lone Wolves from Anders Behring Breivik? *Perspectives on Terrorism, 5*(5–6), 27–42.

Parkin, W. S., & Freilich, J. D. (2015). Routine Activities and Right-Wing Extremists: An Empirical Comparison of the Victims of Ideologically-and Non-ideologically-Motivated Homicides Committed by American Far-Rightists. *Terrorism and Political Violence, 27*(1), 182–203.

Perliger, A. (2012). *Challengers from the Sidelines: Understanding America's Far Right.* West Point NY: Combating Terrorism Center.

Perry, B. (2000). "Button-Down Terror": The Metamorphosis of the Hate Movement. *Sociological Focus, 33*(2), 113–131.

Perry, B. (2001). *In the Name of Hate: Understanding Hate Crimes*. New York: Routledge.

Perry, B., & Blazak, R. (2010). Places for Races: The White Supremacist Movement Imagines U.S. Geography. *Journal of Hate Studies, 8,* 29–51.

Perry, B., & Olsson, P. (2009). Cyberhate: The Globalization of Hate. *Information and Communications Technology Law, 18*(2), 185–199.

Perry, B., & Scrivens, R. (2016). Uneasy Alliances: A Look at the Right-Wing Extremist Movement in Canada. *Studies in Conflict and Terrorism, 39*(9), 819–841.

Petrou, M., & Kandylis, G. (2016). Violence and Extreme-Right Activism: The Neo-Nazi Golden Dawn in a Greek Rural Community. *Journal of Intercultural Studies, 37*(6), 589–604.

Pollard, J. (2016). Skinhead Culture: The Ideologies, Mythologies, Religions and Conspiracy Theories of Racist Skinheads. *Patterns of Prejudice, 50*(4–5), 398–419.

Poynting, S. (2006). What Caused the Cronulla Riots? *Race and Class, 48,* 85–92.

Rosenfeld, R. (2004). Terrorism and Criminology. In M. Deflem (Ed.), *Terrorism and Counter-Terrorism: Criminological Perspectives* (pp. 19–32). Boston: Elsevier.

Schafer, J., Mullins, C., & Box, S. (2014). Awakenings: The Emergence of White Supremacist Ideologies. *Deviant Behavior, 35*(3), 173–196.

Sheffield, C. (1995). Hate Violence. In P. Rothenberg (Ed.), *Race, Class and Gender in the United States* (pp. 432–441). New York: St. Martin's Press.

Simi, P. (2010). Why Study White Supremacist Terror? A Research Note. *Deviant Behavior, 31,* 251–273.

Simi, P., & Futrell, R. (2015). *American Swastika: Inside the White Power Movement's Hidden Spaces of Hate* (2nd ed.). Lanham, MD: Rowman and Littlefield Publishers.

Simi, P., Futrell, R., & Bubolz, B. F. (2016). Parenting as Activism: Identity Alignment and Activist Persistence in the White Power Movement. *The Sociological Quarterly, 57*(3), 491–519.

Simon, J. D. (2013). *Lone Wolf Terrorism: Understanding the Growing Threat*. New York: Prometheus Books.

Tanner, S., & Campana, A. (2014). *The Process of Radicalization: Right Wing Skinheads in Quebec* (No. 14-07). Vancouver: Canadian Network for Research on Terrorism, Security and Society.

Toronto Star. (2015, March 15). *Terrorism Threat Runs Broad 'Gamut'*, p. 1.

Treadwell, J., & Garland, J. (2011). Masculinity, Marginalization and Violence: A Case Study of the English Defence League. *The British Journal of Criminology, 51*(4), 621–634.

U.S. Department of Homeland Security. (2009). *Rightwing Extremism: Current Economic and Political Climate Fueling Resurgence in Radicalization and Recruitment.* Washington, DC: U.S. Department of Homeland Security and the Federal Bureau of Investigation.

Webb, J., & Cutter, S. (2009). The Geography of U.S. Terrorist Incidents, 1970–2004. *Terrorism and Political Violence, 21,* 428–449.

Wigerfelt, A., & Wigerfelt, B. (2014). *A Challenge to Multiculturalism: Everyday Racism and Hate Crime in a Small Swedish Town.* Retrieved from http://muep.mau.se/handle/2043/17654.

Wojcieszak, M. (2010). 'Don't Talk to Me': Effects of Ideological Homogenous Online Groups and Politically Dissimilar Offline Ties on Extremism. *New Media & Society, 12*(4), 637–655.

Wooden, W. S., & Blazak, R. (1995). *Renegade Kids, Suburban Outlaws: From Youth Culture to Delinquency.* Belmont, CA: Wadsworth.

Young, I. M. (1990). *Justice and the Politics of Difference.* Princeton, NJ: Princeton University Press.

2

Tracing the History of Right-Wing Extremism in Canada

Historical Context

The 1920s marked the era in which the *Ku Klux Klan (KKK)* established its roots in Canada. At the time, three separate Klan organizations emerged: (1) the *Ku Klux Klan of Canada*; (2) the *Kanadian Ku Klux Klan*; and (3) the *Ku Klux Klan of the British Empire*. The Klan's presence was particularly pronounced in Ontario, British Columbia, Alberta and Saskatchewan, and they promoted anti-Catholic, anti-immigration and racist sentiment. Anti-Catholic sentiment was already entrenched in Canada with the presence of the *Orange Order*, a protestant fraternal organization formed in 1830, and the *KKK* emerged in areas where the *Order* was firmly established (Barrett 1987: 21). As such, the Klan's strength was in Western Canada, particularly in Saskatchewan. At the height of its power in Saskatchewan alone, the Klan boasted of the allegiance of nearly 40,000 members, even joining with that province's Conservatives to dislodge the Liberal Party (Kinsella 2001). *The Church of the Creator* was also founded during this era. Through the movement, founder Ben Klassen promoted his

© The Author(s) 2019
B. Perry and R. Scrivens, *Right-Wing Extremism in Canada*,
Palgrave Hate Studies, https://doi.org/10.1007/978-3-030-25169-7_2

anti-Christian and racist organization from 1925 to 1945 (Michael 2006).

The *KKK*'s endeavours were as short-lived as they were dramatic in Canada, and by the 1930s, the group became a fatigued force. As the Klan shrank, a pre-World War II fascist and Nazi movement grew. Adding to Jewish concerns was the development of fascist groups across Canada that included the *Toronto Swastika Club*, the *Swastika Association of Canada*, the *National Social Christian Party*, *Deutsche Bund* and the *Canadian Union of Fascists* (Lauder 2002). In Quebec, Adrien Arcand's antisemitic *Parti National Society Chretien* enjoyed a great deal of success and ultimately expanded to Toronto, ON. Under the group name *National Christian Party of Canada*, later known as the *National Unity Party*, Arcand initially chose John Ross Taylor to lead the Ontario branch. However, he was soon replaced by Joseph Farr, a sergeant major in the British Army and member of the *Orange Order* (Barrett 1987).

Following World War II, the 1940s–1960s were known as "the sanitary decades" for the RWE movement in Canada. Fascism became a dirty word, as the world had seen enough racism and antisemitism (Barrett 1987). Although antisemitism declined slightly from the late 1940s through the 1950s and 1960s, Canada experienced a small but steady trickle of organized RWE activity. For example, the *Orange Order* continued to exist in Canada, but with little clout (Barrett 1987). In 1949, Adrien Arcand attempted to reassert his political power with the *National Unity Party*, but was never fully successful in doing so. Ron Gostick established an Ontario-based antisemitic publication, *Canadian Intelligence Publications*, in the late 1940s, and later created the *Christian Action Movement* in 1963. John Ross Taylor also created an extreme-right-wing mail-order business called the *Natural Order* during this era (Barrett 1987). In Toronto, ON, John Beattie founded the *Canadian Nazi Party* in 1965. Paul Fromm, Leigh Smith and Don Andrews established the *Edmund Burke Society*, which lasted from 1967 to 1972 (Lauder 2002).

In the 1970s and 1980s, Canada saw an explosion of RWE activity. The atrocities of World War II and Hitler's antisemitism had begun to dim; major changes in Canada's immigration laws were introduced; and unemployment and inflation were rampant (Barrett 1987). Together, these factors created a powder keg of pent-up frustration and anxiety. Influenced by Britain's far right-wing party *National Front Political* and British white power rock and punk music (i.e. the band *Skrewdriver*), neo-Nazi skinheads began to appear in the United States and Canada in the late 1970s, springing up in numerous urban settings, including Montreal's east end, Vancouver's Granville St. Mall and Robson, Edmonton's Jasper Avenue, and Calgary and Toronto's downtown core (Young and Craig 1997). Such racist skinhead groups included: (1) *Longitude 74*; (2) the *White Federation*; (3) the *Aryan Resistance Movement (ARM)*; and (4) the *United Skinheads of Montreal* (Ross 1992). Furthermore, changing immigration patterns and harsh economic realities in Canada added to the appeal of neo-Nazism, especially for young people (Kinsella 2001), and among the most important organizations to emerge during this time were: (1) the *Western Guard*; (2) the *Nationalist Party*; (3) the *KKK*; (4) *Aryan Nations*; (5) *Concerned Parents of German Descent*; (6) *Campus Alternative*; (7) *Alternative Forum*; and (8) *Citizens for Foreign Aid Reform (C-FAR)* (Barrett 1987).

While the *KKK* remained the grandfather of most modern white supremacist groups in Canada, it was not successful in attracting many new recruits in Canada's Western provinces in the 1970s and 1980s. With the exception of Tearlach Mac a'Phearson and Bill Harcus's success in the Klan, other groups such as the *Aryan Nations* and the *Heritage Front* surpassed the various Klan cells in both membership and visibility (Kinsella 2001). In the 1970s, the *Western Guard*, a white supremacist group founded in 1972 and derived from the *Edmund Burke Society*, was very active, carrying out a series of public attacks and attempts to manipulate public opinion through its propaganda and recorded telephone hate messages (Ross 1992). In the 1980s, *Aryan Nations*, led by Terry Long in Canada, built a training camp in Caroline, AB, bringing together different extremists, as well as staging a major rally and cross burning in Provost, AB. *Heritage Front* a neo-Nazi white supremacist organization was founded in 1989 by former *Nationalist Party of Canada* members Wolfgang Droege, Gerry Lincoln, Grant Bristow and James Dawson and disbanded in 2005. The group also formed an alliance with *World Church of the Creator* and its

Canadian leader George Burdi, as well as with Canadian extreme-right ideologues Paul Fromm and Ernst Zundel. During the 1980s, the neo-Nazi alternative music scene started to develop and became visible in Calgary, AB, Toronto, ON, and Ottawa, ON from the 1980s onwards (Kinsella 2001).

Canada continued to see a rise in neo-Nazi activity in the 1990s, particularly around the neo-Nazi skinhead music scene. The birth of the Internet also increased RWE' visibility, potential for recruitment, and lone actor and "leaderless resistance" activity from groups such as *Combat 18* (C-18). In addition, Don Black established *Stormfront* in 1995, which continues to be one of the most infamous RWE online communities, featuring news stories, community discussion boards and scholarship competitions (Conway 2016). Such websites and other similar sites provided connections among RWEs and groups (Bowman-Grieve 2009).

During this time, the *Heritage Front*, led by ultra-violent Wolfgang Droege, continued to grow in power, making its mark in urban centres such as Toronto (Kinsella 2001). In Montreal, QC, various Hammerskin groups including the *Northern Hammerskins* and the *Vinland Hammerskins* made their presence known, engaging in a series of assaults and weapons offenses. George Burdi's band *RaHoWa* formed in 1989, and the Canadian branch of the *World Church of Creator* was heavily involved in the RWE movement, pushing the white power music scene across the country (Kinsella 2001). In 1993, Burdi, who still maintained a close bond with Droege, attempted to advance white power music by launching *Resistance Records*. He also organized *Church of the Creator* paramilitary training with a former member of the *Canadian Forces Airborne Regiment* (Michael 2006). In Alberta, Terry Long, leader of the *Aryan Nations* in Canada, and Kelly Scott Lyle, founder of Calgary's *Final Solution Skinheads*, gained media attention in a series of racist activities. Matt McKay member of the Manitoba Klan and the *Final Solution Skinheads* in Winnipeg was involved in a murder and a number of assaults, and Carney Nerland of Saskatchewan's *Aryan Nations* led the group in a series of violent crimes (Anti-Racist Canada 2014).

Entering the twenty-first century, the *KKK, Church of the Creator* and racist skinhead groups such as *Aryan Guard/Blood & Honour* have maintained their presence in Canada, promoting bigotry, intolerance and hate-motivated violence. The *Aryan Guard/Blood & Honour*, however, appear to be amongst the most active and violent groups in the current movement. The *Aryan Guard*, a neo-Nazi group, was founded in Alberta in late 2006, staging counter rallies against anti-racists, disseminating discriminatory fliers and engaging in an array of violent activities. Kyle McKee was the founder and spokesperson for the group and has been arrested and charged numerous times for weapons offenses and violent offences (One People's Project 2009). In 2010, two ultra-violent white supremacist groups, *Western European Bloodline (WEB)* and *Blood & Honour*, replaced the *Aryan Guard*. Both groups were allegedly founded in Alberta by McKee and co-founded by Dallas Price and Robert Reitmeier, two other extremely violent individuals (Jarvies 2012; One People's Project 2011). In 2011, Robert Reitmeier and Tyler Sturrup of *WEB* were charged with second-degree murder in a deadly and brutal attack in Calgary, AB (CBC News Calgary 2011), and four affiliates of *Blood & Honour* were charged during a sequence of racial assaults in Calgary (Edmonton Sun 2011). In addition, *Blood & Honour* members in Vancouver, BC were charged for a series of attacks in 2011, one in which a Filipino man was set on fire in the downtown core (Anti-Racist Canada 2014).

Additionally, the racist skinhead movement remains active in parts of Quebec and includes two types of groups. One branch is known as anarchist skinheads, fighting against fascism, racism and capitalism, and they have existed predominantly in Montreal since the mid-1990s. The second type, the more extreme of the two, defines themselves as "nationalists". They promote RWE beliefs and ideals and engage in an array of criminal activities that revolve largely around the racist skinhead music scene. Such violent groups include *Légitime Violence*, the *Dead Boys Crew, Légion Nationaliste*, the *Quebec Radical, Ragnarok, Ragnarok Vinland, Vinland Front* and the *Vinland Warriors* (Tanner and Campana 2014).

Contemporary Categories of Right-Wing Extremism in Canada

Three clear classes of RWEs emerged during our fieldwork: (1) variants of white supremacists/neo-Nazis/racist skinheads; (2) anti-authority communities; and (3) what we will frame as "ideologues", gurus" and "lone actors". This is not to say that there are no other strands of extreme-right sentiment. There is something here that can be loosely thought of as a "religious right" in Canada. While not as widespread or successful as their American counterparts, the associated churches and congregants here are similarly evangelical in nature and rally around the common foes of feminism, the sexual revolution, abortion and homosexuality (Fetner, forthcoming). Marci McDonald (2011) chronicled the creeping rise of religious right in Canada, arguing that they have been "emboldened" by a broader turn to the right in federal politics.

The religious right finds its voice in the context of particular single issues. Across parts of Western Canada, in particular, the home-schoolers movement is frequently associated with Christian fundamentalism (Basham et al. 2007). This faction is most renowned for their resistance to educational reforms that would have required them to explicitly address human rights issues in their curriculum. The West is also a strong base for a viable anti-abortion/pro-life faction, largely grounded in fundamentalist visions of morality and gender roles (Williams 2015). However, they have not been associated with violence in Canada since the beginning of the millennium.

There is also a strong thread of homophobia across the country, but it hardly reflects any organizational footing outside of particular churches. Trinity Western University, for example, has come under fire for its proscription against same-sex relationships. There are also movements where the two themes come together, in fact decrying any and all "subversions" of the proper moral order and gender roles. Donald Andre Bruneau, a self-proclaimed pro-life advocate, manages the website Aborterrorism.ca, on which he rails equally against abortion, homosexuality—"the gay agenda"—and contraception. Similarly, *Human Life*

International, which has a Canadian presence, has a wide-ranging platform of morality linked to racism, sexism and homophobia. A Catholics for Choice (2011: 1–2) report alleges a history of abuse and incitement to violence grounded in an array of exclusionary tenets, including

> concerns that Asians, Latinos and Muslims will overrun the world; proclaiming that Jews were responsible for abortions worldwide; labeling homosexuality and feminism as degraded and satanic, respectively; and condemning black leaders in the anti-apartheid movement.

Reminiscent of the nativist movements of the 1920s, anti-immigrant groups were also apparent in Canada in the mid-2010s. Emboldened by recent federal shifts in immigration rhetoric and practice, bodies like *Immigration Watch Canada (IWC)* were and continue to be very active. One of the Greater Toronto Area's (GTA) most diverse communities, Brampton, ON, was host to a campaign of hate, characterized by pamphleting and flyer posting in 2013 and 2014. One such poster featured an old photo of a group of white people, presumably dating from the early part of the twentieth century, alongside a contemporary photo of a group of Sikhs. The caption asks "Is This What You Really Want?" referring to Canada's history of immigration as a "social engineering experiment". *IWC* calls for Euro-Canadians to take back "their" country. While offensive and hurtful, however, there does not seem to be any indication that *IWC* intends to cross the line into violence any time soon.

Notwithstanding the individuals profiled below, these extreme-right-wing elements noted above do not tend to rise to the threshold of what might be considered serious threats, either numerically or otherwise; nor are they generally on the radar of law enforcement or intelligence communities. In contrast, white supremacists, sovereigntists and extreme-right ideologues are worthy of attention, either because of their direct involvement in criminality and extremist violence, or the indirect impact of their discourse on others.

White Supremacists/Neo-Nazis/Racist Skinheads

By far the most commonly noted category of RWE in Canada is that associated with neo-Nazism, racist skinheads or white supremacy. The anti-Semitism and racism that characterize so many hate groups—and not just the Identity Churches—can be traced to the theocratic principle of Christian Identity. On the basis of a creative reading of biblical scripture, those advocating this perspective claim the white race to be the direct descendants of Ancient Israel, and therefore God's chosen people:

> WE BELIEVE that Adam, man of Genesis, is the placing of the White Race upon this earth. Not all races descend from Adam. Adam is the father of the White Race only. (Aryan Nations, online)

Consequently, only the "White Race" is truly blessed and thereby part of God's Kingdom in Heaven. Frequent references are made to the assurances by God's law and natural law that the white race is the covenant race, and therefore to be jealously protected. The *World Church of the Creator* (online) reminds its followers that

> what is good for the White Race is the highest virtue, and what is bad for the White Race is the ultimate sin. We have come to hold these views by observing the Eternal Laws of Nature...The highest Law of Nature is the survival of one's own kind...It is therefore logical and sensical (sic) to place supreme importance upon the Race and to reject all ideas which fail to do so.

In contrast to the glorification of the white race, Jews are seen to be the source of all evil, spawned as they are by the Devil himself:

> WE BELIEVE that there are literal children of Satan in this world today...WE BELIEVE that the Canaanite Jew is the natural enemy of our Aryan (White) Race. The Jew is like a destroying virus that attacks our racial body to destroy our Aryan culture and the purity of our race. (Aryan Nations, online)

Kyle McKee, leader of *Blood & Honour* in Alberta, made the following statement about Jews on *Stormfront* in 2007:

> The jews do alot more behind the sceans and I would almost belive that the jews would try and push the idea that these other races are the ones that need to be delt with first. But the thing is that these other races only are what they are they for the most part are not bright enough to master mind the destruction of a race. they are like rats the are all running out of this hole on the deck of your boat, now you can try and catch them all and trow them over board or you can try and stop the flooding that they are all runing from and I'l bet if you stop the flood then you'll find that the flood was caused by some termights/jews. When people find this out we can get out the pest control. (Anti-Racist Canada 2007)

A natural extension of Christian Identity ideology is that of white supremacy. Whether God-given or biologically derived, the white race is deemed inherently superior to all others. The creation of race categories and valuations represents a means of identity construction for both whites and other races. Race is seen as an "essence" which carries with it inherent differences between groups, differences which are claimed as justification for "natural" hierarchies. The *National Alliance* (online) summary statement of beliefs makes this apparent:

> We see ourselves as part of Nature, subject to Nature's law. We recognize the inequalities which arise as natural consequences of the evolutionary process...We accept our responsibilities as Aryan men and women to strive for the advancement of our race in the service of Life.

They go on to state that

> (O)ur world is hierarchical. Each of us is a member of the Aryan (European) race, which, like other races, developed its special characteristics over many thousands of years during which natural selection not only adapted it to its environment but also advanced it along its evolutionary path.

A similar claim is made by the longest-lived white supremacist group, the *KKK*:

> Our main and fundamental objective is the Maintenance of the Supremacy of the White Race in this Republic. History and physiology teach us that we belong to a race which nature has endowed with an evident superiority over all other races, and that the Maker in thus elevating us above the common standard of human creation has intended to give us over inferior races a domination from which no human laws can permanently derogate. (cited in Sapp et al. 1991: 123–124)

Canadian *Stormfront* member, Skogarmadur, posted his thoughts on mixing races in 2007:

> Race Mixing is treason - I myself believe that in the future once a National Socialist government is put into play any sort of interracial "affairs" should be considered treason. And treason should be treated with the death penalty. Not only is it betraying your race and kin, but it is ruining the future of the white race and if people continue to do so it will be the bringer of destruction of all that is Aryan blood. (Anti-Racist Canada 2007)

Inevitably, the white race is presumed to be at the top of this hierarchy, followed by the Jews and the "mud-people" (i.e. people of colour). Blacks are typically placed on the lowest level. Ultimately, the ideology of white supremacy seeks to restore the white privilege that RWE claim has been lost.

In certain regions of the country, specifically Quebec and the Western provinces, the RWE movement takes particular aim against Aboriginal communities. Collectively, anti-Aboriginal groups and individuals foment hostility towards Canada's First Nations people, by claiming that tribal bodies exploit "public sympathies" and "historical white guilt" in an effort to gain access to natural resources, including water, wildlife, fish and especially land. Ostensibly premised on the notion of "equal rights for all", these arms of the RWE movement deny the legitimacy of Aboriginal rights claims.

Unfortunately, the posture of entitlement recently taken by First Nations activists in places like Caledonia, ON and Oka, QC is often seen as an affront to white dominance, in that the activists are perceived to be violating the anticipated rules of behaviour—that is, the rules of Canadian apartheid. Instead of accepting their subordination, they resist it. In such a context, incidents of racial violence may escalate in retaliation. To paraphrase, the only good Indian is a quiet Indian. Should they step outside the permissible boundaries that define "a good Indian", they become vulnerable to reactionary violence.

Significantly, anti-Aboriginal actors often posit competing nationalisms—white Canadian vs. Aboriginal—in ways that demonize the latter as "freeloaders" and exploitative. Gary McHale founded *Canadian Advocates for Charter Equality (CANACE)*, in large part, to challenge Aboriginal rights. His rhetoric revolves around such themes as "native lawlessness", "land claim terrorism" and "race-based policing"—by which he means, ironically, "excessive" policing of those who threaten or attack Aboriginals.[1] Consequently, anti-Native groups have engaged in quite tangible violations of *human* rights, through ongoing harassment and violence against Aboriginal people. This is a continuation of the historical legacy by which Aboriginals are kept "in their place".

Anti-Authority Community

During the time that we conducted our study on RWE in Canada, no better source of information on the anti-authority community in Canada could be found than that delivered in Associate Chief Justice Rooke's decision in Mead v. Mead. In his decision, Rooke, in fact, coins a phrase, labelling them as "Organized Pseudolegal Commercial Argument" litigants (OPCA). Alternatively, he refers to the loose collection of individuals and small cells as "vexatious litigants". Rooke also highlights the heterogeneity of these followers, observing that they

---

[1]See http://joincanace.wordpress.com/about-2/.

do not express any stereotypic beliefs other than a general rejection of court and state authority; nor do they fall into any common social or professional association. Arguments and claims of this nature emerge in all kinds of legal proceedings and all levels of Courts and tribunals. This group is unified by:

1. A characteristic set of strategies (somewhat different by group) that they employ,
2. Specific but irrelevant formalities and language which they appear to believe are (or portray as) significant, and
3. The commercial sources from which their ideas and materials originate.
4. This category of litigant shares one other critical characteristic: they will only honour state, regulatory, contract, family, fiduciary, equitable, and criminal obligations if they feel like it. And typically, they don't.

The decision provided us with important insight into the diverse nature of the sovereigntist movement in Canada, identifying five core parts of the movement: (1) Detaxers; (2) Freemen or Freemen-on-the-Land; (3) Sovereign Men or Sovereign Citizens; (4) Church of the Ecumenical Redemption International (CERI); and (5) Moorish Law.

While each of these has a slightly unique focus, the core that holds them together is the rejection of the authority of the federal state. They are bound, they say, only by the principles of "natural law", not human law. In a rambling statement of obligations The *FreeMan Society of Canada*, for example, urges members and prospective members

> To maintain a non-consent posture as to the Governments Rule - Powers, to Judge, question, approach, demand, any reasons, answers to your Decision to Claim your Rights, under and on behalf of, for the Purpose to Maintain Self Rule Under, on behalf of all members and families of The FreeMan Society of Canada to promote freedom, truth, peace and abundance in Common Law Jurisdiction. Which makes you Free Men on the Land, and not Subjected to any --Statues, Bylaws, Rules of any Governments of Canada or Agencies there in. (http://freemansocietyofcanada.webs.com/)

The Canadian anti-authority movement is largely decentralized, eschewing the recreation of bureaucratic hierarchies. Nonetheless, there are what Rooke calls "gurus" who provide the inspiration and rhetoric. Robert Menard (profiled elsewhere in this book) has been one of the leading spokespersons of the movement since the early 2000s. Founder of the World Freeman Society, Menard, has travelled the country hosting public seminars, and touting his "instructional" videos.

Ideologues, Gurus and Lone Actors

Not all Canadian extremists are explicitly affiliated with particular groups. Nonetheless, they contribute extensively to the "movement", especially in terms of providing ideological fodder on which others may feed. Some—like Paul Fromm—do not claim membership in extant RWE groups but are known to associate with them, attending their rallies or other public events. In addition, there are what might be described as lone actors who "independently" feed their hunger for extreme-right-wing rhetoric by following related websites, or collecting propaganda, for example. The following are examples of some of Canada's more visible individual actors (more can be found in Appendix A).

Ideologues

The extreme right—just like the extreme left—plays out along a continuum of belief and action. As suggested by the definitions offered above, there can be wide variation in the focus of different adherents' ideological worldviews. So, too, is there considerable difference in the ways in which they may be engaged with RWE, either informing, or being informed by it. The ideologues we note at the outset often eschew—or profess to—direct membership in RWE groups. Nonetheless, they serve to provide the intellectual underpinnings and conceptual tools that are taken up by others who may be more explicitly involved in RWE groups and RWE violence.

Douglas H. Christie (1946–2013), a graduate of the University of British Columbia's law school and founder of the *Canadian Free Speech League*, was one of Canada's most well-known and controversial lawyers who advocated for what he called "freedom", or more specifically, encouraged individual liberty and free speech. Critics, however, regarded him as dishonourable, labelling him as the "battling barrister" for the antisemites, the white supremacists, the Holocaust deniers and individuals charged with hate crimes (Watts and Dickson 2013). For example, Christie represented some of Canada's most reviled hatemongers, including James Keegstra (Alberta teacher, convicted of promoting hatred against Jewish people), Ernst Zundel (a Toronto-based publisher, Holocaust denier and Nazi sympathizer, who printed and distributed an array of antisemitic literature), Paul Fromm (white supremacist and self-proclaimed Nazi sympathizer), Malcolm Ross (antisemitic conspiracy theorist), white supremacists Doug Collins, John Ross Taylor, and Terry Tremain, Michael Seifert (Nazi prison guard, convicted of war crimes), Tony McAleer (white supremacist and founder of *Canadian Liberty Net*) and Nazi war criminal Imre Finta.

Understandably, critics believed that Christie's views were in line with those of the RWE movement, and that he maintained similar views on Nazism and antisemitism as did his clients. Nonetheless, Bernie Farber, the former head of the *Canadian Jewish Congress*, was skeptical of Christie's beliefs, noting that while he may have been a fellow traveller with the white power movement, he was also a passionate defender of one's right to free speech (Boeveld 2013). Pete McMartin (2013), a *Vancouver Sun* columnist, also believed that Christie's legal battles were less about his moral compass and more about maintaining a loner's natural inclination for defiance and defending free speech. Christie was always careful not to publicly support the views of his clients (Watts and Dickson 2013).

Ezra Levant (1972–present), Calgary-raised lawyer and far-right pundit, is Canada's best-known conservative analyst, political activist and TV host and has been involved in several legal cases and controversies on free speech issues in Canada. Levant was parliamentary assistant to Preston Manning and member of the editorial board of the *National Post*, and his areas of expertise during this time included national politics, the Supreme Court and the Middle East (Speakers' Spotlight 2014). Levant was also the founder and former publisher of the *Western Standard* magazine, Canada's only media outlet to publish the Danish cartoons of Mohammed. The magazine was eventually charged with two counts of hate speech offenses, which went before the Alberta government's human rights commission. Levant's battles against those attacking freedom of speech resulted in significant changes to how Canadian human rights commissions operate, and he later wrote a book, titled "Shakedown", on what he perceived as the illiberal nature of Canadian human rights commissions (Speakers' Spotlight 2014). He is also the author of the best-seller "Ethical Oil: The Case for Canada's Oil Sands", and the new book "Groundswell: The Case for Fracking".

Levant was also a Canadian media personality, broadcaster and columnist for *Sun Media*. He was the host of *Sun TV*'s now defunct controversial daily news programme *The Source*, on which he discussed controversial issues such as multiculturalism, immigration, human rights, political correctness, the ethics of oil and other political events of the day (Speakers' Spotlight 2014). Levant also faced a defamation lawsuit as a result of allegedly Islamophobic comments made in a series of blog posts towards Khurrum Awan, the then law student who published an article in *Maclean's* magazine in 2006 titled "The Future Belongs to Islam" (Jones 2014). In 2015, he established *Rebel Media*, a far-right outlet that regularly features global and domestic "stars" of the nationalist movement.

William (Bill) Whatcott (1967–present), resident of Weyburn, SK, is a Canadian social conservative activist and religious anti-gay activist. Whatcott is a born-again Christian who discovered religion following an early adulthood of drugs, crime and homosexuality (CBC News 2013). With the goal of making both abortion and homosexuality illegal, Whatcott is known as an awkward revolutionary, a sexual purist and Christian fundamentalist who regrets his own homosexual and criminal conduct, denouncing it as filthy and corrupt (Brean 2013).

In his adolescent years, he lived on the streets, at times having sex with men to support his drug addiction. In his adult years, he repeatedly ran for mayor in Regina and Edmonton, losing each and every race. Whatcott's relentless pursuit of media attention landed him an appearance on *The Daily Show* with John Stewart, but it was soon revealed that he was hosting a Heterosexual Family Pride Parade, and was mocked as a closeted gay man (Hoffmann 2013).

Whatcott has protested at various gay pride celebrations and outside of abortion clinics. Eventually, however, Canada's anti-gay crusader was charged with distributing flyers that promoted gay men as sodomites and paedophiles, one titled "Keep homosexuality out of Saskatoon's public schools", and the other "Sodomites in our public schools" (Canadian Press 2013). The leaflets, which were being handed out on the University of Saskatchewan's campus, resulted, initially, in a hearing with the Saskatchewan Human Rights Commission, which ruled against him. The Saskatchewan Court of Appeal overturned that ruling, which led Whatcott to the Supreme Court. The Supreme Court of Canada, however, unanimously ruled that these flyers constituted hate speech, in that they promoted hatred against gays and lesbians (Canadian Press 2013).

Gurus

There is also an array of Canadian RWE activists who seek to lead the movement towards greater visibility and resonance with the broader public. These are often people who take to the stage and the airwaves to freely share their condemnation of all that they see as wrong about contemporary Canada: immigration, multiculturalism, government regulation or lack thereof, etc. Like the ideologues, they provide rhetorical fodder for the movement, but are much more directly engaged with it. They often provide the guidance and mentorship that young, emerging local leaders seek.

Frederick Paul Fromm (1949–present), Canada's core RWE leader and one of Canada's most notorious white nationalist activists, is recognized for his relentless critique of and attacks on foreign aid, inflation, unemployment and government spending sprees, to name but a few. His most noteworthy group associations were with the *Edmund Burke Society*, *Western Guard* and *Campus Alternative*, and he is currently the leader of the *Canadian Association for Free Expression (CAFE)*, and *Citizens for Foreign Aid Reform (C-FAR)*. Here, his beliefs include a God-centred moral order, the fundamental importance of family, individual freedom, limited government, a free society, law and order, and uncompromising opposition to communism (Barrett 1987). Fromm has also been known to rail against the ban on capital punishment, abortion, gun control legislation and "insane"—i.e. liberal—immigration policies. He has spoken at a number of white power rallies, such as the 1989 Toronto Skinheads "Domination Day celebration", and many *Heritage Front* rallies, including a December 1990 rally commemorating the death of *Silent Brotherhood* leader Robert Mathews (Kinsella 2001). He has also shared the stage with Holocaust denier David Irving and has organized Canadian rallies to support Holocaust denier Ernest Zundel.

In 1967, University of Toronto students Paul Fromm and Leigh Smith formed the ultra-conservative *Edmund Burke Society*, a group of approximately 1000 individuals mostly from the Toronto region, who opposed immigration, sex education, homosexuality, abortion, welfare, big government and Pierre Trudeau (Kinsella 2001). The group infiltrated left-wing organizations, countering groups with violence, and some members were eventually convicted of break-ins, thefts, vandalism, arson, countless assaults and even bomb threats. In 1972, the *Edmund Burke Society* converted to the *Western Guard*; however, founders Fromm and Leigh left the group, as they were concerned with the racist and pro-Nazi elements of the new group (Kinsella 2001).

Although Fromm resigned from the *Western Guard* in 1972, over the years he has been involved in RWE activity in Canada. For example, Fromm became editor of a new publication, titled *Countdown*, which was targeted at a growing anti-communist movement in Ontario, serving as a means to preserve Western Christian Civilization (Barrett 1987). Fromm also established a new organization in 1973, *Campus Alternative*, providing opportunities for conservative students to discuss their views counter to what was discussed by left-wing academics at the University of Toronto. The organization later branched out to York University and the University of Waterloo, and *Countdown* and *Campus Alternative*—which was not much different than the *Edmund Burke Society*—continued to gain popularity, promoting borderline racist messages that opposed communism, socialism and welfare-state liberalism (Barrett 1987). By the end of the 1970s, Fromm's messages became subtler and quite mild, and this was echoed in the organizations in which he then became involved: *Alternative Forum*, *C-FAR* and the *Cornerstone Alliance*.

Robert Menard (1953-present) is the Director of the *World Freeman Society* and a "guru" or "poster boy" for the loosely knit *Freeman-on-the-Land* movement in Canada. As a former stand-up comedian, construction worker and four-year member of the *Royal Canadian Regiment*, some consider him a leader who helped advance the movement in Canada in the early part of the twenty-first century. Freemen such as Robert Menard have been caught driving without license plates or phoney plates, and when brought before justice, they use common law to argue that courts have no jurisdictions over them, for example. This method is known as "paper terrorism", as they clog the court system with a large number of idiosyncratic documents and use jargon that is recommended by movement gurus such as Menard (Bell 2010).

Menard became involved in the movement when a government agent allegedly denied him access to the courts by threatening an infant with harm, and he felt deeply betrayed by the Canadian government. As a result, he began to study the law and soon engaged in what some call a "harmless fringe movement" (CBC News 2012c; Zerbisias 2013). Menard notes that the Freemen movement, which takes certain ideologies from the Bible, "embraces the law" and "spiritual libertarianism" and defines the group as one which promotes less intrusive government and greater freedom. Law enforcement agencies, however, define them as an anti-government group of "sovereign citizens" and "detaxers" who refuse to be governed by human laws, disrupt court operations and frustrate the legal rights of governments, corporations and individuals (Bell 2012). Police are also concerned that this group, which preaches endlessly online, is growing in numbers as the economy worsens, and predict that they may become increasingly violent (CBC News 2012c).

Keith Francis William Noble (1976–present), also recognized as "Exterminance" or "Leto Atreides II" on racist websites, message boards and forums, is well known to law enforcement officials for spreading messages of "white pride", becoming a fixture on the *Stormfront* and *Vanguard National News* forums, as well as the now obsolete *Western Canada For Us (WCFU)* forums. He is also a member of the *National Socialist Party of Canada* and was the founder of the now-defunct *National Progressivist Party of Canada*. It is also alleged by *Simon*

Wiesenthal Centre (SWC) researchers in Toronto and Los Angeles that Noble registered the *Aryan Guard* website on 17 June 2007, and that he was behind a popular flyer campaign targeting immigrants in Calgary, AB (CNW 2007).

In his early years of becoming a neo-Nazi, Noble styled himself after his idol, the Fuhrer, trying to recruit skinheads in Fort Saint John's, BC but was not successful (One People's Project 2009). He did however gain attention from the British Columbia (BC) Hate Crimes division, and his apartment was raided in February of 2005. Unhappy about this event, paired with the fact that he could not find like-minded others locally, Noble left BC and settled in Edmonton, AB, a community known for its concentration of white nationalists (One People's Project 2009).

While he had a strong presence on the World Wide Web, Noble did not show a significant presence in the racist movement until he moved to Alberta (One People's Project 2009). Here, he met and lived with former *WCFU* leaders Glenn Bahr and Nathan Touchette, eventually joining the *Aryan Guard* movement in Calgary, AB. He then became part involved with the group in 2006, but was not concerned with physical aspect of the movement (One People's Project 2009).

In 2006, Bill Noble was arrested in Edmonton and charged with violating s. 319(2) of the *Criminal Code of Canada* (wilful promotion of hatred), the result of his material posted on his website (www.exterminance.org) and similar white pride websites. In 2008, he was sentenced to four months in prison, three years probation, and his computer was seized and destroyed by the Crown (One People's Project 2009). He was released in April of 2008 and has since been quiet in public and on the Internet.

Christian Waters, known online as "BOK Canada" online, is a Regina resident and "Grand Dragon" of the *KKK* in Saskatchewan. He is also a high-ranking officer with the Canadian branch of *Brotherhood of Klans (BOK)*, which is the largest Klan group in North America. Waters has attracted new members in Saskatchewan over the past few years, causing unease, say anti-racist activists (CBC News 2007b).

Rooted in the post-Civil War in southern United States, *BOK* has shown concern for what they call Canada's "open door" immigration policies, arguing that Canada is a "haven for terrorism". Notably, Waters was drawn to the white-only group when he saw crime rates in inner-city Regina neighbourhoods rise steadily, blaming aboriginal gangs for this increase (CBC News 2007b). Waters, however, argues that *BOK* is not a hate-based organization, nor is it associated with skinhead or neo-Nazi groups. Instead, Waters insists that *BOK* is a Christian-based organization, occasionally holding private gatherings; most of their interactions are online (Leader-Post 2007). Waters also notes that the group is not violent, but rather, is committed to staging rallies that support stricter immigration policies and harsher punishments for violent crimes (CBC News 2007b). Royal Canadian Mounted Police (RCMP) spokesperson Heather Russell has also claimed that *BOK* Canada's website and activities are considered legal (Leader-Post 2007).

Lone Actors

Increasing attention is being paid to lone actor extremists of all stripes. Bruce Hoffman (2003: 17) remarks that

> Increasingly, lone individuals with no connection with or formal ties to established or identifiable terrorist organizations are rising up to engage in violence. These individuals are often inspired or motivated by some larger political movement that they are not actually a part of, but nonetheless draw spiritual and emotional sustenance and support from. Indeed, over the past 10 years or so—with the exception of the two World Trade Center attacks and that on the Pentagon—all of the most significant terrorist incidents that occurred in the United States were perpetrated either by a lone individual or very tight two- or three-man conspiratorial cells.

By their very nature, lone actors are difficult to identify until they act on their radicalized beliefs. In the Canadian context, it is chilling to note that perhaps the most infamous contemporary RWE lone actor—Anders Breivik—made frequent references to Canada in his online manifesto. Some of the notes were critical (e.g. sexual immorality); some were laudatory (increasing social conservatism) (Toronto Star 2011). During the time of our study, Canada's most recent home-grown and notorious RWE lone actors were Justin Bourque and Norman Raddatz.

Justin Christian Bourque (1990–present) was accused of murdering three RCMP officers and injuring two others on 4 June 2014 in Monton, NB and later charged with three counts of first-degree murder and two counts of attempted murder (Brean 2014). Bourque was known for his anti-establishment Internet rants. To illustrate, his *Facebook* page portrayed him as a gun enthusiast and libertarian with an anti-authoritarian mindset, and his account was awash with pro-gun, cop-hating and liberal-bashing propaganda (CBC News 2014). His *Facebook* page also contained a reference to the widening gap between the rich and the poor, and an antisemitic cartoon depicting Jacob Rothschild with a hook-nosed, huge teeth and beady eyes (Terry 2014). Most interestingly, a *Globe and Mail* reporter found a large Confederate flag in Bourque's mobile home (CBC News 2014).

Many have argued that Bourque was a self-motivated ideologue, a lone actor, and had no ties to any larger organization (see Perry and Scrivens, forthcoming). Bourque used social media to educate himself on far-right libertarian preoccupations, such as the "militarization" of police, anti-authoritarianism, survivalism, "crownless kings", confiscation of guns and Canada's readiness for a Russian invasion (Brean 2014). Sophie Bourque, the sister of Bourque, claims that he battled with substance abuse issues (i.e. alcoholism and drug use), relationship troubles and job insecurity, and in turn was paranoid that someone would take away his guns (Carlson 2014).

Norman Walter Raddatz (1973–2015), was the alleged shooter in the death of an Edmonton police officer on 8 June 2015. When members of the hate crime unit visited Raddatz's home to serve him with an arrest warrant and court documents, the man refused to come outside. Officers left to get a Feeney warrant and returned with a battering ram, all in an effort to gain access to the West Edmonton residence. Upon entry, the suspect unloaded a high-powered rifle on officers, killing Constable Daniel Woodall, 35, on scene and injuring 38-year-old Sgt. Jason Harley. The house was later set ablaze, most likely by the suspect, and his body was located in the basement of his burned-out home (CBC News 2015).

Police officers had no reason to foresee such an act of violence, as Raddatz was merely being served with court documents relating to criminal harassment charges and an arrest warrant for by-law infractions (Canadian Press 2015). The paranoid man was suspected of harassing a local Jewish man and his family for a year-and-a-half, intimidating them with increasingly hateful and violent messages (Simons 2015). Raddatz was also known as "Dino Stomper" on *Facebook*, and he had a lengthy criminal record of hate-related offenses. However, he did not have a significant criminal record beyond the harassment charges, and it is unclear whether he was affiliated with a particular RWE group. Still, he was clearly an antisemite, anti-government homophobe, posting hateful messages about "sodomites" and "f-bomb Jews", and sharing crude jokes about the film "Brokeback Mountain". Public Safety Minister Steven Blaney described the lone-offender as a member of the extreme right (Kornik 2015), and an individual who was battling alcoholism and depression. Raddatz had recently been divorced, lost his business and motor home and was in the process of losing his bungalow (Canadian Press 2015).

Distribution of Right-Wing Extremist Groups

The findings of our project highlight the importance of examining the Canadian RWE movement on a national rather than local scale. Locally, study participants generally had some—albeit limited—sense of the level of RWE activity in their communities or their regions. Few people were able to comment on the national or even provincial distribution of related groups. In short, they were unable to identify anything that might be characterized as a "movement". The necessarily myopic perspective had barred them from seeing the bigger picture. It is when we look at the cumulative data that we can see that the presence of RWE activists is much more diffuse and that they are much more numerous than any of the study participants thought to be the case. Drawing on the expertise of those in the field, media reports and social media

Table 2.1 Distribution of right-wing extremist groups in Canada[a]

Region	Estimated number of groups	Estimated number of members per group	Target community
Maritimes	6–8	10–15	Aboriginal Black
Quebec	20–25	15–25 to 80–100	Aboriginal Jewish Immigrant Muslim LGBTQ
Ontario	18–20	3–5 to 15–25	Aboriginal Black Jewish Immigrant Muslim LGBTQ
Manitoba	8–10	5-10	Aboriginal Black
Saskatchewan	6–8	5–10 to 40–50	Aboriginal Immigrant
Alberta	12–15	10–15	Aboriginal Black Jewish Immigrant Muslim Asian LGBTQ
British Columbia	12–15	5–10	Aboriginal Black Jewish Immigrant Muslim Asian LGBTQ
Total	82–101		

[a]For a list of historical and contemporary extreme-right groups in Canada, see Appendix C

activity, we are able to provide broad estimates of activity coast to coast, as illustrated in Table 2.1. We suggest that these are probably very conservative estimates given that our focus was primarily on the urban areas of Ontario, Quebec, Alberta and British Columbia. There is no doubt considerable activity in rural areas across the country (Fig. 2.1).

Fig. 2.1 Distribution of right-wing extremist groups in Canada

The data might not give cause for concern at the provincial level—after all, there are some regions, such as the Maritimes collectively, that see very little activity from the extreme right. However, in light of the connectivity among groups nationally that we discuss in Chapter 3, the combined significance of the findings is cause for concern. The collated data suggest the presence of at least 100 RWE groups across the country. What these numbers cannot account for are those who have been driven underground and remain off of the radar, or those lone actors who may not be visible at all. At any rate, in tracking all reported incidents of RWE activity in Canada (see Appendix B), the vast majority of activity was in south-western Ontario, southern Quebec, as well as southern Alberta.

Nature and Threat of Right-Wing Extremist Violence

We were also able to piece together a picture of the nature of the violence associated with Canadian RWEs during the time of our fieldwork. It was relatively consistent across the country. It tended to involve sporadic, largely unplanned and opportunistic attacks. The perpetrators would say that it is reactive violence—that they were provoked by the behaviours or speech of their victims. RWE violence in Canada, then, does not much resemble its counterpart in the United States or in Europe, where it can be highly methodical and well planned. Moreover, it tends to be individualistic rather than collective. Both the perpetrators and the intended targets are individuals, or small groups of 2–4 for the most part. Rare are the sorts of conspiracies like those uncovered in the United States, where plans are laid to bomb or burn synagogues, or mosques, for example. However, this is not to say that there is no threat. While RWE in Canada did not at the time involve mass violence, it is nonetheless part of the fabric of the lives of its diverse targets. It is a consistent threat of which Canada's diverse communities are very much aware (Perry and Alvi 2011). Moreover, the very unpredictability of violence here may make it all the more disturbing. It is difficult to assess precisely when an attack might occur, or what might motivate it. It is especially challenging, then, to anticipate or counter the violence. In addition, online messaging on web-forums such as *Stormfront* does tend to highlight the calls for violent responses to perceived threats, so the potential is very real.

It is important to distinguish between the types of criminality and violence in which RWEs engage. As a meta-analysis by Gruenewald et al. (2009) reveals, RWEs is typically involved in a broad array of crimes including violent and non-violent crimes, and ideological and non-ideological crimes. In the current study, we found that, generally speaking, the criminality of RWE individuals and groups fall into 3 clusters: (1) non-violent crime; (2) criminal violence; and (3) extremist violence. Largely as a result of their connections to criminal groups and organizations (discussed more fully below), some RWE groups engage in profit-motivated crimes—drug dealing, in particular. This was the case with the *White Boys Posse* in Alberta, for example. Established as a neo-Nazi group, the members drifted into drug dealing, and in fact ultimately transitioned into what was allegedly a drug gang. There are also occasional forays into armed robbery, as was the case for alleged neo-Nazis Ian Michael Butz, 28, and his brother Jason Avery Butz, 26, who were suspected in two armed roberies at a gas station and a convenience store in the Peace River region of Alberta in 2011 (CBC News British Columbia 2011).

More common were forms of criminal violence. Typically, the violence involved brutal beatings, with fists, boots, baseball bats and other similar weapons. Knives were occasionally wielded, while guns were rare. There were several cases involving pipe bombs and arson. For example, in Fort St. John, BC in 2009, Peter Houston, known for his involvement in the Canadian racist movement, was convicted of building a potentially deadly pipe bomb that was planted in a highway restroom in north-eastern BC (Anti-Racist Canada 2014; CBC News British Columbia 2009). Arson was among the charges against Tony Laviolette, a 19-year-old neo-Nazi who was convicted in Charlottetown, PE in 2007 for setting fire to a building and a vacant home, and for three break and enters, including one at a skating rink which he vandalized with a swastika and racial slurs (Anti-Racist Canada 2014; CBC News 2007a; Mayne 2007).

A considerable amount of the violence that RWE individuals and groups engage in seems to be unrelated to their ideological positions. Rather, it is random brutality, apparently for its own sake. A case in 2010 in Calgary, AB saw 55-year-old Dave Burns—known as "The Nazi" and white supremacist around his office—walk into his workplace and started shooting, killing a co-worker and himself. No ideological motive for the attack was reported (Anti-Racist Canada 2014; CBC News Edmonton 2010). Apparently even more common is retaliatory violence within or across RWE groups, as in Calgary in 2009, when Tyler Sturrup, a member of *Western European Bloodlines (WEB)*, and Carolyne Kwatiek, a white nationalist, were targets of two home-made pipe bombs allegedly planted by 17-year-old *Aryan Guard* founder Kyle McKee (Anti-Racist Canada 2014; Canoe.ca 2010). Similarly, Jessie Lajoie, a former *Aryan Guard* member, was charged with aggravated assault, disguise with intent and conspiracy for his alleged attack on a victim presumed to be affiliated with *Blood & Honour*, in 2013 in Kitchener, ON.

However, most disturbing—and relevant here—is violence targeting racialized, religious and gender minorities. Extremist violence was widespread, with particular concentration in Alberta, southern BC and western Ontario. It is puzzling, then, that so little attention is paid to the patterns of RWE violence in Canada. As Vidhya Ramalingham (2014: 4)—previously from the *Institute for Strategic Dialogue (ISD)* and currently with *Moonshot CVE*—asserts,

> While high-profile and high-impact events hit the headlines, the bulk of the threat posed by the far right is felt through smaller-scale localized harassment, bullying and hate crime by extremists targeting minority communities. These kinds of incidences often go undetected, and indeed they are hard to quantify. They manifest in the sectioning off of some local areas as no-go zones for ethnic minorities, graffiti of far-right symbols on mosques and synagogues, or threats received by individual members of the community.

There is some variability in the targets of RWE violence in Canada. In line with the prevailing Christian Identity influence, the targets of both verbal and physical attacks are predominantly Muslims, Jews and people of colour, Afro-Canadians, Asians and South Asians especially. In the Western provinces, Aboriginal individuals and communities are common targets. In all areas, members of LGBTQ communities may also be at risk. An extensive list of such incidents is included in Appendix B; we offer just one illustrative example here. In 2008, a 17-year-old *Aryan Guard* member attacked a 26-year-old Japanese woman in Calgary, AB. The youth first made disparaging comments about Asians and then followed her as she left a bar, drop-kicking her in the back of the head with steel-toed boots, and continuing to kick her after she hit the ground (Anti-Racist Canada 2014; Calgary Herald 2009).

What is especially noteworthy is that there are several instances of "campaigns" of extremist violence targeting particular communities. St. John, NB was the site of several attacks against Chinese students in 2007. Initially, four students were attacked with baseball bats and wooden sticks. Days later, two more Chinese students were attacked, and a bus stop was spray-painted with the words, "Gooks go home". The assaults and vandalism took place in the same neighbourhood where Chinese students were attacked with eggs, ice and fireworks two years prior. A 19-year-old male and two youth with neo-Nazi affiliations were charged with the 2007 assaults (Anti-Racist Canada 2014; Canwest News Service 2007). A similar spree of racially targeted violence was reported in Montreal, QC in 2008, when neo-Nazi Julien-Alexandre LeClerc, 20, and a male youth attacked several people in a series of racially motivated assaults, first against a group of Arab men. After stabbing two of them, the offenders continued by insulting and assaulting two successive cab drivers, one Haitian and one of Arab descent (Anti-Racist Canada 2014; CTV Montreal 2011).

Aside from identifiable minority groups, two other groups are vulnerable to RWE violence in Canada: those involved in anti-racist organizing, and law enforcement officers. *Anti-Racist Action (ARA)* activists Bonnie Collins and Jason Devine have been singled out on several occasions (see Appendix B). Anti-racist activists and journalists we interviewed in Saskatchewan spoke about their own experiences of threats, harassment and violence at the hands of white supremacists. One described her experience in her workplace—a correctional institution—where some of her colleagues appeared to be, at the very least, sympathetic to local neo-Nazi activists. She was routinely threatened and harassed by these colleagues when it became apparent that she was involved in anti-hate efforts. At one point, she was told by her human resources department that it was "unsafe" for her to return to work.

The threat to police officers was most apparent in Justin Bourque's murders of three RCMP officers, described above. Law enforcement officials are also especially likely to encounter aggressive postures taken by sovereigntists. Movement adherents in Canada have not yet risen to the level of violence seen in the United States, where six police officers have been killed by sovereign citizens (Law Society of British Columbia 2012). Nonetheless, an RCMP spokeswoman is quoted in the *Huffington Post* saying that

> Individuals associated to this movement are a concern because some followers advocate violence to promote their views and this may involve violence toward police officers. There are officer safety concerns when dealing with followers of this movement during routine police interaction. (Moore 2013)

The same article refers to a series of "hard take-downs" in British Columbia. A case that made it to the courts involves Daren Wayne McCormick, who was convicted in Nova Scotia for uttering threats towards officers. His argument was that, as a *Freeman-on-the-Land,* he had freed himself of the *Criminal Code* and federal gun laws were soundly rejected by the court (Moore 2013).

The data we have uncovered warrant closer attention being paid to RWE in Canada. They suggest that the movement is active and is engaged in violent, targeted activities. The threat is not negligible. Ironically, Public Safety's (2013) *2013 Public Report on the Terrorist Threat to Canada* stated that no attacks by Islamist extremists occurred in Canada in 2012 (or any other year); nor have any Canadians been killed on domestic soil by *al-Qaeda* or similar extremists. Nonetheless, the report highlights a number of foiled or disrupted jihadist plots in Canada as well as the scope of those attacks that were being planned in many of these cases, warning that "homegrown violent extremists still pose a threat of terrorist attack in North America". The report also goes on to say the "homegrown violent extremism can be based on other causes"—aside from the *al-Qaeda* influences—"but is more limited in scope and scale than the activities of terrorist entities listed under the Criminal Code". While this may be the case globally, the opposite appears to be true in North America. An *Anti-Defamation League (ADL)* report in 2018 (Anti-Defamation League 2018) revealed that, between 2009 and 2018, 73.3% of extremist-related murders were committed by RWEs, and just 23.4% by Islamist-inspired extremists. In Canada, the data presented here provide stark evidence that Canadian extreme-right-wing adherents have also been responsible for ongoing violence domestically, including arson, assault and homicide. Yet the threat has been dismissed out of hand, thereby running counter to available evidence. The fact that the violence is perhaps more spontaneous does not make it any less dangerous or less of a threat. Indeed, several participants in our study suggested that the unpredictability of RWE violence is itself troubling.

References

Anti-Defamation League. (2018). *Murder and Extremism in the United States in 2018*. Washington, DC: Anti-Defamation League.

Anti-Racist Canada. (2007). *A Neo-Nazi Group in Alberta: The Aryan Guard*. Retrieved from http://anti-racistcanada.blogspot.ca/2007/12/aryan-guard-members-and-associates.html.

Anti-Racist Canada. (2014). *A History of Violence: 1970–2014*. Retrieved from http://anti-racistcanada.blogspot.ca/2011/10/history-of-violence-1989-2011.html.

Barrett, S. R. (1987). *Is God a Racist? The Right Wing in Canada*. Toronto, ON: University of Toronto Press.

Basham, P., Merrifield, J., & Hepburn, C. (2007). *Home Schooling: From the Extreme to the Mainstream*. Studies in Educational Policy: Fraser Institute Occasional Paper. Vancouver: The Fraser Institute.

Bell, S. (2010, October 29). Who Are Canada's 'Freemen'? *National Post*. Retrieved from http://www.activistpost.com/2010/10/who-are-canadas-freemen.html.

Bell, S. (2012, September 28). Judge's Scathing Ruling Against Alberta 'Freeman' Could Signal Clampdown on Anti-Government Movement. *National Post*. Retrieved from http://news.nationalpost.com/news/canada/judges-scathing-ruling-against-alberta-freeman-could-signal-clampdown-on-anti-government-movement.

Boeveld, S. (2013, March 12). Controversial Free Speech Defender Douglas H. Christie, Lawyer for Canada's Most Prominent Hatemongers, Dead at 66. *National Post*. Retrieved from http://news.nationalpost.com/2013/03/12/controversial-free-speech-defender-douglas-h-christie-lawyer-for-canadas-most-prominent-hatemongers-dead-at-66/.

Bowman-Grieve, L. (2009). Exploring "Stormfront": A Virtual Community of the Radical Right. *Studies in Conflict and Terrorism, 32*(11), 989–1007.

Brean, J. (2013, February 26). How Former 'Street Kid' William Whatcott Became the 'Deliberately Provocative' Spark Behind the Supreme Court Hate-Speech Ruling. *National Post*. Retrieved from http://news.nationalpost.com/2013/02/26/how-former-street-kid-william-whatcott-became-the-deliberately-provocative-spark-behind-supreme-court-hate-speech-ruling/.

Brean, J. (2014, June 6). Justin Bourque's Alienation Nurtured in the Old Confines of Social Media. *National Post*. Retrieved from http://news.nationalpost.com/2014/06/06/justin-bourques-alienation-nurtured-in-the-cold-confines-of-social-media/.

Calgary Herald. (2009, January 28). *Attack on Visitor Linked to Aryan Guard.* Retrieved from http://www.canada.com/calgaryherald/news/city/story.html?id=79a32d0b-7b3d-403e-8fb1-08512d8240b4.

Canadian Press. (2013, April 18). William Whatcott's Anti-Gay Flyers Case Won't Be Re-Open: Supreme Court. *Huffington Post.* Retrieved from http://www.huffingtonpost.ca/2013/04/18/william-whatcott-anti-gay-flyers-saskatchewan_n_3110097.html.

Canadian Press. (2015, June 9). Edmonton Police Release Details About Deadly Shootout. *Huffington Post.* Retrieved from http://www.huffingtonpost.ca/2015/06/09/edmonton-police-officer-k_n_7540386.html.

Canoe. (2010, May 19). *Purported Neo-Nazi Admits to Making Explosives.* Retrieved from http://cnews.canoe.ca/CNEWS/Crime/2010/05/18/13995161.html?cid=rssnewscanada.

Canwest News Service. (2007, August 10). Racial Attacks on Chinese Students Linked to Skinheads. *Ottawa Citizen.* Retrieved from http://www.canada.com/ottawacitizen/news/story.html?id=f3b7dbc5-a6d0-4553-872c-3aed9de90a11&k=80416.

Carlson, K. B. (2014, June 12). Sister of Justin Bourque Speaks of His Troubled Life, Paranoia. *The Globe and Mail.* Retrieved from http://www.theglobeandmail.com/news/national/sister-of-justin-bourque-speaks-of-his-troubled-life-growing-paranoia/article19131608/.

Catholics for Choice. (2011). *An Investigative Series on Those Who Oppose Women's Rights and Reproductive Health.* Washington, DC: Human Life International.

CBC News. (2007a, August 13). *Friends of Simon Wiesenthal Center Advises of Calgary-Based Neo-Nazi's Recent Activity.* Retrieved from http://www.newswire.ca/en/story/155641/friends-of-simon-wiesenthal-center-advises-of-calgary-based-neo-nazi-s-recent-activity.

CBC News. (2007b, August 27). *Klan Plans Fall Rally in Sask., Says Leader.* Retrieved from http://www.cbc.ca/news/canada/saskatchewan/klan-plans-fall-rally-in-sask-says-leader-1.690030.

CBC News. (2012a, March 18). *1 Killed in Surrey Stabbing.* Retrieved from http://www.cbc.ca/news/canada/british-columbia/1-killed-in-surrey-stabbing-1.1165838.

CBC News. (2012b, March 19). *Surrey Stabbing Victim ID'd.* Retrieved from http://www.cbc.ca/news/canada/british-columbia/surrey-stabbing-victim-id-d-1.1155340.

CBC News. (2012c, February 29). Finding the Freemen. *The National.* Retrieved from http://www.cbc.ca/news/canada/freemen-movement-captures-canadian-policeattention-1.1262159.

CBC News. (2013, February 27). *Top Court Upholds Key Part of Sask. Anti-Hate Law.* Retrieved from http://www.cbc.ca/news/politics/top-court-upholds-key-part-of-sask-anti-hate-law-1.1068276.

CBC News. (2014, June 5). *Justin Bourque: Latest Revelations About Man Charged in Moncton Shooting.* Retrieved from http://www.cbc.ca/news/canada/new-brunswick/justin-bourque-latest-revelations-about-man-charged-in-moncton-shooting-1.2665900.

CBC News. (2015, June 9). *Norman Raddatz Had Extensive Police File for Hate Crimes.* Retrieved from http://www.huffingtonpost.ca/2015/06/09/edmonton-police-officer-k_n_7540386.html.

CBC News British Columbia. (2009, June 9). *B.C. Man Convicted of Building Bomb Planted in Highway Restroom.* Retrieved from http://www.cbc.ca/news/canada/british-columbia/b-c-man-convicted-of-building-bomb-planted-in-highway-restroom-1.861498.

CBC News British Columbia. (2011, September 4). *Fugitive Brothers Arrested Near U.S. Border.* Retrieved from http://www.cbc.ca/news/canada/britishcolumbia/fugitive-brothers-arrested-near-u-s-border-1.1037138.

CBC News Calgary. (2011, June 1). *2 Men Charged in Deadly 2010 Attack.* Retrieved from http://www.cbc.ca/news/canada/calgary/2-men-charged-in-deadly-2010-attack-1.1017160.

CBC News Edmonton. (2010, March 13). *Edmonton Shooting Suspect a Racist: Co-Worker.* Retrieved from http://www.cbc.ca/news/canada/edmonton/edmonton-shooting-suspect-a-racist-co-workers-1.940915.

CNW. (2007, August 13). *Friends of Simon Wiesenthal Center Advises of Calgary-Based Neo-Nazi's Recent Activity.* Retrieved from http://www.newswire.ca/en/story/155641/friends-of-simon-wiesenthal-center-advises-of-calgary-based-neo-nazi-s-recent-activity.

Conway, M. (2016). Determining the Role of the Internet in Violent Extremism and Terrorism: Six Suggestions for Progressing Research. *Studies in Conflict and Terrorism, 40*(1), 77–98.

CTV Montreal. (2011, March 22). *22-Year-Old Found Guilty of Assault.* Retrieved from http://montreal.ctvnews.ca/22-year-old-found-guilty-of-assault-1.621919.

Edmonton Sun. (2011, March 8). *Edmonton Police Lay Charges over Alleged Hate Crimes.* Retrieved from http://www.edmontonsun.com/news/edmonton/2011/03/08/17540196.html.

Gruenewald, J., Freilich, J., & Chermak, S. (2009). An Overview of the Domestic Far-Right and Its Criminal Activities. In B. Perry & R. Blazak (Eds.), *Hate Crime: Issues and Perspectives, Vol. 4 Offenders* (Vol. 4, pp. 1–22). New York: Praeger.

Hoffman, B. (2003). *Al Qaeda, Trends in Terrorism, and Future Potentialities: An Assessment*. Santa Monica: RAND Corporation.

Hoffmann, D. (2013, March 13). Ultraconservative Bill Whatcott Clashes with U of S Students in Wake of Supreme Court Ruling on Hate Crime. *The Sheaf*. Retrieved from http://thesheaf.com/2013/03/13/ultraconservative-bill-whatcott-clashes-with-u-of-s-students-in-wake-of-supreme-court-ruling-on-hate-speech/.

Jarvies, M. (2012). How Neo-Nazis Think: Photojournalist Spends Three Years Following Skinheads' Lives (with Photos). *Calgary Herald*. Retrieved from http://www.calgaryherald.com/news/Nazis+think+Calgary+photojournalist+spends+three+years/7208326/story.html.

Jones, A. (2014, March 7). Ezra Levant, Sun News Host, Explains Trial 'Bombshell Moment'. *Huffington Post*. Retrieved http://www.huffingtonpost.ca/2014/03/07/ezra-levant-libel-lawsuit_n_4922214.html.

Kinsella, W. (2001). *Web of Hate: Inside Canada's Far Right Network*. Toronto: HarperCollins.

Kornik, S. (2015, June 11). Social Media Highlights Norman Raddatz's Hatred of Authority. *Global News*. Retrieved from http://globalnews.ca/news/2048798/social-media-highlights-norman-raddatz-hatred-of-authority/.

Lauder, M. A. (2002). *The Far Rightwing Movement in Southwest Ontario: An Exploration of Issues, Themes, and Variations*. The Guelph and District Multicultural Centre.

Law Society of British Columbia. (2012). The Freemen on the Land Movement. *Benchers' Bulletin*, 4. Retrieved from https://www.lawsociety.bc.ca/page.cfm?cid=2627&t=Practice-Tips-The-Freeman-on-the-Land-movement.

Leader-Post. (2007, August 25). *KKK Revived, with Strong Regina Ties*. Retrieved from http://www.canada.com/reginaleaderpost/news/story.html?id=326a8ced-8c75-4c1b-acdc-7bcd8e090ffb.

Mayne, L. A. (2007, December 20). Laviolette Given 30 Months. *Journal Pioneer*. Retrieved from http://www.journalpioneer.com/Justice/2007-12-20/article-1389852/Laviolette-given-30-months/1.

McDonald, M. (2011). *The Armageddon Factor: The Rise of Christian Nationalism in Canada* (2nd ed.). Toronto: Vintage.

McMartin, P. (2013, March 13). Doug Christie—Defender of Free Speech, Symbol of Democracy. *Vancouver Sun*. Retrieved from http://www.vancouversun.com/news/Pete+McMartin+Doug+Christie+defender+free+speech+symbol+democracy/8093191/story.html.

Michael, G. (2006). RAHOWA! A History of the World Church of the Creator. *Terrorism and Political Violence, 18*(4), 561–583.

Moore, D. (2013). 'Freeman on the Land' Movement Concerns Police, Notaries. *Huffpost British Columbia*. Retrieved from http://www.huffingtonpost.ca/2013/09/02/freemen-on-the-land_n_3856845.html.

One People's Project. (2009). *Bill Noble*. Retrieved from http://onepeoplesproject.com/index.php/en/rogues-gallery/14-n/128-bill-noble.

One People's Project. (2011). *Kyle McKee*. Retrieved from http://www.onepeoplesproject.com/index.php?option=com_content&view=article&id=663:kyle-mckee&catid=13:m&Itemid=3.

Perry, B., & Alvi, S. (2011). "We are All Vulnerable:" The *In Terrorem* Effects of Hate Crime. *International Review of Victimology, 18*(1), 57–72.

Public Safety Canada. (2013). *2013 Public Report on the Terrorist Threat to Canada*. Retrieved from http://www.securitepublique.gc.ca/cnt/rsrcs/pblctns/trrrst-thrt-cnd/trrrst-thrt-cnd-eng.pdf.

Ramalingham, V. (2014). *On the Front Line: A Guide to Countering Far-Right Extremism*. London: Institute for Strategic Dialogue.

Ross, J. I. (1992). Contemporary Radical Right Wing Violence in Canada: A Quantitative Analysis. *Terrorism and Political Violence, 4*(3), 72–101.

Sapp, A., Holden, R., & Wiggins, M. (1991). Value and Belief Systems of Right-Wing Extremists: Rationale and Motivation for Bias-Motivated Crime. In R. Kelly (Ed.), *Bias Crime: American Law Enforcement and Legal Responses* (pp. 105–131). Chicago IL: Office of International Criminal Justice.

Simons, P. (2015, June 11). Police Constable Fought to Protect Edmonton from Hate. Sadly, Hate Killed Him. *Edmonton Journal*. Retrieved from http://www.edmontonjournal.com/news/edmonton/Simons+Police+constable+fought+protect+Edmonton+from/11127592/story.html#__federated=1.

Speakers' Spotlight. (2014). *Ezra Levant*. Retrieved from http://www.speakers.ca/speakers/ezra-levant/.

Tanner, S., & Campana, A. (2014). *The Process of Radicalization: Right Wing Skinheads in Quebec* (No. 14-07). Vancouver: Canadian Network for Research on Terrorism, Security and Society.

Terry, D. (2014). *Canadians Hunt Gun Control-Hater in Cop-Killing Rampage. Southern Poverty Law Center.* Retrieved from http://www.splcenter.org/blog/2014/06/05/canadians-hunt-gun-control-hater-in-cop-killing-rampage/.

Toronto Star. (2011, July 26). *Gunman Saw Canada as Potential Junior Partner.* Retrieved from http://www.thestar.com/news/world/2011/07/26/gunman_saw_canada_as_potential_junior_partner.html.

Watts, R., & Dickson, L. (2013, February 26). Victoria Lawyer Doug Christie, Who Defended Zundel and Keegstra, Is Dying. *Times Colonist.* Retrieved from http://www.timescolonist.com/news/local/victoria-lawyer-doug-christie-who-defended-zundel-and-keegstra-is-dying-1.80575.

Williams, C. (2015). *Campus Campaigns Against Reproductive Autonomy: The Canadian Centre for Bioethical Reform Campus Genocide Awareness Project as Propaganda for Fetal Rights.* Retrieved from https://www.uleth.ca/dspace/bitstream/handle/10133/3645/WilliamsCampusCampaignsAgainstReproductiveAutonomyDec2014.pdf?sequence=1.

Young, K., & Craig, L. (1997). Beyond White Pride: Identity, Meaning and Contradiction in the Canadian Skinhead Subculture. *The Canadian Review of Sociology and Anthropology, 34*(2), 175–206.

Zerbisias, A. (2013, September 29). Talking with the Guru of the Freemen on the Land. *Toronto Star.* Retrieved from https://www.thestar.com/news/canada/2013/09/29/talking_with_the_guru_of_the_freemen_on_the_land.html.

3

Looking In: Group Dynamics of the Canadian Right-Wing Extremist Movement

In spite of the historical and contemporary patterns noted in the previous chapter, we have seen little current scholarship or systematic analysis on the state of the right-wing extremism (RWE) movement in Canada (notable exceptions include Parent and Ellis 2014; Perry and Scrivens 2015; Tanner and Campana 2014). Indeed, there is a limited perspective on the threat posed by members of the extreme right, despite the fact that some officials have identified this movement as a significant threat. For example, in the 2015 *National Security and Defense Committee* report "Countering the Terrorist Threat in Canada: An Interim Report", the Sûreté du Québec is cited as saying that the majority of their extremism files are associated with the right wing.

In the latter part of the twentieth century, the Canadian extreme-right-wing movement was the focus of a mere handful of studies. Barrett (1987) interviewed members of the radical movement and described the membership, ideologies and actions of its groups and fringe right figures. Ross (1992) measured the likelihood of right-wing

Portions of this chapter are reprinted by permission from Taylor and Francis: Studies in Conflict and Terrorism, Uneasy Alliances: *A Look at the Right-Wing Extremist Movement in Canada*, Barbara Perry and Ryan Scrivens, 2016.

© The Author(s) 2019
B. Perry and R. Scrivens, *Right-Wing Extremism in Canada*,
Palgrave Hate Studies, https://doi.org/10.1007/978-3-030-25169-7_3

actors to engage in violence using a chronology of events methods, and Kinsella (2001) interviewed members and provided a journalistic account of the web of hate. The same era also saw some accounts of the Canadian racist skinhead subculture, including interviews with violent youths involved in racist skinhead street gangs in Vancouver, BC (Baron 1997), and an in-depth understanding of racist skinhead culture via participant observation and interviews with racist skinheads living in a city in Western Canada (Young and Craig 1997). More recently, Tanner and Campana (2014) have offered an assessment of the radicalization process of racist skinheads in Quebec using social media scans and interviews with current extreme-right-wing activists; Parent and Ellis (2014) penned a brief overview of the current state of RWE in Canada, comparing it with radical right-wing movements in the United States and Europe. Interestingly, what emerges from the latter report is the implication that while the Canadian right wing has close connections to the US movement, it is distinct by virtue of being more "secular" in its ideological foundations. Hence, it is perhaps more akin to European movements, shaped as they are by the politics of immigration and multiculturalism.

The purpose of this chapter is to explore the endogenous factors that shape the development of right-wing hate groups in Canada, and that make them more or less likely to plan, engage in or incite violence towards targeted objects and communities. Informed by Black's framework (2004), we identify a number of key characteristics that shape group membership, sustainability and organizational capacity, as well as group or individual violence, such as saliency/immediacy of the perceived grievance, and organizational capacity of the hate group. Ultimately, we observed that RWE groups in Canada were connected domestically and globally via the Internet, and that members were often lured in by a number of what might initially seem to be "appealing" features of the groups. However, it is also the case that they were generally weakly organized, and prone to rapid phases of morphing and collapse.

Building Solidarity

Creating the Façade of Legitimacy

The visible face of the extreme-right-wing, the one that we typically envisage, is the tattooed, snarling, angry young white male. There is a great deal of truth to that image, as some of the most active and in fact dangerous representatives of the movement do offer a malevolent presentation of self. Selfies and other photos posted to RWE websites and social media accounts, for example, often feature images that reflect "tough guy" postures. Yet these are the storm troops, the front lines. Behind the lines stand others who seek to further their cause through slightly more subtle means, in a way that makes it more palatable, more acceptable to a public sensitized by a generation of discourses of equality, multiculturalism and diversity. In a word, hate is increasingly "mainstream", and thus increasingly legitimate. In part, this has been accomplished by toning down the rhetoric, and doing away with the white robes and brown shirts. But it has also accomplished by forging links with the ultimate authority: the state.

In Ontario, the 2014 election year was unusual for the slate of extreme-right-wing actors who entered the race. The Greater Toronto Area (GTA), for example, had such candidates as Jeff Goodall (*Edmund Burke Society*, a right-wing populist organization) running for Oshawa City Council (Anti-Racist Canada 2014), John Beattie (former Nazi leader) vying for municipal office in Minden (Humphreys 2014) and Paul Fromm, one of Canada's most notorious RWE, running for mayor of Mississauga (Mississauga News 2014). Even Don Andrews, founder and current leader of the *Nationalist Party of Canada*, an extreme-right-wing political party, threw his hat in the ring for Toronto's mayoralty (Hong 2014). As we discuss more fully in our concluding chapter, this was a trend that would be amplified in subsequent elections.

While the electoral success of these extremists was limited, they nonetheless made their mark at the level of political discourse; they injected a note of intolerance into political debate. As part of the official political apparatus, they created the appearance of legitimate actors with valid interpretations of the state of economic and cultural relations throughout the country. They were the visible and audible presence of RWE and intolerance within the machinery of the state. They brought ideals to "the people" in hopes of spreading the word and strengthening the movement.

This is part of a much longer trend—within some elements of the extreme right—by which the movement has sought to establish some "mainstream" credibility and thus greater appeal. As long ago as the 1980s and 1990s, former Louisiana *KKK* "Grand Wizard" David Duke recognized that legitimacy could only come with moderation and respectability, apparent in his exhortation for Kluxers to "get out of the cow pasture and into hotel meeting rooms" (Anti-Defamation League 1996: 36). So smooth was his presentation of self that Duke's often imitated style became known to journalists as "rhinestone racism" or "button-down terror". Rejecting the in-your-face aggression of traditional white supremacists, Duke instead adopted what Ridgeway (1995: 166) refers to as "the persona of the boyishly good-looking white rights activist". Who could be threatened by this benevolent and compassionate seeker of justice?

Web of Hate

The Internet in general and social media platforms in particular are important conduits for the dissemination of messages of hate and intolerance. The results of our project indicate that inexpensive, easy to use communication technologies enhance the reach of the Canadian RWE movement. For those who subscribe to RWE ideologies (among other ideologies), the Internet serves as a space in which users—from around the globe—typically find their views supported, reinforced and mirrored by others, rather than challenged by anti-racist sentiments, for example. In addition, users are able to freely communicate racist, xenophobic, sexist or other sorts of views that might be unpalatable in other contexts, especially in the offline world. During the time of the project, there were multiple e-venues, including social media platforms such as *Facebook*, *YouTube* and *Twitter*, that users could access for purely social purposes. Among these was *Stormfront*—which is arguably the most conspicuous RWE discussion forum (see Bowman-Grieve 2009; see also Scrivens et al. 2018)—as well as private discussion forums that were hosted by hate groups such as *Hammerskins*, *Blood & Honour*, *Volksfront* and *National Vanguard*. In addition to the social networking sites that are widely used by the broader public (e.g. *Facebook*, *YouTube* and *Twitter*), RWE discussion forums were among the most popular online spaces in which Canada's movement connected and communicated with like-minded others during the time of our project.

Nevertheless, it also became apparent that, regardless of the online space, the Internet was not only a "tool" or "resource" for disseminating ideas and products; it was—and still is—a site of important "identity work", accomplished interactively through the *exchange* of ideas. In other words, white supremacists' use of the Internet is not passive; rather, participants actively and discursively construct collective identities. The collective identity is one such illustration of what Adams and Roscignio (2005: 760) refer to as a "process that allows a disparate group of individuals to voice grievances and pursue a collective goal under the guise of a 'unified empirical actor'". It is, in short, key to the capacity of hate groups to mobilize both individually, but also collectively across the globe in ways that enhance their sense of "oneness" and unity.

Increasingly, social media platforms and networking sites allow ongoing dialogues among and between members of the RWE movement, which reflects an active engagement in the process of constructing a shared identity; they are expressive exchanges that affirm and reaffirm the stated position. In short, such exchanges announce the collective agency of the adherents. The carrier of white nationalist culture is managed within cyber-culture. It provides like-minded individuals with a meeting place in which they can define themselves as belonging to a distinct nationalist setting and position themselves within a shared racial lineage. It gives them a place to express and connect with others on the basis of national chauvinism. As this implies, the Internet allows this shared project to cross the global rather than simply the local or national landscape. It is readily acknowledged and exploited as a central node for extremists to exploit as they come together under the banner of "White Pride Worldwide" (see Perry and Scrivens 2016).

Given the geographical diffusion of hate groups across Canada, and indeed the world, Internet communication helps to close the social and spatial distance that might otherwise thwart efforts to sustain a collective identity across Canada's RWE movement. Without having to travel great distances or incur great costs, members in Ottawa, ON and Kamloops, BC, as well as Munich, Toronto, ON and Oslo, for example, can engage in real-time discussions, to share the ritual and imagery that bind the individuals to the collective. Virtual conversations on interactive platforms, as well as ready access to websites that contain radical content, strengthen the resolve of adherents by constructing a foundation for a shared sense of both peril and purpose—oftentimes by asserting the shortcomings of the Other. These platforms, on the surface at least, provide isolated and atomized members with the façade of cohesion and collective security, as well as a collective vision of shared fears, values and ideologies (Perry and Scrivens 2016).

Furthermore, not only does the Internet enhance the connectivity of domestic RWE groups with one another; the Internet facilitates global communication and the exchange of information and rhetoric. To illustrate, many Canadian RWE groups—during the time of our project—had direct links to American and European counterparts. For example, the international *Hammerskin Nation* website included a link to *Vinland Hammerskins* in Quebec. Similarly, numerous links to international groups, such as the *British Nationalist Party (BNP)*, and *American Creativity* groups, were featured on the *Creativity Movement Toronto* site, paired with regularly posted interviews with well-known "white racialists" from beyond Canadian borders: Matt Hale, Craig Cobb and members of the Croatian racialist band *Invictus*, among others. In addition, not only were RWEs from all across Canada frequent contributors on *Stormfront*, but members of the Canadian movement also hosted their very own sub-forum and online radio shows. Having said this, regardless of national affiliation, Internet communication allows RWE from across the globe to share in the celebration of a common race. The Internet and social media also facilitate ideological affirmation, recruitment and connectivity, publication and dissemination of materials, and an array of other strategies for RWE in Canada and worldwide.

Online platforms also have the potential to incite violence. Law enforcement and intelligence officers that we spoke with during our project often suggested that it was the online calls for violence that drew their attention to particular RWE groups. One officer, for example, voiced his concern about websites he came across during his investigations of the RWE movement, one of which urged its audience to "kill the Aboriginals, kill the Jews, kill the blacks, kill the gays". Other law enforcement officials in our project expressed similar concerns about the violent discourse that they too had found on RWE sites and further noted that the Internet is exploited by the extreme right as a mobilizing force. A cursory look at some of these spaces reveals that site visitors and members are called upon to put words into action. As but one example, a post on *Stormfront*'s "Events" page urges fellow travellers to "Get out from behind your computer, and go to the streets! Stand up for OUR people". Alongside the grandiose calls for *RAHOWA* or other armed battles are more realistic incitements to collective action. *Stormfront*, which was by far the most popular platform for Canada's RWE movement during the time of our project, has dedicated thousands of threads for both "Events" and "Activism" that invite adherents to join in celebrations of white heritage, to engage in local white pride marches or to attend upcoming white power concerts. Each of these activities encourages members to come together to express their racial pride and commitment.

By design, online dialogue spills over into real-world action. Some of this is relatively benign, as on "singles" sites that result in dates, even long-term relationships. *Stormfront*, for example, has an internal "White Singles" sub-forum, which has two main threads: "Talk" and "Dating Advice"—both of which generate considerable user discussion. Worth highlighting, however, is that the banality of such sites should not overshadow their importance. The promotion of "Aryan coupling" is, in fact, intended to ensure endogamous relationships and the subsequent reproduction of the white race, in line with the "14 Words" doctrine shared by so many white power activists: "We must secure the existence of our people and a future for white children". This credo—widely expressed in multiple ways online—provides the very foundation for mobilizing action around the protection of a global white identity.

On the other hand, RWE websites also feature less benign calls to action. Here, the posturing of aggressive adherents revolves around the active expulsion of the "common enemies" noted throughout. A *Golden Dawn* adherent, for example, is explicit about both the targets and strategies to be used against them:

People, fight against those criminal and ignominious plans and sleazy plans. Stop being cowards, rise as one man, shoulder to shoulder, fight them courageously. Go get the plutocrats and their subservient corrupt governments and organizations. Organize a wide front of military attack on them, get them, punish all of them, hang them, get the power in your hands, reorganize future economy according to other new principles. Kick all aliens from Europe and other similar countries back to their own continents. Europe is for Europeans. Crush the vermin. (Anonymous, October 6, 2013, http://golden-dawn-international-newsroom.blogspot. ca/p/our-identity.html)

The overlapping belief systems documented herein lead many hate groups to the conclusion that, through organized action, the white race can and must reverse the trends represented by the myriad forms of white racial "suicide", "homicide" and "genocide". Web communities such as *Stormfront* are also magnets for the most aggrieved white people, and media in which to rally around extreme-right-wing ideals, and to strategize around preserving them in the real world. Aggressive posturing around racial defence is common online. For example, as one user wrote on the *Vanguard News Network Forum*:

If as a White man you are not by now an extremist, then you are quite simply nothing but a cowardly traitor. JEWS KILLING GERMANS, NOTHING IS EVER ACHIEVED BY BEING 'NICE.' KILL THE JEW OR HE KILLS YOU. (August 8, 2014)

As the ultimate testament to their racial loyalty, such extremists offer a fight to the death—theirs or the enemy's.

Solidarity Through Music

Of particular value to the RWE movement is their music, now typically found online. White power music is that which is purposefully created and disseminated with the aim of promoting a white supremacist agenda. Moreover, as Dyck (2015: 159) noted, white power musicians use pro-white racist and/or European ultra-na-tionalist symbols and express pro-white racist ideas intentionally, creating music that they hope will draw new believers to racist and ultra-national-ist ideologies.

It is well established that this music provides sympathetic listeners with a sense of pride, dignity and pleasure that may not be found else-where (Cotter 1999; Futrell et al. 2006; Macklin 2013; Shaffer 2013). Naturally, then, white supremacists have long used popular music to spread their ideology, recruit, indoctrinate and integrate people into their subculture and reproduce the ideology of existing members (Dyck 2015). While there is clearly a profit motive, producers of white power music are perhaps most interested in sustaining the "movement" through recruitment of successive generations of like-minded activists (Kim 2006). By popularizing the ideology of the white power movement, this industry, its musicians and their anthems may have a pernicious influ-ence on its participants. In 2012, for example, Wade Michael Page, head of white power band *End Apathy*, started to "figure out how to end peo-ple's apathetic ways" and "be the start towards moving forward", shoot-ing ten people at a Wisconsin-based Sikh Temple, killing six and injuring four (Hogan 2012). This incident highlights the convergence of white power music and real-world terrorism by a RWE.

Canada was once the site of one of the most successful white power music distributors: *Resistance Records*. The enterprise was founded by Ontario native George Burdi who was at the time a key member of the *World Church of the Creator*, and part of the band *RAHOWA*, an abbreviation of "**RA**cial **HO**ly **WA**r" (Talty 1996). However, thanks to the Internet, hate music now circulates freely on RWE sites, *YouTube* and other similar social media sites. In fact, a quick *YouTube* search for "white power music" returns thousands of RWE videos with titles like "Spirit of 88 - White Power Skinheads", "English Rose - My Life - My Fate", "Blackout - This is My Country" and "Celtic Warrior - White Resistance". These videos are even hyperlinked to popular white power music channels, such as "Skrewdriver" and "Hammerskins", and are widely viewed and promoted by extreme-right adherents from around the globe.

During the time of our project, Quebec appeared to be the centre of the white power music scene in Canada. Tanner and Campana's (2014) exploration of the racist skinhead movement in Quebec identified at least 19 racist skinhead music crews, mostly in Montreal and Quebec City; however, one of their informants indicated that there could be as many as 45 crews in Quebec City alone. Similarly, a former extreme-right activist in our study noted that Alberta is a hotbed for a subtler form of white power music: black metal. While the song lyrics are encrypted and not overtly xenophobic, it is the pro-apocalyptic nature of the music that brings street-level racist skinheads and veteran members from the *Church of the Creator*, for example, into the same venue, bridging extremist ideologies. Band members dress in German military fatigue, display the Nazi salute and re-enact the fall of the economic system, a result of Jewish conspiracies.

White power music—both online and offline—is intended to fulfil a number of functions, chief among them being engagement and mobilization of movement adherents and, to a lesser extent, recruitment of new "brethren". Judging by the number of views, likes, shares, and the quantity and quality of comments posted in response to white power music videos posted on *YouTube*, for example, these aims may well be achieved. Consideration of one playlist alone (i.e. Mix-Combat 18—Terrommachine) highlights this. Quantitatively, of the 27 hate-inspired anthems on the list, there were 21 videos—nearly 80%—that had more than 100,000 views. "Working Class Heroes" had 1,189,162 views, and "Pulling on the Boots" had a staggering 2,206,827 views. They also drew in significant numbers of "subscribers", ranging from 138 ("My Life - My Fate"), to as many as 7448 ("Blood and Honour"). Likes far outnumbered dislikes across all of the videos by a wide margin. This was mirrored in the comments ($n = 203{,}418$). The featured songs certainly drew commentary from both proponents and opponents, although comments were predominantly supportive of the messages informing the music. Several corroborative "mantras" reappear across videos. One of the most common is the classic 14 Words. White Pride Worldwide (or WPWW) also came up frequently, as did Zieg Heil, Heil Hitler and 14/88 (14 Words/Heil Hitler)—all of which are defining slogans of the white power movement.

Not surprisingly, the comments were not all in English. Rather, support was posted in an array of languages including German, Polish, Swedish, Norwegian, French and Russian. In short, these *YouTube* videos seem to capture a large and in fact international audience of viewers/listeners.

It comes as no surprise that one of the dominant themes that arises in the videos is that of the need to share in a collective identity, specifically, the universal white man (Back 2002; Caiani and Kröll 2014; Perry and Scrivens 2016). As proclaimed in *My Life, My Fate*, "I'm a proud white man and they all know". What stands out is their allusion to a collective "we" that transcends national boundaries: "One for all and all for one, One for all and all for one" (*Einer für alle*). At first glance, it seems paradoxical that those coming together through their music should be characterized as white *nationalists*. They pledge allegiance to particular nation states: Sweden, Germany or the United States, for example. Each refers to their imagined nation as the great white homeland. The chorus of "White Power", for instance, is decidedly British:

> White Power! For England
> White Power! Today
> White Power! For Britain

However, otherwise diverse nationalists pledge a more profound allegiance to the mythic *white* nation, wherein nationality comes to be defined not by state, geography or citizenship, but by race. More than pan-American, or pan-European, the appeal is to join the fraternity of pan-Aryanism, wherein extremists assert a common lineage, traceable to white Aryan cultures of Western Europe. This is particularly evident, certainly in the very name of the song "White Pride World Wide", but also in its lyrics, with its reference to a nation that transcends local borders:

> We fight in the name of Odin! We fight in the name of Thor!
> We want a European Nation where we live in unity…
> Victory! White Pride World Wide

Interestingly, white nationalism is also tied up with notions of aggressive masculinity—a tough "guise"—in some of the white power music.

It is white working-class masculinity that is reflected in the music: "Proud to be a different breed, we're the working class, all we get is victimised, given loads of strife" ("He's a Skinhead"). In one of the few "proper" music videos, we see the band (i.e. *Working Class Heroes*) playing against a backdrop of images of hard-working white men—idyllic images that celebrate a glorious past for white men.

Lyrics celebrate typically dominant male activities as shows of strength. The very title "I'm Still Standing" itself speaks to nationalists' stamina. In that particular song, part of the focus is "recreational", with its references to berserking:

> I like to drink and I like to fight, I love to party on all night. I go to shows and I go to gigs, I love loud music and guitar licks.

However, more typical are the frequent assurances that they will not be beaten down, but stand proudly and fiercely against whatever threats come their way:

> You want to scare me, hohohoho! But hear my laughter. Hahahahaha!
> ("Hu Ha Antifa")

> An independent voice against my foes...
> I rock against the reds any chance I get,
> they wanna see me gone but still ain't yet. ("My Life - My Fate")

So, too, do several of the video and still images reflect this toughness. The independence and strength of RWE adherents is represented symbolically by such images as pit bulls, wolves, World War II Nazis, but also by the very stance of neo-Nazis or racist skinheads who are prominently featured. The CD cover that fronts "Alonzo", for example, shows us one of the band members yielding a baseball bat. The CD cover for "Burn the Koran" features a cartoon image of two unarmed but fierce neo-Nazis standing against a circle of what are presumably meant to be armed "Islamists".

Solidarity in the face of threats like the "Islamists" noted above is core to the musical messaging. Indeed, the forces that threaten the hard-won place of the white race are myriad. Communists, Marxists (a proxy for Jews), race traitors, immigrants and Muslims come under fire in the videos included in the selected mix list, both in visual form and in the lyrics; the porous borders that correspond to Zionist inspired policies of multiculturalism have allowed crime, violence, immorality and a host of other social and cultural threats to prevail. "This is My Country" refers to the "parasites" that have left a "stench that filled my valley's streets". It is accompanied by a still shot of what appears to be a neo-Nazi demonstration, with one adherent holding a sign that demands "Islam Out of Britain". "White Power" reacts against the impacts of immigration:

> I stand watch my country, going down the drain
> We are all at fault, we are all to blame
> We're letting them takeover, we just let 'em come
> Once we had an Empire, and now we've got a slum

As the title suggests, "Rock Against Islam" is a tirade directed specifically at the dangers unleashed by the spread of Islam in the West. It raises the usual images of terrorism, religious fundamentalism, foreign languages and accents, and dangerous cultural practices. The chorus, which is repeated eight times over the course of the video, sums up the common perception of Muslims:

> Number one threat nowadays,
> A religion so vile and dumb
> We won't yield for it's twisted ways
> Or for the scumbags that it's coming from…
> Rock against Islam!

It is the task of white nationalists, then, to join together to defeat the threats—foreign and domestic—that challenge white supremacy.

Connectivity

These common grievances, as portrayed in white power music, are the foundations that bring white people together within the movement and that sustain them. While some activists are drawn into the movement by "accidental" contact at music venues or online, individuals continue to be lured in by people they know personally according to the results of our project. Our contemporary focus on social media should not blind us to the persistence of face-to-face recruitment. Group members are often friends or associates—sometimes even relatives of potential recruits—prior to joining. Those already engaged in the movement may, over time, drop hints about "what's wrong with the world". Or, when their "targets" are experiencing personal, financial or legal problems, they may swoop in to assure them that their problems are linked to disturbing trends like non-white immigration, affirmative action or the extension of rights to previously marginalized communities. Recruits are thus encouraged by people they know and presumably trust. This may, in part, account for the apparent clustering of RWE groups in particular areas in Canada. For example, the *KKK* and assorted variants of *Aryan Guard* remain visible in the Western regions. A close cousin of the *KKK*—the *Creativity Movement*—continues its lengthy tenure with an active voice in Ontario, and racist skinhead groups are especially prevalent in Quebec.

What is the appeal, though, of these groups? Like so many other similar subcultures—gangs, Islamist extremists, etc.—RWE groups provide a place to belong. One officer in our study suggested that members are "lone wolves looking for a pack". Another officer described the process by which young men, typically, "try on different coats to find one that fits". He also characterized some groups as "anti-social social clubs" that provided a space to connect with others over beer, shared grievances and machismo. The ideologies that are introduced to new recruits provide a frame for understanding personal experiences. Their own employment struggles can be attributed to "immigrants stealing jobs"; their social isolation and failed relationships can be blamed on "frigid feminazis"; or their lack of identity can be blamed on the "multi-culti communists". The groups can harness recruits' anxiety, hostility, and aggression around shared experiences, and a shared identity. The careful crafting of "us" vs. "them" makes members part of something bigger than the self.

The notion of connecting with like-minded others plays out in other ways within the RWE movement in Canada. We referred above to the ways in which the exploitation of the Internet has enabled the building of a global network. There are a number of other important "connections" that shape the extreme right in Canada, again enabling a powerful sense of being part of something "bigger". Drawing on and building alliances with other disparate yet sympathetic subcultures enhances the ideological and strategic strength of the extreme-right movement. One of the most important points of engagement is with the military. The Canadian Armed Forces (CAF) host a number of RWE sympathizers, if not activists within their midst (Pugliese 2012), ranging from Cpl. Matt McKay's military scandal involving the death of a teenager (Farnsworth 1993), to the armed heist by Sgt. Darnell Bass of the *Canadian Airborne Regiment* (CBC News 1998). The highly publicized torture of Somali citizens by CAF members in 1993 is also attributed to perpetrators' affiliation with extreme-right ideologies and activities (Whitworth 2004). A Canadian report also warned of the increase in white supremacist membership within this country's armed forces. The Quebec-based extreme-right group *La Meute* (the *Wolf Pack*), which was established just as we were releasing our report in 2015, was founded by two former military men. The *Three Percenters* are also widely believed to include a number of active and former military and law enforcement personnel. Kazz Nowlin, founder of the British Columbia *Three Percenters*, posted on their *Facebook* page that "we are military ... ex military ... first responders ... police members".

Again, this linkage implies a risk associated with the combination of RWE ideology and the capacity for lethal violence. This should come as no surprise, as the two subcultures share some affinity, especially the hypermasculinity noted above, along with traits such as authoritarianism, need for "brotherhood" and, of course, engagement in violence. Indeed, a review of the New America Foundation's data set on homegrown extremists found that "military service among right-wing extremists is correlated with an increase in rates of violent incidents compared to those without military service" (Sterman 2013: 2).

While RWE groups may feed the needs of some recruits, the opposite is also true. There is value in enlisting members who bring with them the skills honed in the military. Johnson (2012) speaks directly to the purposive recruitment of military personnel to the extreme-right movement. Specifically, he argues that they target law enforcement and military personnel for their training experience (particularly weapons and explosives training), their disciplined way of life, leadership skills, and access to weapons, equipment, and sensitive information. (Johnson 2012: 79)

These skill sets clearly have the capacity to increase the groups' lethality, and from their perspective, their likelihood of success in the "inevitable" and "imminent" race war.

Equally worrying relative to association with "legitimate" organizations are the linkages between Canadian RWE groups and "traditional" criminal groups such as outlaw biker gangs and drug gangs. Law enforcement officers in Quebec and in Saskatchewan, especially, highlighted the apparent links between bikers and the RWE movement in those provinces. Police officers in different regions of Saskatchewan both observed that the remnants of the *KKK* in that province appeared to be attempting to strengthen their position by aligning themselves with outlaw bikers. Interestingly, more than one officer in the study suggested that white supremacists "age into" the biker gangs. They leave the ideological realm behind them, but find solidarity in a masculinist, potentially violent alternate subculture.

Indeed, biker gangs share similar subcultural characteristics, such as slang, language, dress and a propensity for violence. For example, a former extreme-right activist in the study described his relationship with outlaw biker gangs in Vancouver, BC as a seamless fit, noting how he—and others—served club members in various ways. He had acted as an enforcer for the club, collecting money from low-level criminals and drug addicts, and a doorman at the club's locally owned taverns. The risk of this sort of affinity is the mixing of far-right ideologies with the armed violence often associated with biker gangs.

Another trend that Canadian law enforcement—especially in Western provinces and Quebec—was observing at the time of the study was a frequent "morphing" from white supremacist to drug gangs. For example, the *White Boys Posse*, which was present in Alberta and Saskatchewan, was initially affiliated with white supremacy, as their chosen name implies. Established as a neo-Nazi group, their membership reached as high as 50–100, and by 2008 they were more closely aligned with *Hells Angels*. Consequently, the activity of this puppet group shifted towards illegal markets, as evidenced by police seizure of drugs, weapons and cash. They also became a very violent faction of the Canadian RWE movement, with criminal activity ranging from attempted murder to three gruesome and shocking homicides (Wittmeier 2012). A similar small collective in Saskatchewan—the *Waffen SS*—was thought by law enforcement there to be equally engaged in white supremacist, biker and drug gangs.

In Toronto, ON, an anti-authority element of the RWE movement has also been characterized by law enforcement in the study as closely linked to gang activity. The *Moors* follow a racially charged variant of Sovereign Citizenship that centres around issues and ideas involving African Canadian/American identity. A lawyer interviewed for our study also suggested that anti-authority tenets were "…being grabbed onto by what looks to me to be gang culture, gang and criminal culture. Nasty stuff". Officers who we interviewed in Toronto concur, arguing that the chapter of *Moors* who are active in the city is generally thought to be a "smokescreen" for illegal activities. Officers were of the mind that they are hiding their motives behind religious and *Freeman-of-the-Land* ideologies. They also suggest that the estimated 40–50 members are virtually all gang affiliated, and most have criminal records for violent offences, including homicide.

The Culture of Violence

Many of those like-minded individuals in the Canadian RWE movement share another significant trait: the propensity for violence. Several study participants—i.e. law enforcement, intelligence, former RWE activists—made reference to the inherent violence of the movement, in fact, the glorification of violence. This is also readily apparent from social media accounts, where images of fights, bloodied faces and weapons were commonly featured. Violence was also often celebrated in white power music and related videos. As noted in Chapter 2, this included both ideological and non-ideological violence. Indeed, it appeared to be common for members of the Canadian

RWE movement to ring up lengthy criminal histories both before and during their engagement with identifiable groups. Violent offences were especially common, running the gamut from harassment to armed robbery to attempted murder and murder. For example, Robert Reitmeier, co-founder of *Western European Brotherhood (WEB)* in Alberta, has a lengthy history of violent activity. His most recent arrest in 2011 was for a brutal homicide that did not appear to be hate-related (Humphreys 2014). With this sort of profile, it is perhaps not surprising that such figures are attracted to the inherent violence of the movement.

It is also the presence of this extreme form of violence that unifies and facilitates RWE in Canada. Members showcase their love for violence in an environment that is both accepting and laudatory. Fights within the group—often staged like "cage-fighting"—were frequently posted on social media platforms, testament to the machismo and toughness of the combatants. Additionally, many members of the movement, especially in the Western provinces, were thought to be involved with the Mixed Martial Arts (MMA) culture. Key informants in our study noted the extent to which MMA became a rallying point for a number of RWEs, providing both an outlet and training grounds for violence.

We also documented dozens of incidents of violence directed towards those perceived to be a threat, whether in racial or cultural terms. In 2009, for example, Lacey Dan Snyder, 22, and Dylan Alfred Trommel, 23, were charged in a racially motivated attack on 32-year-old Congolese student Valentin Masepode. The two confronted Masepode in a convenience store, calling him a "nigger" and telling him "this is our country nigger" before dosing him in the face with bear spray. Trommel, who had a swastika tattoo on his back, blamed the assault on the fact that he was drunk (Blais 2010). In early 2013, a neo-Nazi march in Edmonton, AB was followed by a spree of targeted violence against visible minorities. These kinds of attacks represent a forceful expression of the "us" vs. "them" mentality that binds the movement. They are stark reminders of the relative place assigned to groups who do not correspond to the ideal "Canadian".

A final variant of "defensive" violence intended to preserve the primacy of the Canadian RWE movement is violence between activists and their challengers. It was common to find calls to action on RWE social media, exhorting adherents to physically challenge anti-fascists. Indeed, the *Proud Boys'* fourth level of initiation demands the physical assault of a member of the *Antifa*. Officers who we interviewed in Western provinces, in particular, expressed their concern that this sort of retaliatory violence was a real risk whenever RWE groups made public their plans to appear on the street. Neo-Nazis frequently clashed with members of *Anti-Racist Action (ARA)* in Calgary, AB in the 2000s and 2010s. *ARA* members have also been targeted outside of public contexts. For years, members Jason and Bonnie Devine have been subjects of a series of attacks, allegedly by RWE assailants, in retaliation for their ongoing anti-racist activism. In 2010, two years after the couple's home was firebombed by suspected *Aryan Guard* members, Jason was brutally beaten with a hammer when a group of what were alleged to be *Blood & Honour* members broke into his house (CBC News Calgary 2010). Quebec police reported similar incidents directed towards the anti-fascist movement in that province. There, however, the violence tended to go both ways, with counter-attacks from both sides.

Destabilizing the Movement

Ideological Commitment

While there are some in Canada's RWE movement who, regardless of the consequences, are staunch supporters of "the cause", the results of our project suggest that there is an overall lack of commitment to the professed ideologies associated with particular groups. This lack of commitment, however, is not the case for all group members. In fact, there is a small assembly of those who, regardless of the consequences, have remained committed to the causes. To illustrate, a number of Canadian ideologues and propagandists, including—but indeed not limited to—Paul Fromm and a key figure in the movement who works closely with him, Marc Lemire, have dedicated much of their lives to spreading anti-immigrant sentiment, among other hateful rhetoric. This level of commitment is evident in the cases involving RWEs being the target of lawsuits and arrests. Founder of the ultra-violent *Heritage Front*, Wolfgang Droege (see Kinsella 2001), for example, and founder of the ultra-violent *Aryan Guard* in Alberta, Kyle McKee (see Gundlock 2013), continued to maintain close relationships with their so-called former neo-Nazi colleagues despite having to serve a number of prison sentences. Similarly, despite being deported from Canada and the United States for disseminating antisemitism and holocaust denial propaganda and later convicted in Germany in 2007 on 14 charges relating to the incitement of racial hatred, German publisher Ernst Zundel continued to correspond with other holocaust deniers while serving time in prison (CBC News 2007).

These cases, however, are outliers; within the Canadian RWE movement, it is uncommon to find someone who, over a reasonable period of time, remains loyal to the cause. According to one police officer in our project, many extreme-right adherents seem to be "trying on different coats". This officer and others further described how these adherents are typically youths looking for a place to belong and seeking explanations for their hardships in life. Also explained to us was how these adherents may—just as easily—have been drawn into other types of violent groups, such as street gangs or drug gangs, had the opportunity been available to them. This parallels Totten's (2014) research on violent gang members; the need to belong underlies the appeal of an array of local gangs (see also Young and Craig 1997). At a critical time in their lives, the presence and activity of a racist skinhead group, for example, may provide them with that initial sense of belonging. Having said this, regardless of whether individuals are drawn into the movement because of the radical ideologues, or friends in the movement, or the music, our findings suggest that potential recruits buy into the messages of hate but often for a short period of time. It is the initial appearance of solidarity that they find some comfort in.

In addition, other police officers in our project claimed that it is the sense of community, grounded in hate and not the hatred itself, that holds groups together. One officer even noted that, during her interactions with individuals who left the Canadian RWE movement, they consistently described the challenges of having to justify—on a daily basis—why they were racist, or homophobic or antisemitic, and they were constantly tired of having to manage those contradictions. To them, "hating was exhausting". A former RWE in our project expressed similar views, describing how he eventually realized that others were not truly committed to the cause, and that the movement was essentially a "sham". Other RWE adherents in our project noted that, while in many ways it was the radical ideologies holding the groups together, their events were much more social than they were political. In other words, it was as much the party aspect of the gatherings as it was the discussions about race and identity that drew members in.

Lastly, this lack of commitment to the cause—and the subsequent frailty of RWE groups in Canada—is further highlighted by the transitions like those experienced by the *White Boy Posse*. That is, for those who were searching for a sense belonging and a new identity, a supremacist ideology may have had some initial appeal, but it was the biker or drug culture—which included a violent element as well as a profit element—that was more attractive than the ideology.

Ideological Infighting

It should come as little surprise that the previously discussed "revolving door", as one officer in our project put it, has an impact on the sustainability of the RWE groups themselves. In short, most RWE groups in Canada have a shelf life of no more than a few months and certainly no more than a year (notable exceptions include *KKK, Church of the Creator* and *Aryan Guard* organizations). In fact, Canada's contemporary RWE movement, especially the neo-Nazi and racist skinhead groups, is plagued by conflict and consistent infighting, with members regularly jockeying for power and status. This mirrors the volatility of the white power movement in the United States, which has been described as fragmented and prone to ongoing tension (see Freilich et al. 2009). Similar to the US movement, many extreme right adherents in Canada will jump from group to group and, as a result, groups will oftentimes morph and splinter into new factions. A key illustration of this is the recent account of the *Aryan Guard, Blood & Honour* and *WEB* groups. The latter two were born out of the original *Aryan Guard* group, which was initiated by Kyle

McKee, after a lengthy conflict among its members (see Stop Racism and Hate Collective 2015).

Law enforcement officials in our project suggested that contemporary RWE groups quickly shift and transform depending on intra-group dynamics and in many ways are "moving targets". One police officer described it most effectively, observing that "they hate so much and so many that they start to hate one another – that is why they splinter". Other key informants in our project often referred to physical altercations within the RWE groups, noting that the hostility between group members was not only among their ideological foes, but among their peers as well. At times, this activity, according to a number of informants in our project, is designed as a form of "entertainment", wherein adherents will pit contestants against one another in unarmed combat. Violence also emerges naturally as a result of disagreements, usually fuelled by alcohol. In both cases, the after-effects of the violence have been captured in videos and posted on *YouTube*, *Facebook* and RWE sites.

At the extreme end of the spectrum are rival RWE groups targeting one another or acting in retaliation for some presumed slight. The list of these events is long and disturbing. In 2006, for example, a member of the Ottawa *Hammerskins*, Stephen Long, 22, was murdered by up and coming white supremacist Christopher Broughton, 29. In retaliation for an event earlier in the evening, Long was brutally attacked with a baseball bat while he was sleeping (Ottawa Citizen 2006). In 2009, member of *WEB*, Tyler Sturrup, and white supremacist Carolyne Kwatiek were targets of two home-made pipe bombs allegedly planted by *Blood & Honour* leader Kyle McKee (Martin 2010). In 2012, a woman was mistakenly murdered by members of the *White Boy Posse* when a hit was ordered on a man who left the gang (CBC News 2015). In 2013, a man who was allegedly a guest of the McKee-aligned *Blood & Honour* was attacked by former *Aryan Guard* member Jessie Lajoie, 24, with an edged weapon in Calgary, AB.

Transience/Mobility

Internal squabbles between some members of the Canadian RWE movement have resulted in a degree of mobility associated with the movement. In fact, we uncovered an extensive record of RWEs "jumping between western Ontario and Western provinces – Alberta in particular", as one law enforcement official in our project explained. In some of these cases, movement adherents were trying to separate themselves from other group members. In other cases, members would move back and forth between cities—or provinces—as a form of outreach, all in an effort to recruit new members or establish a new chapter. In the early 2000s, *Blood & Honour* in Edmonton, AB, for example, offered incentives for those who wanted to make the trek out to Western Canada to join their comrades in Alberta. In turn, a small number of adherents headed westwards with promises of paid rent and travel, and assistance with job seeking, among other assurances. It appeared, though, that financial incentives were much more attractive than the ideological message. A number of participants in our project made similar observations.

In most cases, however, the transience associated with RWE movement in Canada is connected to law enforcement officers "turning up the heat" in specific cities, according to several law enforcement officials in our project. As an example, adherents may move to Edmonton, AB when it becomes uncomfortable in Calgary, AB. When that becomes too risky, they may relocate provinces—to Vancouver, BC or London, ON, for example. Key illustrations of this transience include the biographies of Nathan Touchette of *Combat 18* and Kyle McKee of *Blood & Honour*. Both made news when they flew a Nazi flag over the men's apartment in Kitchener, ON. When they later publicized their intent to move to Calgary for one of the many construction jobs available, the mayor of Calgary publicly declared that they were not welcome in the city. Undeterred by this, the men moved to Calgary but their stay was short-lived. Touchette, within just a few months of arrival, moved back to Ontario, then returned to Alberta to live in Edmonton and eventually left that city under a cloud of suspicion regarding a number of assaults and arson. McKee, on the other hand, spent a number of months in an Alberta prison for assault, possession of a weapon, and disguising his identity. McKee also moved back to Ontario upon release, but he eventually returned to Calgary. There he co-founded the *Aryan Guard* and later *Blood & Honour*, as well as impregnating his 16-year-old girlfriend (Anti-Racist Canada 2007). On the whole, the Canadian

RWE movement struggles to maintain a collective presence, especially when members move on a regular basis, thereby destabilizing Canada's already unstable RWE movement.

Weak/Loss of Leadership

The results of our project revealed that the weakness of the leadership within Canada's RWE movement further destabilizes group membership. Indeed, the previously discussed infighting has a negative impact on group members' ability to mobilize and unify Canada's RWE movement. In short, current leaders are oftentimes challenged by other members in a display of hypermasculinity, or leaders themselves are not leadership material. A number of law enforcement officials and RWE adherents in our project highlighted this particular limitation, claiming that, in most cases, members of Canada's RWE movement are uneducated and unintelligent—even among leaders. Participants in our project further noted that movement leaders, despite their strong, tough and charismatic traits, oftentimes cannot articulate themselves—or are not strategic enough—to maintain group cohesion.

For the (very few) leaders who manage to maintain a level of stability, it is oftentimes the leaders themselves who—mistakenly—make themselves highly visible. In turn, they become "known to police" and fall under ongoing surveillance. According to a number of law enforcement officials in our project, it is common for Canadian police officers to have "a chat with the leaders" of the movement, as one study participant put it, in an effort to let them know that they are being watched. This level of pressure can weaken their position within the group. However, much more common is for leaders to eventually engage in illegal behaviour and find themselves under arrest. Noted earlier, Kyle McKee followed this trajectory; as the leader of *Blood & Honour*, McKee was arrested on assault and weapons charges and was subsequently chased out of Kitchener, ON by police activity. The group later collapsed when he was in prison because there was no worthy second in command. Similarly, the earlier trajectory of Wolfgang Droege, the leader of *Heritage Front*, parallels that of McKee's. Following Droege's arrested for his involvement in "Operation Red Dog" in 1981, Canada's RWE movement saw a decline in activity and adherents began to lack urgency and commitment to the cause. Yet soon after Droege was released from prison, *Heritage Front* once again became a significant component of Canada's RWE movement (Lauder 2002).

Lone Actors

In the light of the fact that many RWE groups in Canada are neither cohesive nor well organized, they remain a cause for concern. Tragic events such as the slaying of 77 civilians in Norway by Anders Breivik (Feldman 2012), the killing of nine black parishioners in Charleston by Dylann Roof (Capehard 2015), and in the Canadian context, the murder of three police officers in New Brunswick by Justin Bourque (Boutilier 2015) highlight the significant risks associated with RWE lone actors. In short, they are generally individuals who act on their own but may or may not be affiliated with identifiable RWE groups. While they are unlikely to engage in group activities such as marches or rallies, they do, however, find inspiration from the tenets of some element of the movement.

A number of key informants in our project indicated that, through various investigations, they were aware of local individuals who they believed fit the above-mentioned profile. These individuals, according to several informants, were "loners" who adhered to RWE ideologies and took their cue from related RWE websites. Also described by several officers in our project were those who went so far as to showcase white power symbols in their home windows, but that was the extent of their commitment to the movement. Officers from Quebec also described one disturbing case of an individual who, despite self-identifying as a committed racist skinhead, had allegedly never met any other racist skinheads; instead, he became radicalized through his use of the Internet. This adherent had a desire to generate enough money to purchase an AK-47 and "kill a bunch of blacks". It was unknown, however, as to whether he had the will or capacity to carry out this act.

The cumulative effect of this constellation of inhibiting factors is that the Canadian RWE movement appeared, at the time of the study, to be distinctly unorganized. The fact that a handful of law enforcement officers in our study refer independently to hate "groups" in disparate communities as something like "three man wrecking crews" says volumes about the nature of the organizational capacity of Canadian RWE groups. Interestingly, some of these groups have the appearance of being organized, often by virtue of their websites. Kevin Goudreau of Ontario, for example, manages a *White Nationalist Front* website (Bell 2011), which offers the appearance of being a hub for the group's activities. However, there is no concrete evidence that he is anything more than a community of one. Certainly, there are people who are attracted to his site, but not necessarily enough to take their beliefs any further. In fact, site visitors are as likely to engage him in a "war of words" as they are to support his views.

It is evident that Kinsella's (2001) now classic phrase—and title— "Web of Hate" continues to resonate, to the extent that the Canadian RWE movement has a greater capacity to connect and share than ever before. In many respects, the Canadian RWE "movement" of 2015 was no more or less fluid or heterogeneous than the racist skinheads interviewed by Craig and Young in 1997. If anything has changed, it is probably their online versus offline presence, and not necessarily their structure or lack thereof.

We noted an inherent tension within the Canadian RWE movement at the time of our study. As this chapter has likely implied, while the movement tends towards frequent morphing and in-fighting, this should not be taken to mean that they don't then represent a threat. Yes, it appeared that the movement was decidedly *un*organized and constituted by small loosely linked cells, lone actors, or as more than one police officer suggested, "three man wrecking crews". But on the other hand, it was also sustained, collectively, through their mobilization online and across subcultures. Moreover, we cannot discount the physical threat they pose to targeted communities, given their propensity for violence, highlighted both here and in Chapter 2. We remain optimistic, however, that the weaknesses noted here can nonetheless be exploited in order to further diminish their capacity, as we take up again in Chapter 5. Before that, however, we turn to examine the contextual factors that shape the capacities of the Canadian extreme right, that is, exogenous factors that constitute permission to hate.

References

Adams, J., & Roscigno, V. (2005). White Supremacists, Oppositional Culture and the World Wide Web. *Social Forces, 84*(2), 759–778.

Anti-Defamation League. (1996). *Hate Groups in America*. New York: ADL.

Anti-Racist Canada. (2007). *A Neo-Nazi Group in Alberta: The Aryan Guard*. Retrieved from http://anti-racistcanada.blogspot.ca/2007/12/aryan-guard-members-and-associates.html.

Anti-Racist Canada. (2014). *A History of Violence: 1970–2014*. Retrieved from http://anti-racistcanada.blogspot.ca/2011/10/history-of-violence-1989-2011.html.

Back, L. (2002). Aryans Reading Adorno: Cyber-Culture and Twenty-First Century Racism. *Ethnic and Racial Studies, 25*(4), 628–651.

Baron, S. (1997). Canadian Male Street Skinheads: Street Gang or Street Terrorists? *Canadian Review of Sociology and Anthropology, 34*(2), 125–154.

Barrett, S. R. (1987). *Is God a Racist? The Right Wing in Canada*. Toronto, ON: University of Toronto Press.

Bell, S. (2011, August 6). A Hater Among Us. *National Post*. Retrieved from http://news.nationalpost.com/news/canada/a-hater-among-us.

Black, D. (2004). Terrorism as Social Control. In M. Deflem (Ed.), *Terrorism and Counter-Terrorism: Criminological Perspectives* (pp. 9–18). Boston: Elsevier.

Blais, T. (2010, May 13). Racist Man Bear-Sprayed Student. *Canoe*. Retrieved from http://cnews.canoe.ca/CNEWS/Crime/2010/05/13/13929911.html.

Boutilier, A. (2015, March 15). CSIS Highlights White Supremacist Threat Ahead of Radical Islam. *Toronto Star*. Retrieved from https://www.thestar.com/news/canada/2015/03/15/csis-highlights-white-supremacist-threat-ahead-of-radical-islam.html.

Bowman-Grieve, L. (2009). Exploring "Stormfront:" A Virtual Community of the Radical Right. *Studies in Conflict and Terrorism, 32*(11), 989–1007.

Caiani, M., & Kröll, P. (2014). The Transnationalization of the Extreme Right and the Use of the Internet. *International Journal of Comparative and Applied Criminal Justice, 39*(4), 331–351.

Capehard, J. (2015, June 19). Dylan Roof: 'White Supremacist Lone Wolf'. *The Washington Post*. Retrieved from https://www.washingtonpost.com/blogs/post-partisan/wp/2015/06/19/dylann-roof-white-supremacist-lone-wolf/?utm_term=.13d019dc9898.

CBC News. (1998, December 1). *Soldiers Blame Airborne for Robbery*. Retrieved from https://www.cbc.ca/news/canada/soldier-blames-airborne-for-robbery-1.166500.

CBC News. (2007, February 15). *Ernst Zundel Sentenced to 5 Years for Holocaust Denial*. Retrieved from http://www.cbc.c/new/worl/ernst-zundel-sentenced-to-5-years-for-holocaust-denial-1.659372.

CBC News. (2015, June 9). *Norman Raddatz Had Extensive Police File for Hate Crimes*. Retrieved from http://www.huffingtonpost.ca/2015/06/09/edmonton-police-officer-k_n_7540386.html.

CBC News Calgary. (2010, November 8). *Calgary Anti-Racism Activists' Home Invaded*. Retrieved from https://www.cbc.ca/news/canada/calgary/calgary-anti-racism-activists-home-invaded-1.902197.

Cotter, J. M. (1999). Sounds of Hate: White Power Rock and Roll and the Neo-Nazi Skinhead Subculture. *Terrorism and Political Violence, 11*(2), 111–140.

Dyck, K. (2015). The (Un)Popularity of White-Power Music. In S. A. Wilson (Ed.), *Music at the Extremes: Essays on Sounds Outside the Mainstream* (pp. 157–177). Jefferson, NC: McFarland.

Farnsworth, C. (1993, May 17). Canada Investigates Reported Ties of Rightist Militants and Military. *The New York Times*. Retrieved from http://www.nytimes.com/1993/05/17/world/canada-investigates-reported-ties-of-rightist-militants-and-military.html.

Feldman, M. (2012, August 27). Viewpoint: Killer Breivik's Links with Far Right. *BBC News*. Retrieved from http://www.bbc.com/news/world-europe-19366000.

Freilich, J., Chermak, S., & Caspi, D. (2009). Critical Events in the Life Trajectories of Domestic Extremist White Supremacist Groups: A Case Study Analysis of Four Violent Organizations. *Criminology and Public Policy, 8*(3), 497–530.

Futrell, R., Simi, P., & Gottschalk, S. (2006). Understanding Music in Movements: The White Power Music Scene. *The Sociological Quarterly, 47*(2), 275–304.

Gunlock, B. (2013, March 12). A New Look at Calgary's Neo-Nazi Movement. *Vice News*. Retrieved from https://www.vice.com/en_ca/article/exkmvz/a-new-look-at-calgarys-neo-nazi-movement.

Hogan, M. (2012, August 6). Alleged Sikh Temple Shooter Was Frontman for White-Power Hardcore Band. *Spin*. Retrieved from http://www.spin.com/2012/08/alleged-sikh-temple-shooter-was-frontman-white-power-hardcore-band/.

Hong, G. (2014, January 17). We Interviewed the White Supremacist Running for Mayor of Toronto. *Vice News*. Retrieved from http://www.vice.com/en_ca/read/we-interviewed-the-white-supremacist-running-for-mayor-of-toronto.

Humphrey, A. (2014, July 29). Canadian Nazi Party Founder Running for Office in Ontario Township. *National Post*. Retrieved from http://news.nationalpost.com/2014/07/29/canadian-nazi-party-founder-running-for-office-in-ontario-township/.

Johnson, D. (2012). *Right-Wing Resurgence: How a Domestic Terrorist Threat is Being Ignored*. Lanham, MD: Rowman & Littlefield.

Kim, T. K. (2006, April 19). A Look at White Power Music Today. *Southern Poverty Law Center*. Retrieved from https://www.splcenter.org/fighting-hate/intelligence-report/2006/look-white-power-music-today.

Kinsella, W. (2001). *Web of Hate: Inside Canada's Far Right Network*. Toronto: HarperCollins.

Lauder, M. A. (2002). *The Far Rightwing Movement in Southwest Ontario: An Exploration of Issues, Themes, and Variations*. The Guelph and District Multicultural Centre.

Macklin, G. (2013). 'Onward Blackshirts!' Music and the British Union of Fascists. *Patterns of Prejudice, 47*(4–5), 430–457.

Martin, K. (2010, May 19). Purported Neo-Nazi Admits to Making Explosives. *QMI Agency*. Retrieved from http://cnews.canoe.co/CNEW/Crim/201/0/1/13995161.html?cidDrssnewscanada.

Mississauga News. (2014, September 17). *Paul Fromm: Mississauga Mayoral Candidate*. Retrieved from December 28, 2015. http://www.mississauga.com/news-story/4865617-paul-fromm-mississauga-mayoral-candidate.

Ottawa Citizen. (2006, April 18). *Murder Charges Laid in Death of Ottawa Man*. Retrieved from http://www.canada.com/ottawacitizen/news/story.html?id=a9f4eaa8-1f44-4217-b988-8ca489147158&k=38214.

Parent, R., & Ellis, J. (2014). *Right Wing Extremism in Canada* (No. 14-03). Vancouver: Canadian Network for Research on Terrorism, Security and Society.

Perry, B., & Scrivens, R. (2016). Uneasy Alliances: A Look at the Right-Wing Extremist Movement in Canada. *Studies in Conflict and Terrorism, 39*(9), 819–841.

Perry, B., & Scrivens, R. (2015). *Right-Wing Extremism in Canada: An Environmental Scan*. Ottawa, ON: Public Safety Canada.

Pugliese, D. (2012, June 17). Canadian Forces Warned of Possible Infiltration by White Supremacist Group. *Ottawa Citizen*. Retrieved from http://www.ottawacitizen.com/life/Canadian+Forces+warned+possible+infiltration+white+supremacist+group/6801966/story.html.

Ridgeway, J. (1995). *Blood in the Face*. New York: Thunder's Mouth Press.

Ross, J. I. (1992). Contemporary Radical Right Wing Violence in Canada: A Quantitative Analysis. *Terrorism and Political Violence, 4*(3), 72–101.

Scrivens, R., Davies, G., & Frank, R. (2018). Measuring the Evolution of Radical Right-Wing Posting Behaviors Online. *Deviant Behavior*. Ahead of Print, pp. 1–17.

Shaffer, R. (2013). The Sound of Neo-Fascism: Youth and Music in the National Front. *Patterns of Prejudice, 17*(4–5), 458–482.

Sterman, D. (2013, April 24). The Greater Danger: Military-Trained Right-Wing Extremists. *The Atlantic*. Retrieved from https://www.theatlantic.com/national/archive/2013/04/the-greater-danger-military-trained-right-wing-extremists/275277/.

Stop Racism and Hate Collective. (2015). *One People's Project: Aryan Guard Knew About Kyle McKee's Involvement in Pipebomb Attack*. Retrieved from http://www.stopracism.ca/content/one-peoples-project-aryan-guard-knew-about-kyle-mckees-involvement-pipebomb-attack.

Talty, S. (1996, February 25). The Method of a Neo-Nazi Mogul. *The New York Times*. Retrieved from http://www.nytimes.com/1996/02/25/magazine/the-method-of-a-neo-nazi-mogul.html?pagewanted=all.

Tanner, S., & Campana, A. (2014). *The Process of Radicalization: Right Wing Skinheads in Quebec* (No. 14-07). Vancouver: Canadian Network for Research on Terrorism, Security and Society.

Totten, M. (2014). *Gang Life: 10 of the Toughest Tell Their Stories*. Toronto: James Lorimer & Company.

Whitworth, S. (2004). *Men, Militarism and UN Peacekeeping: A Gendered Analysis*. Boulder, CO: Lynne Rienner.

Wittmeier, B. (2012, December 9). Money, Drugs and Violence: The Evolution of White Boy Posse—In the Wake of Recent High-Profile Killings, Experts Look at Criminal Gang Behaviour. *Edmonton Journal*. Retrieved from http://www.edmontonjournal.com/news/Money+drugs+violence+evolution+White+Posse/7673689/story.html.

Young, K., & Craig, L. (1997). Beyond White Pride: Identity, Meaning and Contradiction in the Canadian Skinhead Subculture. *The Canadian Review of Sociology and Anthropology, 34*(2), 175–206.

4

Permission to Hate in Canada

In the post-Trump/post-Brexit world, the line between mainstream and extreme is becoming increasingly blurred, more so than it was just three years earlier when we were conducting our study. In the short period of time since the Brexit vote and the election of Trump, we are already beginning to see scholarship exploring the ways in which these particular currents have further mobilized the right-wing extremist (RWE) movement (e.g. Huber 2016; Inglehart and Norris 2016; Komaromi and Singh 2016). This is an extension of a lengthy history of the parallels between "mainstream" xenophobia and "extreme" versions of the same discourse. Indeed, in the current climate, considerable attention has been drawn to the ways in which mainstream political and public discourse have paved the way for the re-emergence of a viable RWE movement—a pattern that was evident as we conducted our own research. It is not, however, a simple linear relationship between politics and extremism. Heitmeyer (2005) observes that both "underreaction and overreaction" to RWE movements can condition their growth and

Portions of this chapter are reprinted by permission from Springer: *Critical Criminology*, A Climate for Hate? An Exploration of the Right-Wing Extremist Landscape in Canada, Barbara Perry and Ryan Scrivens, 2018.

escalation to violence. Failure to respond to RWE can be read as ena-bling, while punitive responses can further marginalize and thus embit-ter adherents, resulting in more rather than less targeted violence.

In what follows, we trace the environmental factors that we were able to identify in the fieldwork as particularly important in facilitating RWE in Canada—in short, conditions that bestow—and challenge—"permission to hate". Reflecting back on the theoretical model addressed in the opening chapter, the hate and hostility that animate the extreme-right groups to which we refer are not to be understood as simple emotive states associated with individuals. Rather, the ani-mosity reflects the assertion of identity and belongingness over and above others—in short, it is about power. It reflects much more than the perpetrator's state of mind. In fact, it reflects the taken for granted, popular notions of identity and hierarchy. We must look beyond indi-vidual motives to unpack the "cultures of racism" or of heterosexism, or of ableism, for example, that condition the possibility of RWE groups (Ray and Smith 2002: 89). The groups to which we refer aspire to social power by which white, Christian, heterosexual males in particular assert a particular version of hegemonic whiteness and/or masculinity. The verbal and physical violence that they perpetrate represents a "will to power" by which the very threat of otherwise unprovoked acts of vio-lence deprives the victims of personal security, and therefore of freedom of movement and engagement.

Normativity/History of Racism

According to Welliver (2004: 251), "Communities have histories of hate". It is these histories, and their contemporary remnants, that lay the foundations for the emergence and growth of a racist RWE move-ment. In short, the persistence of RWE in Canada is generally indica-tive of the broader normativity of racism and other related patterns of exclusion extant in the communities infected with a RWE presence. Moreover, the RWE movement itself has been a part of that normative history of hate in Canada. The *KKK* is not new to Saskatchewan; the

Aryan Guard is not new to Alberta; and racist skinheads are not new to Quebec.

It is striking that we observed such a clustering of RWE activity in just a few areas: Quebec, Western Ontario, Alberta, and the lower mainland of British Columbia (BC). We engaged in several conversations about these concentrations over the course of this project, and the consensus seems to be that there is something about these areas that makes them fertile ground for the cultivation of organized RWE activity. Indeed, one anti-racist activist in our study argued that racism was endemic in the culture, especially in Western provinces, and was evident at all levels of society, across institutions. It is "simply an organized form of what lies under the surface – barely", he claimed.

There are both historical and contemporary foundations for the observable patterns of RWE noted here. This is probably most evident in the "histories of hate" experienced by Aboriginal people, grounded as they are in the legacy of colonialism. In fact, it is impossible to understand the current strains of anti-Native organizing outside of its connection with colonialism (Perry 2008). The broader history of oppression lends itself to modern iterations that continue to privilege the place of straight, white, Christian males. As one Alberta community activist in our study noted, the "prevailing sentiment" in many Canadian communities remains deeply racist, and in many places, deeply religious in a way that also has implications for views on abortion and homosexuality, for example. People still have "hate in their hearts" in a way that enables and encourages conservative values to dominate.

Degradation of the Other is on fertile ground in a culture with a history of—and indeed origins in—a worldview which saw non-whites as heathen savages, for example. Canada is itself a legacy of centuries of persecution of minorities, whether they are First Nations, immigrants, women, or "sexual deviants". Such a history normalizes mistreatment of those who do not appropriately conform to the preconceived hierarchies. That leaves us with a culture reflected in bitter letters to the editor in local and national media, and opinion polls (described below) that seem to tap deep divisions and resentment—fodder for Canada's hate movement. These are the sorts of attitudes that provide fruitful ground for the rhetoric of hate groups. They enable these groups to play on public sentiment, exploiting fears and stereotypes. In short, like other social movements, RWE groups are dependent on the resonance of their claims, that is, the extent to which their messaging is salient and meaningful to the intended audience (Benford and Snow 2000).

In some of the areas most affected by the presence of RWE organizing, there were readily manipulable processes underway during the course of our study. Western Ontario, for example, was undergoing dramatic demographic shifts. Some of the cities in the region, which had been homogeneously white and Christian, were experiencing large influxes of non-white immigrants. For example, one city that has long been host to RWE activity, London, ON saw growth in visible minorities from 8% to over 15% in just over a decade; it was home to approximately 15,000 newly arrived Latin Americans by 2011, and about the same number of Muslims (Statistics Canada 2011). Southern Alberta also saw considerable change in the early years of the twenty-first century. The increase in the visible minority population, between 1996 and 2006, increased at triple the rate of overall population growth. Over the course of the decade, the proportion of visible minorities there rose from 10% to almost 14%. A significant portion of this increase is accounted for by the dramatic growth in the number of Asian and African immigrants, rising by 44%, from 14,000 in 1996 to over 20,000 in 2006. This has had a particular impact on the province's largest cities, Edmonton and Calgary, resulting in high concentrations of visible minorities in both cities (Government of Alberta 2011). While the bulk of the population in these communities is generally either neutral/indifferent or welcoming, there is nonetheless a narrow slice of the population disturbed by these changes. One informant in our study referred to the "lack of preparedness for demographic change" as a key factor in laying the foundation for the emergence of reactionary extreme-right movements. Newcomers are especially likely to be singled out as scapegoats for young, unemployed and under-employed youth drawn to RWE, as they tend to bear the brunt of the hostility of extreme right groups who see the historical homogeneity of their communities challenged. Like this white nationalist on *Stormfront Canada* noted, many adherents

…firmly agree with this post (if the message is to stop immigrants from coming into our beautiful country) […] They seek to make our beautiful Homeland into another Afghanistan, Africa, and/or Mexico. (JIX, June 24, 2007)[1]

Antonio Gramsci (1971), the noted Italian Marxist, asserted that, in the ongoing struggle for hegemonic supremacy, the appeal of any rhetorical formation depends upon "previously germinated ideologies… [which] come into confrontation and conflict, until only one of them, or at least a single combination of them, tends to prevail" (pp. 181–182). This applies to the ability of hate groups to extend their ideologies of hate and intolerance to the broader public and to thus recruit into the RWE movement. In other words, in order to have an impact on the actions of others, hate groups must strike a chord in the broader community; their messages must resonate with their audiences and potential recruits. The message of hate disseminated by RWE groups speaks to existing popular concerns—this is at the heart of the legitimacy of their rhetoric. For example, a *Maclean's* poll report issued just prior to the project (Geddes 2009) underscores the persistence of widespread antipathy towards Muslims, finding that 54% of Canadians held an unfavourable view of Islam, up sharply from 46% in 2006. To put this in perspective, 39% held an unfavourable opinion of Sikhism; all of the other religions were regarded unfavourably by less than 30% of Canadians (see Geddes 2009). The sentiment reached its highest rating in Quebec—a province with extensive racist skinhead activity in particular. A 2015 *EKOS* poll highlighted "an erosion" in support of immigration, revealing that opposition to immigration had doubled since 2005, to 46%. In the same poll, 41% of respondents indicated that they felt there were "too many" visible minorities immigrating to Canada (Graves 2015). An Environics poll, published the same year, indicated that this sentiment was highest in Alberta, BC, and Quebec. Albertans were especially likely to think that immigrants were taking "their" jobs

---

[1]All author names were assigned with pseudonyms to protect user anonymity. All online posts were quoted verbatim.

away. Moreover, respondents in these same provinces were least likely to agree with the notion that multiculturalism was an important Canadian value (see Environics Institute 2015).

In the light of such polling trends, the vitriol of the hate groups is not so much an aberration as it is an albeit extreme reflection of racialist views that permeate society. The sentiments reflected above are exploitable by RWE groups in Canada. It is not at all uncommon for them to target immigrants generally and Muslims specifically in both word and deed, and to challenge the very principles of multiculturalism, which they see as the foundation of the ills associated with these changing demographics. On the *National Socialist Party of Canada* website, for example, the group proclaims that "multiculturalism is the displacement, marginalization, and eventual destruction of the host population – The White Race!!!"[2] An online post associated with the *Canadian Action Party (CAP)* found on *Stormfront Canada* captures the ways in which RWE adherents collapse the threats of multiculturalism, immigration and Islam:

> We are all in agreement that multiculturalism needs to end in this country and in those platforms, the multiculturalism act will be scrapped. It is changing the dynamics of our country and destabilizing the peace in our country. It is not right for any political party to gamble the safety of our current and future citizens by trying to bring in cultures/races/religions that historically have had major anomosity towards each other. We all know what multiculturalism and excess immigration is doing to our country and we're going to try and fix those problems […] I need everyone to phone or email the members of the Canadian Action Party and say your beefs about immigration and cultural issues i.e. language law protection, full face burka bans etc. (VH, October 25, 2012)

Immigration Watch Canada (IWC), which was especially active in the Greater Toronto area, has long been attuned to the public fears of what they see as the negative effects of immigration. The *IWC* website offers a daily diet of "news" and "bulletins" that selectively highlights those threats. Their mission statement reads as follows:

---

[2]See http://nspcanada.nfshost.com.

Immigration Watch Canada is an organization of Canadians who believe that immigration has to serve the needs and interests of Canada's own citizens. It cannot be turned into a social assistance / job-finding program for people from other countries. It should not be a method to suppress wages and provide employers with an unending supply of low-wage labour. It should never be a social engineering experiment that is conducted on Canada's mainstream population in order to make it a minority.[3]

Tapping into prevailing sentiments is a standard strategy for garnering support. It is important to note too that, even if a community may not see itself as a "hateful" place, its reputation as such is still important. An online post on *Stormfront Canada* reveals that one white nationalist, for example, views Quebec through this lens, seeing it as an appealing option for adherents like himself:

> To be honest, from what I have seen Quebec is the only province in Canada standing up to this immigrant flood. Seen they have the power and political power to protect French culture and they seem to be following the trend in France. There have been days recently that I have started to think about moving to Quebec and learning French [...] I am planning a business trip there in the fall and might take a look around while I am there. But Quebec is the only place so far in Canada I have heard of standing up to the Muslims and making them follow the rules and laws of this country. (Delta, March 10, 2015)

Several study participants suggested that Alberta also appears hospitable to RWE activity. It is that province's reputation that lures extreme-right groups and individuals there. Former RWE adherents in our study corroborated this, indicating that it was precisely this image that spurred several neo-Nazis and racist skinheads to leave Ontario for Alberta. Ontario had become "too hot" for them in terms of police surveillance, so they ventured to what they saw as the "promised land" in Alberta, assuming that it would provide a more welcoming environment for their brand of racism and xenophobia. Lund (2006: 181) notes that

---

[3]See https://immigrationwatchcanada.org.

Alberta is "infamous" in that "from the settler colonizing of the West through its history of racist extremism in both fringe and mainstream political movements, Alberta has long been a comfortable place for many who hold negative views on its ever-increasing diversity".

Political/Rhetorical Climate of Intolerance

Across Western nations, a "climate of hate" has historically been conditioned by the activity—and inactivity—of the state. State practices, policy and rhetoric have often provided the formal framework within which hate and hate groups can emerge. Practices within the state, at an individual and institutional level, which stigmatize, demonize or marginalize traditionally oppressed groups legitimate parallel sentiments elsewhere, including among RWE groups. We are concerned, in this chapter, with the ways in which the state, for one, supports the "hegemonic bloc" associated with white, heterosexual male dominance—also the purview of RWEs. Indeed, the state infuses civil society with ideals representative of this core identity, referred to by bell hooks (1994, 1995) as the "white supremacist, patriarchal, capitalist" bloc. To the extent that this is so, there emerges a climate which bestows "permission to hate", through such mechanisms as rhetoric, legislation, policy, the arbitrary use of "legitimate violence" and secondary victimization. The demonization of minority groups is reinforced by the racialized and gendered discourse of politicians, judges, political lobbyists and more. And the targets are diverse: immigrants, gay men and women, Muslims, to name a few—in other words, the very targets of RWE groups. As Perliger (2012: 146) expresses it,

> a contentious political climate and ideological political empowerment play important roles in increasing the volume of violence; thus, it is not only feelings of deprivation which motivate those involved in far right violence, but also the sense of empowerment which emerges when the political system is perceived to be increasingly open to far right ideas.

In short, RWEs benefit from—or are at least informed by—a political culture of possibilities. Much can be learned in this respect from recent

European politics. There, reactionary rhetoric is rampant in viable political parties, some of which are explicitly tied to violent RWE groups. In these cases, fervent nationalism and xenophobic ideologies freely circulate in the public marketplace of ideas, while also coalescing in the ideologies of the extreme right.

What is worrying is that, in some regions of Canada, similar trends were already emerging during the course of our project. At the federal level, the 2010s saw a turn to the far-right unlike any we have seen since at least the early 1900s. Several participants in our study pointed to the impact of conservative politics on the potential for RWE activity, suggesting that it had an empowering effect. Anti-democratic and anti-immigrant rhetoric and practice, and a retreat from the discourse of rights, for example, lend legitimacy to similar strains within the RWE movement. References by then-Prime Minister Stephen Harper to the threat of "Islamization" and to the wearing of hijabs as "offensive" stoked the flames of Islamophobia. The anti-immigrant website, *IWC*, echoed Harper's sentiment, suggesting that British trends were making their way to Canada, wherein "This Islamization programme is in accordance with the duties of Muslims to proselytize".[4] A *Facebook* post by *Patriotic Europeans Against the Islamization of the West (PEGIDA)* Canada included a picture of Harper, overlaid with the comment that "If I were still PM, thousands of possible extremists wouldn't be arriving right now". Among the favourable responses: "Can't believe, how stupid people could be to trade Harper for childish inexperienced Narciss. How all will regret later on! But the harm for our country might be not curable;" and "Harper was 1000 times better than Trudeau".[5] Yet another of his fans—on the *Golden Dawn* international blogspot—celebrated the observation that:

> Canadians traditionally wanted to accept anyone and everyone, but I do see a tide turning. At least the Conservative government has become a

[4] See https://immigrationwatchcanada.org/bulletins/bulletins-since-2010/page/9/.
[5] See https://www.facebook.com/Pegida.canada/photos/a.1534518543491882.1073741828.15 33411596935910/1663626637247738/?type=3&theater.

little more hardline on immigration and even revoked some citizenships. People weren't even living in Canada and were receiving government payments…. (Anonymous, January 20, 2013)

Harper's thwarted efforts to ban face coverings during citizenship ceremonies were also taken as evidence by RWE adherents that he was in their corner, or as one white nationalist on *Stormfront Canada* expressed:

> Lot's of folks are speaking out against the recent ruling on niqabs and burkas for example (being granted the right to vote, with a veil concealing your identity). It would appear that average, everyday people are beginning to wake up to the reality we face as western nation, and let's not forget: Germany, and especially Berlin, became a den of communist leftist debauchery following the first world war, arguably much worse than our current situation, before the people eventually woke up and decided enough is enough. Hang in there. (Magna, October 16, 2015)

Admittedly, during the period of our study, Canada did not see the sort of success of far-right political parties that were so evident in Europe. Nonetheless, the 2014 election year in Ontario was unusual for the slate of extreme-right-wing actors that had entered the race. The Greater Toronto Area, for example, had such candidates as Jeff Goodall, formerly of the *Edmund Burke Society*, running for Oshawa City Council, and former Nazi leader John Beattie vying for municipal office in Minden. Even Don Andrews, founder and current leader of the *Nationalist Party of Canada*, threw his hat in the ring for Toronto's mayoralty. Incredibly, Christopher Brosky, a former racist skinhead thought to have ongoing connections to Don Andrews, ran for Toronto city council. Brosky was convicted in 1993, in Texas, for the murder of a black man. Bob Smith was another candidate, running for Toronto mayor on an explicitly racist platform, as his website makes obvious:

> Who else is standing up for things that our cities and towns need: restoring white community standards and services, now reduced not just in Toronto, but in other cities, to Third World levels, with potholes

everywhere, infrastructure crumbling and no support from provincial and federal governments blowing billions on foreign aid, multicultural programs, and immigrant aid programs, to name just a few stupidities, as Canadians deal with unacceptably low levels of support for the needy and disabled, rising nonwhite crime, years of race-mixer/leftist civic neglect and the deeper digging into our wallets to line their pockets.[6]

While the electoral success of these extremists was limited, they nonetheless made their mark at the level of political discourse. They injected a note of intolerance into political debate or, as Stern (1992: 11) explained it "any success pushes mainstream candidates to imitate them [...] If [they] win even a minor election, they gain credibility, access to the system, and the ability to do better by raising funds from other extremists and those across the country who are too easily taken in by scapegoating".

As part of the official political apparatus, such extremists have the appearance of legitimate actors with valid interpretations of the state of economic and cultural relations throughout the country. They are the visible and audible presence of RWE and intolerance within the machinery of the state. They bring their ideals to "the people" in hopes of spreading the word. Consequently, as more than one key informant stated in our study, the politics of fear mongering creates spaces where it is acceptable to hate. In an environment that has seen the shrinking of funding for human rights groups, the elimination of s. 13 of the Canadian *Criminal Code* (i.e. hate speech protections), increasing restrictions on immigrants and refugees, and much more, the RWE movement finds its positions increasingly reflected in public policy (Mallea 2011; McDonald 2011).

One of the consequences of the demonization of minority groups on the part of politicians is that it finds its way into policies and practices that further stigmatize them. This has been readily apparent in Canada, for example, with respect to Muslims since the September 11 attacks.

---

[6]See http://www.natparty.com/bobsbeat.htm.

Fast on the heels of the attacks, Canada joined the United States and the UK in an ill-considered flurry of legislative activity intended to strengthen anti-terrorism legislation. These revisions allowed for an unprecedented extension of intrusive law enforcement activities on the one hand, and contraction of individual and collective rights on the other. A 2005 *Canadian Council on American-Islamic Relations (CAIR-CAN)* report documents extensive experiences in which law enforcement agents "approached" or "contacted" Arabs and Muslims, often with no explanation for the contact. Of the 467 respondents, 8% had been contacted—the bulk of whom (84%) were Canadian citizens. Moreover, 19% of those who had been contacted indicated that this was not a single event, but one among many.

The effect of such patterns is to draw a line between "law abiding" Canadians and "terrorist" Muslims. It reinforces the public perception that Muslims are questionable with respect to their loyalty to Canada, and with respect to their knowledge of if not involvement in terrorism. However unfounded the police attention may be, it nonetheless leaves a lingering sense of doubt; the pattern of state badgering of Muslims "makes people feel comfortable with their prejudices and grants those who hold pre-existing racist attitudes permission to express those attitudes and expect them to be taken seriously. It empowers individual prejudices and fuels popular fears" (Bahdi 2003: 314). And it empowers RWEs to direct similarly exclusionary language and action towards those Others whom they perceive as a "threat" to Canadian ways of being, as in the following post found on the *Golden Dawn* international blogspot:

> I am rabidly anti-multiculti, not because it weakens my race….but because, by definition, it weakens my culture. A culture I believe superior to those that would hack the genitals off young girls, sell their children into sex-slavery, force women to cover up, allow polygamous families, encourage a culture of taking from society and not giving, spread desease and filth, punish by death, those that wish not to believe in their so-called 'faith', issue 'fatwas', death orders against cartoonists, authors, singers, movie directors… There is NOTHING from any other cultures

that we, as western civilazation need to import…nothing! A mad-as-hell Canadian. (Anonymous, posted May 3, 2013)[7]

The political context in Quebec probably provides the richest illustration of the link between public rhetoric and RWE ideologies, particularly with respect to Islamophobic sentiment. Quebec has long been the "epicentre" for institutional challenges to Muslim identity. There is a lengthening history in that province that would restrict Muslim markers of identity. In the mid-1990s, for example, there was considerable controversy over schools barring women and girls from wearing the hijab in school. Such targeted restrictions, however, reached their zenith under then-Premier Pauline Marois, who first proposed her "Charter of Values" (originally "Charter of Secularism") in 2013. The provision would have banned the wearing or display of religious symbols among public sector institutions. That the Christian crucifix would nonetheless still be allowed in public buildings highlights the selective nature of the proposal (Montpetit 2016a). The rhetoric surrounding the Charter was "dressed in the guise of narratives of gender equality and secular values" (Ameli and Merali 2014: 39). However, it was also clear from the outset that it was targeted at Muslims and their "failure" to have assimilated into the "distinct society" that is Quebec.

It is no coincidence, then, that RWE groups informed by cultural nationalism are probably most visible in Quebec. More so than segments of the movement elsewhere in the country, Quebec hate groups define themselves through the lens of culture rather than race per se, and specifically Québécoise culture (Tanner and Campana 2014). Their rhetoric parallels that of Marois, focusing on the "threat" posed to the French language and culture by the increasing presence of immigrants and especially Muslims. There are countless illustrations of this on Canadian white nationalist sites, including the following posts on *Stormfront Canada*:

---

[7]See http://golden-dawn-international-newsroom.blogspot.ca/p/our-identity.html.

However, all the French speaking immigrants to Quebec include tons of black Africans, LOTS of Muslims from North Africa and Haitians. You can't spend a minute in Montreal without spotting a dozen of women covered from head to tow (sic) with like 4-5 babies yet to be brainwashed. (MTL1488, November 18, 2012)

Disappointed are you, well the garbage they chose to bring to this Country is sickening, looking for work, good luck. If your English forget it, if your black or Muslim its wonderful, I'm sick and tired of hearing how wonderful Montreal is … In any case if your black, Muslim or lord forbid a Jew then you'll fit right in with the rest of the garbage. (Brind, September 24, 2013)

Quebec is also the province in which a German-based Islamophobic group known as *PEGIDA* first made its appearance in Canada (Woods 2015). One of the Quebec group's members told the Toronto Star that "the incompatibility of Islam with the West is flagrant and that's the reason that *PEGIDA* and the Western patriots are rising up. It's not just to counter Islam but to say that if Islam doesn't reform itself, Islam needs to get out of the West" (Woods 2015). Other RWE groups, including the *Soldiers of Odin (SOO)*, had made their presence known in Quebec and in other cities across Canada, patrolling Muslim parts of the city and protecting residents from what they refer to as the "threat" to Canadian values and culture—i.e. Muslim immigrants (Montpetit 2016b). Indeed, these are telltale signs of the undercurrent in Canada, one that opposes the integration of the Muslim community, for example.

Weak Law Enforcement

When asked what they saw as the key factors enabling the emergence and sustainability of RWE groups in Canada, the majority of key informants in our study claimed that the most obvious factor was a weak law enforcement response. This was the sentiment even among police officers, regardless of whether or not they deemed their own department to be vigilant in acknowledging and confronting RWE activity. Members of community-based organizations were also critical of what they saw as police blindness in this respect. They feared that law enforcement was neither well trained nor motivated to confront the movement where it had a presence.

This corresponds more generally to trends in the policing of hate crime. There is a growing body of literature on the role of law enforcement in policing hate crime (Hall 2012), although little that addresses their engagement with RWE specifically. Considerable attention has been paid to ways in which racialized communities, in particular, are both over- and under-policed in this country (CAIR-CAN 2005; Comack 2012). Particularly important in the context of the sort of targeted violence that might be perpetrated by RWE adherents are the ways in which perceived police hostility towards such communities manifests in under-policing (Perry 2009). Selective enforcement is evident in police failure to protect diverse communities from hate crime (Perry 2009), in that police are thought to take less seriously the victimization of minority groups—less seriously than their offending, and less seriously than the victimization of white people. Police officers set the stage for bias-motivated violence by acts of omission, or failure to act on behalf of minority victims. Such violence is explicitly condoned when police fail to investigate or lay charges when victims report assaults motivated by bias (Hall 2012; Perry 2009).

Joshua Freilich, Steven Chermak and their colleagues have focused some attention on policing RWE in the United States. A pair of related papers revealed that police tend to underestimate the threat of RWE (Chermak et al. 2010), and that law enforcement training in the field of terrorism likewise minimizes RWE (Chermak et al. 2010). Kundnani (2012) and Lehr's (2013) assessments in Europe reach similar conclusions, both referring to "blind spots" with respect to how law enforcement and intelligence agencies focus their attention. Our observations in Canada confirm this trend. That terrorism associated with RWEs is largely absent from the public agenda here is evident from even a cursory review of the *Integrated Terrorism Assessment Centre (ITAC)* website, for example. The list of "Terrorist Incidents", while international in scope, includes only one right-wing terrorist incident: Anders Breivik's horrific attacks in Norway in 2011. Justin Bourque's 2014 murder of three RCMP officers, for example, was not included, nor was Alexandre Bissonnette's slaying of six men at an Islamic cultural centre in Quebec

City. Not until 2019 did the list of "Terrorist Entities" include any reference to RWEs or white supremacist organizations, and then added only *Blood & Honour* and affiliated *Combat 18*. Nor do the publications included on the *ITAC* site mention these extremist elements. Rather, the focus tends to be on global, and especially Islamist extremism. Public Safety's (2013) "2013 Public Report on the Terrorist Threat to Canada" stated that no attacks by Muslim extremists occurred in Canada in 2012, nor had any Canadians been killed on domestic soil by *al-Qaeda* or similar extremists until the two 2015 incidents (i.e. Zehaf-Bibeau's long gun attack on Parliament Hill, and Couture-Rouleau's vehicular attack on armed forces personnel in Quebec). Nonetheless, the report warned that "homegrown violent extremists still pose a threat of terrorist attack in North America". The report also goes on to say the "homegrown violent extremism can be based on other causes"—aside from the *al-Qaeda* influences—"but is more limited in scope and scale than the activities of terrorist entities listed under the Criminal Code".[8]

That most Canadian police services share this apathy towards the RWE threat was apparent in our interviews. This is probably most evident in rural areas, where officers suggest that "no one knows" the risk because no one is monitoring activity. But even in urban communities with demonstrable levels of RWE activity, there was a tendency to deny the presence and threat of activists in the community. An officer in one Ontario city that is a known "hot spot" for the RWE activity was worried that "we're not doing enough" to confront the known activists. Another officer in the same community stated outright that "until something happens, we're not looking at them". They also shared an example that illustrated the lack of responsiveness. There had been a gathering of 20–25 neo-Nazis, marching en masse through the streets, replete with White Pride flags and chants. However, there was no police presence to monitor the situation. In fact, neither the officer responsible for hate crime nor the one responsible for diversity was aware of the event, suggesting that they did not have their ears to the ground.

---

[8]Following our three-year study, Public Safety Canada has—in some respects—begun to acknowledge the threat posed by RWEs in Canada, nothing in their 2017 Public Report on the Terrorist Threat to Canada that radical right-wing ideology can fuel terrorism in Canada.

In addition to the neglect paid to any known RWE presence in Canada, some police personnel denied—at least publicly—that there was any risk whatsoever associated with the extreme right. They trivialized their potential for growth and violence. Even in cities where officers admitted to RWE membership numbering in the 100s, the threat was downplayed. Rather, they were much more interested in left-wing extremism, or more likely, Islamist-inspired extremism. Militant groups such as *al-Shabaab* were considered terrorist entities, but violent RWE groups such as *Aryan Nations* or *Blood & Honour* were not. At best, RWE groups were deemed "three man wrecking crews" or "losers without a cause", thereby minimizing the relative threat posed by the latter. Recent reports from CSIS, however, reveal that more lone actor attacks have come from RWEs than from radical Islamists (Boutilier 2015). Moreover, the list of incidents that we generated during the project, one which was in the hundreds between 1980 and 2015, is testament to the fact that these groups are active and are violent. Indeed, contrast this with the fact that only seven incidents of Islamist-inspired violence were recorded during the same time frame. Yet many of those responsible for policing the Canadian RWE movement dismissed them as a minor nuisance.

The possible exception to this lack of attention revolves around the *Sovereign Citizen* or *Freemen-on-the-Land* movement in Canada, which is even less organized, and less likely to be violent than racist skinhead activists, for example (see Perry et al. 2018). Nearly every officer with whom we spoke explicitly stated that this element of the movement was what concerned them the most. Many stated that it was "only a matter of time" before the movement would incubate violent adherents. It was also an area in which they had been most recently and widely trained. However, our subsequent study on related anti-authority movements in Canada found little evidence of violence among adherents within that movement (see Perry et al. 2017). One officer in that study suggested that they might be "…confrontational but not violent;" another observed that they might "…rant and rave, but won't cross the line to physical violence". That was not the general consensus among officers interviewed for this study on RWE in Canada. Again, there is an indication of misplaced priorities in some communities, away from violence that *is* occurring to violence that *might* occur.

This disavowal of the risk posed by RWEs in Canada is attributable to a number of factors. As noted above, it reflects the narrow training around terrorism and extremism in Canada. Yet there are other factors at play as well. Lehr (2013) attributes such trends, first, to the presumptive targets of RWEs, relative to other extremists, such as left-wing or Islamist-inspired extremists. Leftists and Islamists, he argues, are thought to represent a threat to highly symbolic targets such as the state and state (or other) elites. RWEs, in contrast, largely target those "at the fringes" (Lehr 2013: 201). On the one hand "we" are threatened; on the other, "they" are threatened. This is also embedded in the way in which terrorism is defined by security agencies. We saw this in the frequent binary offered by officers we interviewed, who drew a distinction between the "national security threat" posed by Islamist-inspired extremists and the "public order" threat they attributed to RWE. For many, this was the crux of their obsession with the former. This neglects the extent to which targeted violence is intended to terrorize minority groups, and in fact results in a distinct sense of insecurity and fear among those communities (Perry and Alvi 2011). As a result, it is also a threat to national values such as inclusion and respect.

More broadly, Kundnani (2012) traces the blindness to the correspondence between prevailing "security narratives" and those of the far-right extremists. The subject of those narratives in the post-9/11 climate run parallel in many respects. The "stories" embedded in contemporary counter-terrorism discourse, according to Kundnani (2012), may well resonate with RWE groups who exploit the same messaging to lend legitimacy to their own claims. The nature of those narratives in Canada is not so far off from those described by Kundnani in the British context. The "values-identity" narrative he describes is present in both Canadian counter-terror rhetoric and the positions of the extreme right. In particular, both set up "us" vs "them" postulates that enable anti-Muslim constructs in particular. Whether from the state or the extreme-right-wing group, the narrative

> ...introduces three protagonists (us, moderate Muslims and extremist Muslims), whose identities are defined in specific ways (whether or not they share our values), a disturbance (terrorist violence), an explanation

for the cause of the disturbance (extremism) and a suggested resolution (rejecting multiculturalism and asserting our values more forcefully). (Kundnani 2012: 13)

To the extent that Canadian law enforcement is primarily focused on Islamist-inspired extremism, they reproduce tropes of the "dangerous Muslim", just as RWEs takes up the same refrain. The following post on *Stormfront Canada* is especially telling in this respect, as it stresses the "terrorist threat" that the poster sees as inherently connected to current patterns of immigration: "As we know the government is flooding this country with them just for votes. And they would not want to upset the voting apple cart. They don't care if they blow a up or kill a few hundred Canadians, as long as they get the vote and hold power" (Delta, March 10, 2015).

Failure to attend to a RWE presence sends a dangerous message of tolerance. It empowers and emboldens groups and individuals who begin to think that they are under the radar and thus untouchable. Whether this is the reality or the perception is immaterial. If members believe that they can act with impunity, they will be drawn to particular locales. As rational beings, they flee communities where they are under surveillance for those in which they believe they will go unnoticed and unbothered.

Exogenous Inhibiting Factors

Strong and Visible Law Enforcement Response

In the previous section, we noted that a lack of police attention or response was one of the factors that allowed RWE groups to grow in Canada. However, the reverse is also true. That a strong and visible law enforcement response is vital to resisting that growth was also an opinion shared across the interviews. Strikingly, however, there was also a consensus that this was rarely the case. Nonetheless, in the Canadian context, there are two regions that we would like to single out as leaders in dealing with hate crime and extremism: BC and Alberta. Both provinces have developed teams grounded in collaborative, multi-sectoral approaches to hate crime and extremism province-wide. These are intended to facilitate a systematic and coordinated response in both reactive and proactive contexts. This is accomplished by integrating breadth of expertise (e.g. police, policy makers, victim service providers, community organizations), and of reach with respect to audience and clients (e.g. equity-seeking groups, police, policy makers).

These two teams are important and innovative because of the diverse nature of the services they provide, because of their strong engagement with the communities in which they operate, and because of their commitment to policy enhancement. The BC Hate Crime Team has both direct investigative responsibilities as well as engaging in community outreach intended to educate the public and other law enforcement agencies. The Alberta Hate Crime Committee has no direct enforcement role, but is very active in providing guidance and advice to law enforcement bodies that are investigating hate and extremism. It also has a significant community education focus. Both teams are notable for their inclusive memberships and commitment to community involvement. Both are also in the position to offer policy guidance at all relevant levels of decision-making. And, notably with respect to RWE, both services at the time of the study were very much aware of the presence and activities associated with the extreme right and engaged them proactively. Officers in both provinces spoke of their regular interactions with RWE adherents. A Calgary officer, for example, related his response upon receiving a call from an Ontario police service that a known RWE activist was moving from Ontario to Edmonton. The Calgary officer was able to locate the individual in question, and in fact immediately introduced himself just to let him know that the service was aware of his presence and his history.

We would add, too, that Quebec is poised to join this short list of regions actively monitoring and responding to RWE violence in Canada. The Surete du Quebec appears to have made considerable progress in identifying and engaging with RWE organizations in that province in recent years. Their counter-terrorism team was among the most forth-coming and informed participants in the project. They were very active in gathering intelligence about a wide array of RWE groups and activities in the province.

Several law enforcement officers across the country acknowledged the importance of "neutralizing the leadership" of active RWE groups. There were several examples whereby police became aware of RWE presence and/or activity and intervened. In some cases, this was relatively simple—for example, knocking on the door to alert potential RWE activists that police had them in their sights. This was intended to act as a deterrent to action by exploiting their paranoia, as noted by one police officer in our study. However, another means by which to "neutralize" the threat was to "decapitate" the movement by arresting leaders. As noted elsewhere, RWE activists are commonly involved in an array of criminal activities. To the extent that they are under surveillance by attentive law enforcement services, they are eventually subject to some sort of criminal prosecution. This proactive approach serves to rein in the adherents' tendency to openly engage in racist activity. On all fronts, then, there is much to be learned by other police agencies about how to think about their role in policing, preventing and otherwise responding to extremism.

There are also some individual police services that have proven themselves to be proactive in responding to the RWE threat in Canada. In Alberta, Calgary and Edmonton are making strides in this direction, as is York Regional Police Services in Ontario. Each has made some commitment to monitoring hate groups and hate crime more generally. However, this is not the norm. Most police services can learn a great deal from those agencies that acknowledge and respond to the threat. Primary among these lessons is the need to acknowledge the presence, activity and risk of RWE groups and adherents in their communities.

Presence of Anti-Racist Movement

An important source of support for both law enforcement intelligence and counter-extremist initiatives are community partners engaged in anti-racism/anti-fascism work. Indeed, one police officer in our project suggested that rights activists are crucial to counter-extremism initiatives because they "fill in the gaps where police can't go". The BC and Alberta hate crime teams have learned this lesson and rely very heavily on their community partners for intelligence as well as counter-extremism organizing and activity.

Some study participants suggested that Toronto was an interesting location for its apparent ability to resist the emergence of hate groups. Of course, there is considerable disagreement as to whether this was the case. Law enforcement seemed to reject the notion that the city was home to any locally active groups; community activists, and RWE group members in our study countered this assertion. Nonetheless, what is apparent is that there had been relatively few public RWE activities such as marches or demonstrations in that most diverse Canadian city during the time of our study. Participants attribute this to the remarkably rich diversity of the city—recall the mantra "Diversity Is Our Strength" noted above. These informants insisted that extreme-right-wing activity simply would not gain ground, and that there would be immediate media and social media "outing" of extremists. One officer suggested that symbols such as the "Redneck Pride Alberta Wide" image sported on a pickup truck in Alberta would be quickly vandalized in that city.

The community reaction to the *IWC* anti-immigrant pamphleting in Brampton, ON in 2013 and 2014 lends some credence to this proposition. There was zero tolerance shown for this; representatives from an array of faith communities and from different ethno-racial communities were united in their very public condemnation of *IWC*'s activities. The show of solidarity sent a very loud message that such sentiments would not go unchallenged. A similar fate befell *PEGIDA* on the occasion of their first planned march in Quebec in March of 2015. The protestors so far outnumbered the *PEGIDA* contingency that police encouraged them to cancel the event, and in fact, escorted them safely out of the area.

Anti-Racist Action (ARA) and *Anti-Racist Canada (ARC)* represent another illustration of direct challenges to the rhetoric and activities of racist RWE groups in Canada. They engage in ongoing monitoring and "outing" of individuals and groups, as well as directly confronting them in public. This is especially the case for *ARA*, which often gathers members and supporters when RWE marches or demonstrations are planned.

Both make it very difficult for groups to fly under the radar, and for them to gain traction at public events.

The work of the *Southern Poverty Law Center (SPLC)* in the United States provides a model worth emulating. Its former director, Morris Dees, has led dozens of devastating civil rights lawsuits against RWE individuals and groups. Among those he has managed to purge are the *White Aryan Resistance (WAR)*, the *United Klans of America*, and the *Aryan Nations*. Perhaps most notably, he led the case of Berhanu v. Metzger. The best summary of that case can be found on the *SPLC* website:

> In 1988, Tom and John Metzger sent their best White Aryan Resistance (WAR) recruiter to organize a Portland skinhead gang. After being trained in WAR's methods, the gang killed an Ethiopian student. Tom Metzger praised the skinheads for doing their "civic duty."

> Center attorneys filed a civil suit, Berhanu v. Metzger, asserting the Metzgers and WAR were as responsible for the killing as the Portland skinheads. In October 1990, a jury agreed and awarded $12.5 million in damages to the family of the victim, Mulugeta Seraw.

> In 1994, the U.S. Supreme Court refused to review Metzger's appeal, allowing Center attorneys to begin distributing funds from the sale of WAR's assets. The principal beneficiary is Seraw's son, Henock, who receives monthly payments from WAR's bank account. (http://www.splcenter.org/get-informed/case-docket/berhanu-v-metzger)

In Canada, similar efforts have been made to challenge hate and extremism through the law. Alberta's *John Humphrey Centre for Peace and Human Rights* published a report in which they profiled individuals in that province who had also engaged in landmark law suits, some of which involved RWE actors (Clement and Vaugeois 2013). More specifically, attorney Richard Warman has attempted to emulate Dees's strategy. He has used the recently repealed s. 13 of the Human Rights Act to launch legal actions against online hate speech. Early in 2014, for example, in Warman v. Fournier, the Ontario Superior Court found that "The continued publication of libellous material would cause irreparable harm to the plaintiff's reputation and prohibited material has already been found to constitute libel". In consequence, the relevant website, freedominion.ca, was temporarily taken down.

However, there is a fine balance to be struck here. Sometimes, these same strategies can be counter-productive. The legal route, for example, can energize the opposition rather than quelling it. Some study participants feared that flashy trials could have the effect of giving the RWE activists a soapbox from which to preach. Warman's efforts, for instance, have mobilized Ezra Levant into ongoing public diatribes on air and in print. Direct confrontations like those associated with *ARA* can and have induced violence on site as well as subsequent retaliatory violence. Activists engaged in counter-reactive measures need to be fully aware of the potential impacts of their own actions.

Community Resiliency: Lethbridge

We want to close this chapter with something of a case study in community resiliency. On the second research trip to Alberta, we included Lethbridge in the plans, having read and heard that this was one of many small Alberta towns with a deeply embedded history of racism (see Lund 2006). Here, we thought, would be a community ripe for the picking at the hands of extreme-right-wing activists. To our surprise, we found quite the opposite. This was instead a small city that had managed to overcome that history, face racism head-on, and run it out of town.

First, a little background on the community. Lethbridge sits close to the US border, just over 100 kilometres north of Montana. It has a largely white population, numbering just under 100,000. There are still large First Nations and Metis populations in the city—around 5000, or 6%. Nearly 3% of the population is Asian. It is only recently that demographics have shifted noticeably, with a small influx of African immigrants, largely Bhutanese and Somali. There are now more than 30 distinct ethnic communities in the city. More than one study participant—both from Lethbridge and elsewhere—referred to Lethbridge with such labels as the "Canadian Bible Belt", or "Mississippi of Canada". The first refers to the heavy concentration of traditionally conservative denominations such as Catholics, Hutterites and Mennonites. The reference to the "Mississippi of Canada" evokes the history of segregation and racism that has blemished the image of this southern Alberta community (Lund 2006).

These characteristics would seem primed to weave a tapestry with threads of hate. The proximity of Montana and Idaho, with their vibrant RWE presence; the history of marginalization of Indigenous communities; the recent demographic shifts; ongoing residential and labour segregation; and entrenched religious conservatism could easily coalesce as a breeding ground for RWE activism. Apparently, this was also what one particular RWE group anticipated. Each informant we met with in Lethbridge referred to the same episode and the community response to it. In 2010, a small *Aryan Guard* group, presumably based in Calgary, gathered at Henderson Lake, just a short distance from Lethbridge. Ostensibly there for a rally, the members made some attempts at recruiting through invitations to their "party", leafleting, and attempts to make connections in local bars. However, they had no success. In fact, they were met with a wall of resistance. Some informants even suggested that many members of the community made clear their outright anger and hostility towards the group. The backlash was swift and clear. Reminiscent of the successful American initiative, the "Not In Our Town" movement, Lethbridge citizens also insisted "not in our town". In the end, the recruiters returned to Calgary without having gained any traction in the city.

Lethbridge informants attributed their capacity to resist to recent mobilization around "reweaving the fabric of society" in which there was a concerted collective effort. They argued that Lethbridge was a community "equipped to respond" by virtue of the widely shared commitment to address broad problems associated with racism. Study participants described a "really committed cadre" of people addressing the issue in both proactive and reactive ways. This pledge was shared across sectors and layers of the community, from community activists, to a prior mayor, to the chief of police, to schools, to individual citizens. Moreover, the intent to challenge hate head-on was embedded in municipal policy, as evidenced in, for example, "Building Bridges:

A Welcoming and Inclusive Lethbridge—Community Action Plan 2011–2021" (City of Lethbridge 2010). The plan included reference to key objectives, including

- Facilitate positive integration of groups
- Prevent and respond effectively to acts of racism, discrimination and marginalization in the community
- Address systematic barriers faced by racialized and marginalized populations
- Promote a culture that respects and values cultural diversity and inclusion (City of Lethbridge 2010: 10).

To this end, the Action Plan obligates the city to

1. Increase vigilance against systematic and individual racism and discrimination.
2. Monitor racism and discrimination in the community more broadly as well as municipal actions taken to address racism and discrimination.
3. Inform and support individuals who experience racism and discrimination.
4. Support policing services in their efforts to be exemplary institutions in the fight against racism and discrimination.
5. Provide equal opportunities as an employer, service provider and contractor.
6. Support measures to promote equity in the labour market.
7. Support measures to challenge racism and discrimination and promote diversity and equal opportunity in housing.
8. Involve citizens by giving them a voice in initiatives and decision-making.
9. Support measures to challenge racism and discrimination and promote diversity and equal opportunity in the education sector and in other forms of learning.
10. Promote respect, understanding and appreciation of cultural diversity and the inclusion of Aboriginal and racialized communities into the cultural fabric of the municipality (City of Lethbridge 2010: 11).

What is especially significant about Lethbridge's approach is the emphasis that is placed on community-wide capacity building. Resisting the spread of RWE groups was not seen as only the responsibility of law enforcement, or the educational systems, or equity-seeking groups. Rather, it was recognized as the collective responsibility of all elements of the community. It was inclusive of existing structures and organizations, but also of citizens at large. The idea of "voice" appears to be a common refrain. We heard it from study participants, but it is also embedded in policy, as seen in the list above, as well as the following statement of engagement:

> Creating a welcoming and inclusive community will require that a diverse and broad range of partners be identified and engaged in the process. The Inclusion coordinator/CMARD team will contact potential partners that represent a variety of interests such as non-profit organizations, community-based organizations, public institutions, private enterprises, Aboriginal and First Nations organizations, municipalities, regional districts, business organizations, chamber of commerce, faith organizations, government, business, labour, cultural organizations and/or other key partners. (City of Lethbridge 2010: 20)

And again later in the same document:

> Working with others will be one of the key elements that will lead to success. It will be necessary to establish protocols to work with organizations such as human rights tribunals, legal clinics, police services, counseling/advocacy services that can help facilitate prevention, interventions and remedies for those who experience racism and discrimination. (City of Lethbridge 2010: 22)

There are important lessons to be learned from Lethbridge's philosophy and practice. How might larger centres exploit these techniques to enhance their own resiliency? How does any community develop the sorts of multi-sector collaborations that seem to work there?

References

Ameli, S., & Merali, A. (2014). *Only Canadian: The Experience of Hate Moderated Differential Citizenship for Muslims*. Wembley: Islamic Human Rights Commission.

Bahdi, R. (2003). No Exit: Racial Profiling and Canada's War Against Terrorism. *Osgoode Hall Law Journal, 41*(1–2), 293–316.

Benford, R., & Snow, D. (2000). Framing Processes and Social Movements: An Overview and Assessment. *Annual Review of Sociology, 26*, 611–639.

Boutilier, A. (2015, March 15). CSIS Highlights White Supremacist Threat Ahead of Radical Islam. *Toronto Star*. Retrieved from https://www.thestar.com/news/canada/2015/03/15/csis-highlights-white-supremacist-threat-ahead-of-radical-islam.html.

Canadian Council on American-Islamic Relations. (2005). *Presumption of Guilt: A National Survey on Security Visitations of Canadian Muslims*. Retrieved from http://www.caircan.ca/downloads/POG-08062005.pdf.

Chermak, S., Freilich, J., & Shemtob, Z. (2010). Law Enforcement Training and the Domestic Far Right. *Criminal Justice and Behavior, 36*(12), 1305–1322.

City of Lethbridge. (2010). *Building Bridges: A Welcoming and Inclusive Lethbridge—Community Action Plan 2011–2021*. Retrieved from http://www.lethbridge.ca/living-here/Our-Community/documents/community%20action%20plan%202011-2021%20-%20building%20bridges%20-%20a%20welcoming%20and%20inclusive%20community.pdf.

Clement, D., & Vaugeois, R. (2013). *The Search for Justice and Equality: Alberta's Human Rights History*. Edmonton: John Humphrey Centre for Peace and Human Rights.

Comack, E. (2012). *Racialized Policing: Aboriginal People's Encounters with the Police*. Winnipeg, MB: Fernwood Publishing.

Environics Institute. (2015). *Focus Canada: Spring 2015, Immigration and Multiculturalism, Detailed Data Tables*. Retrieved from https://www.environicsinstitute.org/docs/default-source/project-documents/focus-canada-2015-survey-on-immigration-and-multiculturalism/focus-canada-spring-2015—immigration-and-multiculturalism—data-tables.pdf?sfvrsn=2b7b9c30_0.

Geddes, J. (2009, April 28). What Canadians Think of Sikhs, Jews, Christians, Muslims. *Maclean's*. Retrieved from http://www.macleans.ca/news/canada/what-canadians-think-of-sikhs-jews-christians-muslims.

Government of Alberta. (2011). *Demographic Spotlight: The Visible Minority Population: Recent Trends in Alberta and Canada*. Edmonton: Government of Alberta, Demography Unit.

Gramsci, A. (1971). *Selections from the Prison Notebooks*. New York: International Publishers.

Graves, F. (2015, March 12). The EKOS Poll: Are Canadians Getting More Racist? *iPolitics*. Retrieved from https://ipolitics.ca/2015/03/12/the-ekos-poll-are-canadians-getting-more-racist.

Hall, N. (2012). Policing Hate in London and New York City: Some Reflections on the Factors Influencing Effective Law Enforcement, Service Provision and Public Trust and Confidence. *International Review of Victimology, 18,* 73–87.

Heitmeyer, W. (2005). Right-Wing Terrorism. In T. Bjorgo (Ed.), *Root Causes of Terrorism: Myths, Reality and Ways Forward* (pp. 141–153). London: Routledge.

hooks, b. (1994). *Outlaw Culture*. New York: Routledge.

hooks, b. (1995). *Killing Rage: Ending Racism*. New York: Holt.

Huber, L. P. (2016). Make America Great Again: Donald Trump, Racist Nativism and the Virulent Adherence to White Supremacy Amid US Demographic Change. *Charleston Law Review, 10,* 215.

Inglehart, R., & Norris, P. (2016). *Trump, Brexit, and the Rise of Populism: Economic Have-Nots and Cultural Backlash* (Harvard Kennedy School Faculty Working Paper Series RWP16-026).

Komaromi, P., & Singh, K. (2016). *Post-referendum Racism and Xenophobia: The Role of Social Media Activism in Challenging the Normalisation of Xeno-Racist Narratives*. London: Institute of Race Relations.

Kundnani, A. (2012). *Blind Spot? Security Narratives and Far-Right Violence in Europe*. The Hague: International Centre for Counter-Terrorism.

Lehr, P. (2013). Still Blind in the Right Eye? A Comparison of German Responses to Political Violence from the Extreme Left and the Extreme Right. In M. Taylor, D. Holbrook, & P. M. Currie (Eds.), *Extreme Right Wing Political Violence and Terrorism* (pp. 187–214). London: Bloomsbury.

Lund, D. (2006). Social Justice Activism in the Heartland of Hate: Countering Extremism in Alberta. *Alberta Journal of Educational Research, 52*(2), 181–194.

Mallea, P. (2011). *Fearmonger: Stephen Harper's Tough-On-Crime Agenda*. Toronto, ON: James Lorimer & Company.

McDonald, M. (2011). *The Armageddon Factor: The Rise of Christian Nationalism in Canada* (2nd ed.). Toronto: Vintage.

Montpetit, J. (2016a, September 5). *Quebec's Charter of Values, Revisited*. CBC News Montreal. Retrieved from http://www.cbc.ca/news/canada/montreal/caq-quebec-charter-of-values-identity-politics-1.3748084.

Montpetit, J. (2016b, December 14). *Inside Quebec's Far Right: Soldiers of Odin Leadership Shake-Up Signals Return to Extremist Roots*. CBC News Montreal. Retrieved February 13, 2017, from http://www.cbc.ca/news/canada/montreal/quebec-far-right-soldiers-of-odin-1.3896175.

Perliger, A. (2012). *Challengers from the Sidelines: Understanding America's Far Right*. West Point, NY: Combating Terrorism Center.

Perry, B. (2008). *Silent Victims: Hate Crime Against Native Americans*. Tucson: University of Arizona Press.

Perry, B. (2009). *Policing Race and Place: Under- and Over-Policing in Indian Country*. Lanham, MD: Lexington Press.

Perry, B., & Alvi, S. (2011). "We Are All Vulnerable:" The in Terrorem Effects of Hate Crime. *International Review of Victimology, 18*(1), 57–72.

Perry, B., Hofmann, D. C., & Scrivens, R. (2017). *Broadening Our Understanding of Anti-authority Movements in Canada* (The Canadian Network for Research on Terrorism, Security and Society Working Paper Series).

Perry, B., Hofmann, D. C., & Scrivens, R. (2018). "Confrontational but Not Violent": An Assessment of the Potential for Violence by the Anti-Authority Community in Canada. *Terrorism and Political Violence*. Ahead of Print, 1–21.

Public Safety Canada. (2013). *2013 Public Report on the Terrorist Threat to Canada*. Retrieved from http://www.securitepublique.gc.ca/cnt/rsrcs/pblctns/trrrst-thrt-cnd/trrrst-thrt-cnd-eng.pdf.

Ray, L., & Smith, D. (2002). Racist Violence as Hate Crime. *Criminal Justice Matters, 48,* 6–7.

Statistics Canada. (2011). *NHS Profile, London, CMA, Ontario, 2011*. Retrieved from http://www12.statcan.gc.ca/nhs-enm/2011/dp-pd/prof/details/page.cfm?Lang=E&Geo1=CMA&Code1=555&Data=Count&SearchText=London&SearchType=Begins&SearchPR=35&A1=All&B1=All&Custom=&TABID=1.

Stern, K. (1992). *Politics and Bigotry*. New York, NY: American Jewish Committee.

Tanner, S., & Campana, A. (2014). *The Process of Radicalization: Right Wing Skinheads in Quebec* (No. 14-07). Vancouver: Canadian Network for Research on Terrorism, Security and Society.

Welliver, D. M. (2004). Afterword: Finding and Fighting Hate Where It Lives: Reflections of a Pennsylvania Practitioner. In C. Flint (Ed.), *Spaces of Hate: Geographies of Discrimination and Intolerance in the U.S.A.* (pp. 245–254). New York: Routledge.

Woods, A. (2015, March 24). Islam Needs to Reform or Leave, Says Canadian Leader of PEGIDA Movement. *Toronto Star.* Retrieved from https://www.thestar.com/news/canada/2015/03/24/islam-needs-to-reform-or-leave-says-canadian-leader-of-pegida-movement.html.

5

Resisting the Right: Countering Right-Wing Extremism in Canada

There is much to be learned about confronting extreme-right-wing groups from the broader findings represented here. Indeed, as Black (2004: 9) observes in his account of terrorism, "the conditions of its existence finally become the conditions for its demise". Understanding the strengths and weaknesses of the RWE groups themselves can provide leverage for then exploiting them as a means of debilitating such groups. Similarly, understanding the enabling and inhibiting factors in the communities that are challenged by their presence offers guidance on how other locales might immunize themselves from RWE. The task is daunting, and clearly cannot be restricted to a police response. The foundations of RWE are complex and multifaceted, grounded in both individual and social conditions; so too must counter-extremist initiatives be multidimensional, drawing upon the strengths and expertise of diverse sectors: law enforcement certainly, but also education, social services, public health, youth workers and victim service providers to name a few.

Portions of this chapter are reprinted with permission from University of Toronto Press: *Canadian Journal of Criminology and Criminal Justice*, Resisting the Right: Countering Right-Wing Extremism in Canada, Ryan Scrivens and Barbara Perry, 2017.

© The Author(s) 2019
B. Perry and R. Scrivens, *Right-Wing Extremism in Canada*,
Palgrave Hate Studies, https://doi.org/10.1007/978-3-030-25169-7_5

Deschesne (2011: 287) succinctly observes that "Deradicalization is hot". Across disciplines, within and outside the academy, in the media and among politicians, countering violent extremism (CVE) strategies are indeed "hot". An entire industry has sprung up around the project of challenging extremism on the ground and online. Known in academic and government circles as "countering violent extremism", this non-coercive strategy is largely designed to divert individuals from radicalization and violent extremism (Harris-Hogan et al. 2015). The emphasis on these "soft" approaches spring from critical resistance to purely securitized and/or criminal justice responses to extremism, largely because, while neutral on the face of it, they have all too frequently been used to contain Muslims (Ahmed 2015; Parmar 2011). Instead, scholars such as Bjørgo and Horgan (2009), Neumann (2013) and Schmid (2013), for example, draw our attention to factors that account for radicalization to extremism, and by extension, are ripe for targeting for counter-radicalization. Across the western world, government and NGO agencies and centres have likewise set up shop with an eye to developing and implementing novel strategies around counter- and de-radicalization (e.g., the *Institute for Strategic Dialogue (ISD)*, the *International Centre for Counter-Terrorism (ICCT)*, the *National Consortium for the Study of Terrorism and Responses to Terrorism (START)*, and the *Center for Prevention of Radicalization Leading to Violence (CPRLV)*).

For our purposes, however, there are two key limitations to the scholarship and practice of extremism generally and CVE specifically. First, with a handful of exceptions (e.g., *ISD, ICCT, START,* and to some extent, the *CPRLV*), there has been a clear bias towards countering those who are inspired by radical Islam. Indeed, there is even a failure to acknowledge RWE as a phenomenon worthy of attention. The legal label of "terrorist", for example, is far less likely to be applied to RWEs (Perry and Scrivens forthcoming; Simi 2010). From a law enforcement perspective, the activity of the extreme right has not typically been monitored or taken seriously. We found that there is a tendency for officials to deny or trivialize the presence and threat of RWE in Canada.

The second limitation we note is that there has been very little effort to engage in CVE programming of any kind in the Canadian context (a notable exception is the *CPRLV*). Consequently, little research has been dedicated to exploring CVE initiatives in Canada (notable exceptions include Ahmed 2016; Jacoby 2016; Macnair and Frank 2017). A recent policy paper out of the *Canadian Network for Research on Terrorism, Security and Society (TSAS)* describes the landscape here as fragmented and inconsistent (see Thompson et al. 2016). This chapter, then, should be read as a call for a more careful, consistent, and most important, evidence-based approach to thwarting RWE in Canada. Drawing from the key findings from our study of the RWE movement in Canada, we identify several leading agencies, organizations and stakeholders that have attempted to counter RWE in Canada. Our intent is to link our findings to relevant strategies that exploit the limitations and strengths of both RWE groups and their sociopolitical environment. In what follows, we highlight some of our key findings, discussing their implications for intervention, whether proactively or reactively.

We take our cue from the *ISD*, which has established itself as a global leader in research and praxis around RWE. Their 2014 report, "On the Front Line" (Ramalingham 2014), is an invaluable guide to global promising practices around countering RWE. The report is grounded in interviews with more than 120 government and non-government practitioners in the area of tackling RWE, across ten European nations. On the basis of those interviews, the report identifies seven key approaches, each of which is detailed below, with efforts to identify parallel resources in Canada:

1. Diverting people from getting involved.
2. Responding to and countering hate speech.
3. Ending violent behaviour and fragmenting movements.
4. Managing threats to public order.
5. Supporting and empowering victims.
6. Raising awareness of the problem.
7. Pushing public agencies to act.

We would especially like to highlight the need to embark on these diverse strategies in an interactive and collaborative way. This means, first of all, that the various strategies should not be taken as mutually exclusive. We are not recommending an either/or approach. Instead, the mechanisms should be understood as complementary. The cumulative impact of a multi-pronged CVE approach cannot be overestimated, which is a reoccurring theme in the current CVE literature (e.g., Dalgaard-Nielsen 2016; Jacoby 2016; Macnair and Frank 2017).

In addition, it is increasingly clear from the recent studies on CVE initiatives that the locus of action must also be shared across sectors. Multi-sectoral approaches that combine the resources and capacities of several agencies stand the greatest likelihood of success (Dalgaard-Nielsen 2016; Jacoby 2016; Macnair and Frank 2017). Countering right-wing groups—or extremist groups in general—is not just a law enforcement responsibility (Selim 2016). Rather, it also requires the engagement of educators, social service providers, even the media (Cohen 2016). Collaborative action is key to building resilient communities (Dalgaard-Nielsen 2016). We saw this first hand during our project when we visited Lethbridge, AB, as discussed in the previous chapter. Lethbridge informants—including law enforcement, city officials, and community activists—attributed their capacity to resist to recent mobilization around "reweaving the fabric of society" in which there was a concerted collective effort. What is especially significant about Lethbridge's approach is the emphasis that is placed on community-wide capacity building. Resisting the spread of right-wing groups was not seen as only the responsibility of law enforcement, or the educational systems or equity seeking groups. Rather, it was recognized as the collective responsibility of all elements of the community.

Diverting People from Getting Involved

According to the time-worn adage, an ounce of prevention is worth a pound of cure. This is an apt reminder that, in countering RWE, the most effective strategies are preventative rather than reactive. The goal should be to inhibit recruitment to extremist groups. Early intervention is key. Recognizing this, a slate of scholars (e.g., Pressman 2009) and research centres (e.g., *ISD, START* and *CPRLV*) have tasked themselves with creating matrices for identifying the potential for vulnerability to extremist recruitment. Typically, these have been developed in an effort to identify religious extremists, but have some value in providing warning signs of involvement in other types of extremism, including RWE more broadly.

In the course of our study, we identified a number of key strategies and sites that appeared to be central to bringing new members into the fold. Right-wing activists generally indicated that they were very likely to have been lured into the movement by people they knew and presumably trusted. There was also evidence of explicit recruitment initiatives in certain communities, which typically took the form of leafleting in and around schools and universities. The posters or leaflets generally included messages that "explained" the apparent loss of white privilege—immigration, civil rights advances, etc. Recent years have also seen other "street level" attempts by localized RWE groups to render themselves visible. Marches and demonstrations occurred in several cities, including Montreal, London, Hamilton, Calgary, Edmonton and Vancouver. In addition, white power music has long been a powerful recruitment and retention tool among white supremacists, in particular. Thanks to the Internet, hate music circulates freely on RWE sites, as well as on *YouTube* and other similar social media venues. Clearly, the Internet has itself become a key site of engagement for members and potential members.

It is at these points of recruitment that intercessions are necessary, hopefully before individuals become fully engaged with extremist ideologies and/or groups. Fortunately, a number of organizations across the globe—but especially in the UK—focus explicitly on diverting individuals from getting involved in hate movements in the first place. This is done by engaging directly with individuals on a number of difficult issues, promoting dialogue that addressed the grievances underpinning racist or intolerant views. For example, the *Against Violent Extremism (AVE)* network is a global organization that counters extremist narratives and prevents the recruitment of "at risk" youth. Made up of former violent extremists and survivors of violent extremism, *AVE* utilizes the lessons, experiences and networks of those who have experienced extremism first-hand. Here, the aim is to undercut RWE groups' ability to contact and recruit young people.

In Canada, *AVE* developed the "Communitas Project" with the goal of strengthening individuals and communities through social interdependence, active citizenship, dialogue and youth leadership. This project spotlights the various needs of diverse communities and has branched out to Montreal, Ottawa, the Greater Toronto Area, London, Calgary, Edmonton and Vancouver. Another important initiative that attempts to divert Canadians from getting involved in violent RWE—and violent extremism more broadly—is the Montreal-based *CPRLV*. First of its kind in North America, the aim of this non-profit independent organization, among others, is to identify individuals who are in the process of radicalization towards violence, with the overall goal of contributing to individuals' disengagement and stopping the spread of extremism. What is particularly unique about this Centre is that it is led by a multitude of experts in the field, including, but not limited to, social workers, community workers, youth educators, communication advisors and researchers.

Another initiative that is centred on diverting people from becoming involved in extremism is *Life After Hate (LAH)*. This non-profit consultancy and speaker agency provides organizations with the information needed to implement long-term solutions to counter all types of violent extremism and terrorism. Notably, it works with leaders in several sectors, including foreign and domestic governments, military, international security and intelligence, policy makers, law enforcement officials and the private sectors, to name a few. An important feature of *LAH* is its core members—reformed extremists. A key member and motivational speaker, Tony McAleer, is a former RWE, and one of Canada's more notorious members of the movement. He shares messages of hope and compassion to a range of audiences, addressing issues around violence and extremism and offering proactive solutions to divert individuals from entering a life of hate.

Responding to and Countering Hate Speech

Counter-narratives need to target RWE and potential recruits "where they live". They must reflect the interests and day-to-day realities of those directly involved. In particular, contemporary efforts to reach these activists and sympathizers could not do better than to engage through social media and other similar forms. Internet communication helps to close the social and spatial distance that might otherwise thwart efforts to sustain a collective identity across the movement. Given the geographical dispersal of hate groups across the country, and indeed the globe, the medium of cyberspace allows members in Ottawa, ON and Kamloops, BC, as well as Munich, Toronto, ON and Oslo to engage in real-time conversations, to share the ritual and imagery that bind the individuals to the collective without having to travel great distances or incur great costs. Virtual conversations and ready access to web pages, aggressively asserting the shortcomings of the Other, strengthen the resolve of individual members by creating the framework for a shared sense of both peril and purpose. Such sites provide at least the façade of cohesion and collective security, but even more importantly for isolated and atomized members, a collective vision of shared fears, values and ideologies.

Consequently, parallel or even directly engaged online resources must be exploited. For instance, Bailey (2006) would have "antagonists" engaging with the hate movement online. Zickmund (1997) draws attention to the "dance" between racists and anti-racists online, whereby the latter facilitate an "ideological dialectic". A cursory look at some of the publicly accessible white power sites reveals some attempts by anti-racists to challenge right-wing positions. A similar reading of the "comments" sections that follow online news stories about racist or homophobic incidents, for example, also reveals the steps of the "dance" to which Zickmund refers. There are frequent exchanges to be found there between "right"-wing and "left"-wing posters. The most recent Canadian initiative to respond to hate speech, the *Social Media Education Everyday (SOMEONE)* project hosted at Concordia University in Montreal, QC, is a multinational and interdisciplinary team of researchers and practitioners who are dedicated to countering online hate speech, discrimination and radicalization through pedagogical practices: educating youth, educators and the public about the patterns of online hate. The purpose of this initiative, among others, is to build an online portal of educational material that is designed to promote digital knowledge and critical thinking skills.

With youth as the target audience, school-based anti-hate programmes are especially widespread in North America and Europe.

In the UK, for example, the Crown Prosecution Service (CPS), National Union of Teachers (NUT) and the Anthony Walker Foundation (AWF) have produced the "Schools Project: Racist and Religious Hate Crime" to counter prejudice among youth. The scenarios and classroom activities are intended to initiate discussion and increase students' understanding of hate crime and prejudice as a means of challenging them. The programme is intended as inoculation against the development of extremist ideologies through tailored curricula. In addition, the US State Department and *Facebook* have teamed up with EdVenture Partners to create a university competition, titled "P2P: Challenging Extremism". The programme tasks students to develop digital media interventions that counter radicalization to violence (for more on P2P, see Macnair and Frank 2017). In the fall of 2016, three Canadian universities participated, including University of Ontario Institute of Technology (UOIT), Simon Fraser University (SFU) and Concordia University. Dr. Perry's class at UOIT specifically focused on countering RWE and included high school workshops on RWE, and a series of video segments featuring a former RWE adherent.

There are also legal and technical avenues with which to limit both the dissemination and reach of hate speech and incitement, especially those found online. Most western nations have attempted to respond to cyberhate and related Internet phenomena through legal regulation and "take-down" approaches. Legislators have passed new laws to address online extremism, police agencies have trained open source analysts and intelligence officers monitor the online activities of extremists of all stripes. The law enforcement landscape has had to change to come into line with the demands of the evolution of communication technologies.

These dilemmas notwithstanding, western nations have struggled with the legal regulation of cyberhate and extremism online. In many cases, existing legislation has been invoked, as in the case of defamation laws, incitement to hatred policies, and human rights legislation. Bailey (2006) urges the innovative application of intellectual property law, libel law, and even the filing of union grievances in workplaces (e.g., libraries) that are exposed to online hate.

There is another way to use the law to challenge RWE. In the last 20 years, Richard Warman, a Canadian human rights lawyer and activist, has dedicated an enormous amount of his time, energy and resources to monitoring the activity of some of Canada's most notorious and vocal white nationalists, essentially countering hate speech and incitement in the country. His efforts have focused primarily on hate propaganda found on the Internet, with an emphasis on the activity of the extreme right. He also initiated a number of successful complaints against some of Canada's most notorious white nationalist activists. Efforts of individuals like Warman can be effective in challenging hateful narratives online.

The law is not the only—or perhaps even the most effective—weapon available to counter cyberhate. Bailey (2006) suggests additional mechanisms that can supplement legal intervention. The first of these is the simplest and is especially useful in protecting children and specific contexts from hate speech. This is filtering, which allows the prevention of specified content from accessibility. A second option—one that is widely used—is the development of monitoring organizations. Entities like the *Anti-Defamation League (ADL),* the *Simon Wiesenthal Center (SWC)* and the *Southern Poverty Law Center (SPLC)* are powerful examples of this. Not only do they identify and "count" hate sites, they also counter them with high-profile educational campaigns. In Canada, *Anti-Racist Canada (ARC)* monitors and deconstructs the online activities of right-wing hate groups.

Third among Bailey's (2006) suggestions is the use of hate speech hotlines, a slightly more passive means of monitoring online hate activity. Web users report hate sites and incidents of cyberhate, which may then be investigated and passed on to law enforcement or other authorities for official action. Finally, is Internet service provider (ISP) self-regulation, in which service providers assume the responsibility of cleaning up the Web. Canadian and German ISP organizations, for example, have developed codes of conduct for their members. It is not unheard of for ISPs to remove content, and in fact shut down sites, typically in response to public complaints or the actions of anti-racist advocates. Of course, this too raises the spectre of censorship, which is such anathema to free speech advocates.

Ending Violent Behaviour and Fragmenting Movements

Our study findings suggest that there are exploitable weaknesses within Canadian RWE groups themselves. Key limitations of Canada's RWE movement are the incessant group infighting, the general lack of ideological commitment and subsequent weak leadership. Our findings indicate that many individuals seek comfort in the initial appearance of group solidarity, but it is transient and temporary. One-to-one interventions, then, are a logical response to the extreme right, pursuing "softer targets" in the movement and building with rapport with them. In order to extend the gap between them and the movement, interventions should highlight the consequences of their actions, followed by helping them to identify a different life path and supporting them to achieve it.

Most leaders in Canada's RWE movement are tough and charismatic, but they are often uneducated, cannot articulate themselves, and lack a strategic capacity to maintain group cohesion. When leaders are in fact sustainable, they usually become known to the police, which in turn can weaken their position within a group. Our findings suggest that a crucial way for law enforcement officials to manage the threat of the extreme right in Canada is to target their leaders. Doing so will most likely render these unstable groups even more unstable, thus fragmenting whatever group cohesion they already have. RWE groups rarely have a shelf life of more than a few months in Canada, and even less for groups with weak leadership.

European nations have invested a significant amount of resources into counter-narrative initiatives, such as *Exit* programmes in Germany and Sweden, offering violent extremists a means of disengagement. The United States and, to a lesser extent Canada, has also offered individuals structured routes out of extremist movements. In short, these programmes attempt to challenge the belief structures and behavioural aspects of radicalized individuals, offering them pathways out of extremist groups and back into conventional society. According to Ramalingham (2014), these strategies target three processes: group dissolution, disengagement and de-radicalization. Indeed, an entire industry has grown up around de-radicalization. Like the risk assessment strategies, the primary focus of these has been on Islamist terrorism. However, bodies like *Exit*, and *AVE* noted above, specifically target RWE through long-term support.

Managing Threats to Public Order

Key informants, community-based organizations and police officers in our study agreed that a key factor enabling the emergence and sustainability of RWE groups in Canada is a weak law enforcement response. Typically, activities of the extreme right have not been monitored or taken seriously, and while community groups confirmed a level of right-wing activity, there was a tendency for officials to deny or trivialize the presence and threat. In a sense, law enforcement officials have been more reactive than proactive, underestimating right-wing groups as what some police officers described as "three man wrecking crews" or "losers without a cause".

Nevertheless, in contrast, we also identified areas in which law enforcement have taken the lead on combating hate crime and extremism in Canada. British Columbia and Alberta, for example, have demonstrated a strong and visible law enforcement response by developing teams that are grounded in collaborative and multi-sectoral approaches to addressing hate and ensuring that extremists have minimal impact on communities. Here, they integrate and utilize an array of experts, such as police officers, policy makers, victim service providers and community organizations. They are strongly engaged with the communities in which they operate, and they rely heavily on the public to enhance policy. Most police services can learn a great deal from these agencies that acknowledge and attempt to respond to the potential threat of RWE.

It is also clear that, in many communities in Canada, law enforcement officials are closely monitoring and responding to RWE activity. The Sûreté du Québec is clearly cognizant of the diverse RWE groups in that province and keeps a watchful eye on them. Calgary police are also vigilant in their treatment of RWE, keeping the heat on them to the extent that they have successfully "beheaded" some of the most active groups through arrests, or even through surveillance that has gently encouraged activists to move on to other cities. Finally, RWE marches and demonstrations in cities like Montreal, London, Calgary and Vancouver are closely monitored by law enforcement, particularly in the interests of minimizing the likelihood of violent exchanges between RWE and anti-racist activists. The aim is to deter extreme supporters from attending such events, as well as ensuring that demonstrations do not inspire fear within the community, inflame tensions between RWEs and anti-racist activists, for example, or lead to violence.

Supporting and Empowering Victims

During the course of our project, we spoke with members from an array of community-based organizations whose work brought them into contact with communities and individuals who are characterized by RWE groups as "threats" to Canadian culture. These participants often expressed concerns about the lack of attention being paid to the presence and capacity of RWE groups in Canada. They felt that the needs of vulnerable communities were not taken seriously by law enforcement or other similar agencies, nor did they feel that their perspectives were necessarily considered in developing public policy around extremism.

The inclusion of affected groups in relevant conversations on community security is key to the creation of safe spaces and to effective community and victim services more generally (Ahmed 2016; Dalgaard-Nielsen 2016; Jacoby 2016). In short, as community activists with whom we spoke remind us, communities and their members want to be heard, to have a voice in policies, practices and initiatives that affect them. Rather than the paternalistic imposition of programming by a "benevolent" state, anti-hate/extremism initiatives must also be informed by those in the best position to understand what is needed—members of targeted communities themselves, including those who have actually experienced targeted violence. Otherwise, policy makers run the risk of developing counter-productive initiatives or strategies that are far removed from the experiences and informed insights of affected individuals and communities. Consequently, a number of civil society organizations have emerged globally, intended to address the needs of affected communities by acting as a voice for victims of hate crimes, especially by serving as intermediaries with the authorities, and providing practical assistance to victims of hate crimes, such as legal advice, counselling and other services.

Many of these same bodies are actively engaged in providing a diverse array of victim supports, including legal representation or advice, counselling services, and mediation. Programmes and practices that are directed to specific individuals and communities at risk of being targeted by RWE provide skills and awareness that empowers them. These programmes are oriented towards strengthening individuals' capacity to counter the effects if not the incidence of extremist violence.

One such initiative is *Egale Canada*, the nation's lesbian, gay, bisexual, transexual and queer (LGBTQ) human rights organization, advocating equality, diversity, education and social justice. It supports and empowers victims of hate through research, education and community engagement initiatives. *Egale* also has the "Courage in the Face of Hate" (CFH) project, which brings Canadians together to share their experiences with bullying and hate. The purpose of this project is to: (1) reduce isolation among victims of hate; (2) decrease the overall number of hate crimes on the basis of one's sexual orientation, gender identity and/or gender expression; and (3) create a network and community of shared experiences to help victims on their journey of self-restoration, and offer them access to beneficial services and interventions.

As strong advocates of the Jewish community, *B'Nai Brith* is another advocate for victims of hate. It intervenes in courts on behalf of targeted minority groups, forms important strategic alliances with Canadian NGOs and develops Holocaust educational programmes in schools across the nation, to name but a few initiatives. The organization also offers an Anti-Hate Hotline (1-800-892-2624), wherein victims can call 24/7 for frontline counselling and assistance. *B'Nai Brith*'s annual audit of anti-Semitic incidents also provides information on hate crime as well as hate groups. The *National Council of Canadian Muslims (NCCM)* is a non-profit organization dedicated to protecting the rights and liberties of Canadian Muslims, and by extension of all Canadians.

The *NCCM* is a leading voice for the Muslim community. It promotes public interests and challenges Islamophobia and other forms of xenophobia through anti-discrimination and outreach services, as well as media campaigns and public advocacy initiatives.

Another organization that gives victims a voice is the *Anti-Racism Resource Centre (ARRC)*. It was created by the "Community and Race Relations Committee" as a clearinghouse of information for victims of hate, racism and discrimination in Peterborough, ON and surrounding area, and it provides victims with access to justice and education. Similarly, *Victims of Violence* is a Canadian registered charitable organization that promotes public safety and the protection of society. It offers a number of services and referrals; however, the main focus is on conducting research on issues affecting victims of violent crimes, acting as a resource centre for victims and the community, and providing long-term support and guidance to those in need. Overall, these community-based organizations are but a few avenues that should be used to empower victims of extremist hate and discrimination.

Raising Awareness of the Problem

In an environment infused with discourses focused on radical Islam and violence, it has become a daunting challenge for community members, anti-racists, and academics to highlight the presence of the extreme right in Canada. In 2006, on the basis of an extensive series of oral and written submissions on hate crime, the *Ontario Hate Crime Community Working Group* (2006: 32) came to the profound conclusion that:

> hate is so commonplace and institutionalized that is it almost impossible for those outside the vulnerable communities to fully appreciate its magnitude or to recognize it as a scourge on our society as a whole [...] when the public lacks cultural awareness and understanding of difference, this contributes to exclusion, victimization, fear and tolerance of hate crime.

Our study revealed that, while the RWE presence is far more widespread in Canada than generally assumed, groups and individuals associated with the RWE movement had garnered very little attention. Consequently, an important first step in confronting the movement is to convince the broader community that it constitutes a potential threat and, in short, to get RWE on the public agenda. As a starting point for such initiatives, many NGOs, for example, engage in ongoing monitoring of hate incidents and hate groups globally, regionally and nationally. Among these are *Human Rights Watch (HRW), Southern Poverty Law Center (SPLC), B'Nai Brith* and the *Council on American-Islamic Relations (CAIR)*. The readily available reports that are published by these agencies provide an overview of the demographics, distribution and, to a lesser extent, dynamics of hate crime. However, few people go in search of such information, so the key is to find ways to expand the audience by "pushing out" the information. Social media has become crucial to a much broader capacity to share information. Most anti-hate organizations like those noted above are very active on *Twitter, YouTube, Facebook* and other interactive sites. Use of these venues will continue to be key to engaging an otherwise uninformed public.

Anti-Racist Canada (ARC) is a group of like-minded individuals who combat right-wing hatred, bigotry, intolerance and violence through monitoring and reporting to law enforcement officials. In the *ARC* collective, they have documented what they call "A History of Violence: 1970–2019", essentially raising awareness by revealing the activities of the extreme right in Canada. Their website also includes an array of web links that further reveals the dark and often hidden world of the extreme right, including "Nazi Watch Toronto" and "Stand Up To Hate". Similarly, Daniel Gallant, a former RWE and current anti-violence activist in Canada, offers a variety of resources to raise awareness about issues involving the extreme right. The newly launched *Extreme Dialogue* initiative, for example, is a series of short documentary films that share personal stories of Canadians who were affected by violent extremism, one being the story of Daniel. The purpose of the project is to offer young people a positive alternative to the increasing amounts of extremist material found on the Internet and social media outlets. Another former RWE is Maxime Fiset, a former consultant for Montreal's *CPRLV*, who during the time of our study spoke about his experiences in the movement, challenging schools to teach their students to think critically about issues such as Jewish conspiracy theories and misconceptions around Islam (Solyom 2016).

In the United States, a number of initiatives have been developed to shed light on RWE in the communities. *One People's Project (OPP)*, for example, is a US-based initiative that researches and reports on activities of RWE groups and individuals. They are dedicated to being vigilant about the potential threats posed by RWEs, and they encourage communities to follow suit. *OPP* also documents the activity of the extreme-right-wing, raising awareness about the state of the movement across North America. Another US initiative that challenges the extreme right and advocates for social just is *Political Research Associates (PRA)*. In short, *PRA* raises public awareness by producing investigate reports, articles and resource kits, all in the name of advocating for LGBTQ rights, racial/immigrant justice, civil liberties and economic justice. They challenge stereotypes about particular minority groups targeted by the extreme right, with the goal of changing public opinion on diversity issues.

Pushing Public Agencies to Act

A subsidiary component of many of the anti-racist/anti-hate initiatives noted above is their role in challenging public officials to take a public stance against RWE in Canada. Our findings reveal the enabling impact that contemporary conservative politics has on Canadian RWE, wherein anti-democratic and anti-immigrant rhetoric and practices lend legitimacy to hate mongers in Canada. In Ontario, for example, we noted a wave of far-right extremists entering the political arena, including Jeff Goodall's battle for Oshawa City Council and Don Andrews's run for Toronto mayoralty. Inflammatory actions and statements by public figures exacerbate the tensions that already exist in some communities. Justice Eliana Marengo's refusal to hear the case of a woman who appeared in court in a hijab plays to the Islamophobia apparent in Quebec. That the then-Prime Minister of Canada, Stephen Harper, supported the action—calling the wearing of hijabs "offensive"—rather than reproaching it is even more problematic and was challenged by an array of politicians, media commentators, academics and community-based groups (Bryden 2015). Collectively, those interested in social justice have a responsibility to continue to pressure government leaders to refrain from exclusionary language and practices.

Our study also revealed neglect—if not outright derision—of the very idea that there is anything like a RWE threat in Canada. This was evident across the board, from law enforcement to the federal government. Police officers in our study often were unaware of or unconcerned about potential RWE activity in their jurisdictions. Two highly publicized incidents reveal the federal government's vision of RWE: neither Justin Bourque's killing of three Royal Canadian Mounted Police (RCMP) officers, nor the Halifax mall shooting conspiracy were considered acts of terrorism or even RWE. The Minister of Justice at the time of the Halifax incident explicitly stated that the plot was not considered "terrorism" because it was "not culturally motivated". This was in spite of the evidence of the suspects' extensive development and use social of media sites rife with Nazi propaganda and symbolism. Ironically, however, the Minister's statement was made just a month before the Toronto Star (2015) publicized an internal CSIS document asserting that lone actor RWEs represented a greater risk than lone actor Islamist extremists.

The CSIS report just noted is a welcome sign. Prior reports tended to downplay the risk of RWE. A 2012 CSIS report, for example, stated that the extreme-right-wing was marginal and "do not overtly propose serious acts of violence" (Canadian Security Intelligence Service 2012: 8). The findings from our project belie that assessment. Given the number of attacks on Canadian minority groups, along with the aggression that often accompanies police interactions with *Freemen-on-the-Land*, there is a need to acknowledge the presence and impact of RWE groups and individuals. This study was one such effort to lay the groundwork for further assessments of the RWE movement in Canada. Emerging research consortiums—like *TSAS*—have an important role to play in nurturing and publicizing work in the area. As noted at the outset, there has not been much academic interest in the field since the late 1990s. This generation of scholarship has considerable ground to make up in creating and mobilizing knowledge on RWE in Canada.

There are other signs of public agencies invested in challenging RWE in Canada. Our study found that those bodies that have acted against the RWE movement have been met with a degree of success. For example, the persistent surveillance and subsequent imprisonment of ultra-violent neo-Nazi skinhead leaders Kyle McKee and Robert Reitmeier minimized the level of extreme-right-wing activity in Alberta. The formation of the British Columbia (BC) Hate Crime Team has both raised awareness of issues relating to the extreme right and has prompted other law enforcement agencies to be proactive agents of change. And a police presence—in partnership with anti-racist groups—during extreme-right-wing marches and demonstrations in various Canadian cities have made it challenging for hate mongers to gain footing at these public events.

A promising new federal initiative is on the horizon in Canada. In 2016, the Ministry of Public Safety and Emergency Preparedness launched the *Canada Centre on Community Engagement and Prevention of Violence (CCCEPV)*. With a five year, 35-million-dollar budget, the office is to "provide leadership on Canada's response to radicalization to violence, coordinate federal/provincial/territorial and international initiatives, and support community outreach and research" (Canadian Association of Chiefs of Police 2016). It is to be hoped that the office will not bring with it a narrow understanding of "radicalization", but that it will be inclusive of RWE.

Conclusion

In response to the limited national perspective on the threat posed by RWE in Canada, one that has been infused with CVE discussions almost exclusively on violent Islamists, we have offered here insights into challenging the far-right extremist movement in Canada. Springboarding from the key findings of this project, this chapter identifies some of the leading organizations and stakeholders—domestically and internationally—that have attempted to resist the extreme right. We identified a number of agencies and organizations that acknowledge and attempt to counter the presence, as well as context and impacts of a loose RWE movement in Canada and abroad. While there are clearly challenges to overcome in getting RWE on the public agenda and in subsequently confronting elements of the movement, there are also encouraging signs. Organizations like those noted here will no doubt continue to lead the way in nurturing the development of much needed research, theorizing and policy making in Canada.

The ultimate goal of any research in the field of RWE should be to facilitate efforts to nurture safe and inclusive communities. To that end, we argue for the necessity of multi-agency efforts coordinated around acknowledging and responding to the extreme right. The divisive rhetoric and damaging violence associated with this movement are shaped by and in turn shape the communities around them. The motivations for the formation of RWE beliefs derive from the confluence of multiple social processes and institutions. It is imperative, therefore, that CVE efforts not only be seen as a law enforcement or intelligence issue (Cohen 2016; Selim 2016). It is a social issue (Dalgaard-Nielsen 2016; Jacoby 2016; Macnair and Frank 2017). We stress the need for law enforcement officials in Canada to partner with various anti-hate community organizations and human rights activists, sharing both knowledge and ideas for change. Lethbridge, AB, for example, was cited as a strong example of the impact that multi-agency coalitions can have on resisting the encroachment of RWE. We urge policy makers, law enforcement and community-based organizations to redouble their collaborative efforts in enhancing and/or developing the sorts of initiatives identified in this chapter. As was noted previously, the choices are not either/or—rather, multiple programmes operating at the level of the individual, the group and the broader social context can and should operate simultaneously.

References

Ahmed, K. (2016). Radicalism Leading to Violent Extremism in Canada: A Multi-level Analysis of Muslim Community and University Based Student Leaders' Perceptions and Experiences. *Journal for Deradicalization, 6,* 231–271.

Ahmed, S. (2015). The 'Emotionalization of the "War on Terror"': Counter-Terrorism, Fear, Risk, Insecurity and Helplessness. *Criminology and Criminal Justice, 15*(5), 545–560.

Bailey, J. (2006). Strategic Alliances: The Inter-Related Roles of Citizens, Industry and Government in Combating Internet Hate. *Canadian Issues*, 56–59.

Bjørgo, T., & Horgan, J. (Eds.). (2009). *Leaving Terrorism Behind: Individual and Collective Disengagement*. London: Routledge.

Black, D. (2004). Terrorism as Social Control. In M. Deflem (Ed.), *Terrorism and Counter-Terrorism: Criminological Perspectives* (pp. 9–18). Boston: Elsevier.

Bryden, J. (2015). Trudeau Calls Harper's Niqab Comments 'Pandering to Fear' of Muslims: 'It's Unworthy of Someone Who Is Prime Minister'. *National Post*. Retrieved from https://nationalpost.com/news/politics/trudeau-calls-harpers-niqab-comments-pandering-to-fear-of-muslims-its-unworthy-of-someone-who-is-prime-minister.

Canadian Association of Chiefs of Police. (2016). *Federal Budget*. Retrieved from https://cacp.ca/index.html.

Canadian Security and Intelligence Service. (2012). *Intelligence Assessment: 2012 Domestic Threat Environment in Canada (Part I): Left-Wing/Right-Wing Extremism*. CSIS IA 2011-12/115.

Cohen, J. D. (2016). The Next Generation of Government CVE Strategies at Home: Expanding Opportunities for Intervention. *The ANNALS of the American Academy of Political and Social Science, 668*(1), 118–128.

Dalgaard-Nielsen, A. (2016). Countering Violent Extremism with Governance Networks. *Perspectives on Terrorism, 10,* 135–139.

Deschene, M. (2011). Deradicalization: Not Soft, but Strategic. *Crime, Law and Social Change, 55,* 287–292.

Harris-Hogan, Shandon, Barrelle, K., & Zammit, A. (2015). What Is Countering Violent Extremism? Exploring CVE Policy and Practice in Australia. *Behavioral Sciences of Terrorism and Political Aggression, 8*(1), 6–24.

Jacoby, T. (2016). How the War Was 'One': Countering Violent Extremism and the Social Dimensions of Counter-Terrorism in Canada. *Journal for Deradicalization, 6,* 272–304.

Macnair, L., & Frank, R. (2017). Voices Against Extremism: A Case Study of a Community-Based CVE Counter-Narrative Campaign. *Journal for Deradicalization, 10,* 147–174.

Neumann, P. (2013). Options and Strategies for Countering Online Radicalization in the United States. *Studies in Conflict and Terrorism, 36,* 431–459.

Ontario Hate Crime Community Working Group. (2006). *Addressing Hate Crime in Ontario*. Retrieved from https://www.attorneygeneral.jus.gov. on.ca/english/about/pubs/hatecrimes/HCCWG_full.pdf.

Parmar, A. (2011). Stop and Search in London: Counter-Terrorist or Counter-Productive? *Policing and Society, 21*(4), 369–382.

Pressman, E. (2009). *Risk Assessment Decisions for Violent Political Extremism*. Ottawa: Canadian Centre for Security and Intelligence Studies, Carleton University. Retrieved from http://www.publicsafety.gc.ca/cnt/rsrcs/pblctns/2009-02-rdv/2009-02-rdv-eng.pdf.

Ramalingham, V. (2014). *On the Front Line: A Guide to Countering Far-Right Extremism*. London: Institute for Strategic Dialogue.

Schmid, A. (2013). *Radicalisation, De-radicalisation, Counter-Radicalisation: A Conceptual Discussion and Literature Review*. The Hague: International Centre for Counter-Terrorism.

Selim, G. (2016). Approaches for Countering Violent Extremism at Home and Abroad. *The ANNALS of the American Academy of Political and Social Science, 668*(1), 94–101.

Simi, P. (2010). Why Study White Supremacist Terror? A Research Note. *Deviant Behavior, 31,* 251–273.

Solyom, C. (2016, November 14). The Trump Effect and the Normalization of Hate in Quebec. *Montreal Gazette*. Retrieved from http://montrealgazette.com/news/national/the-trump-effect-and-the-normalization-of-hate.

Thompson, K., Hiebert, D., & Brooks, L. (2016). *Policy Brief: On the Creation of the Office of the Community Outreach and Counter-Radicalization Coordinator*. Canadian Network for Research on Terrorism, Security and Society.

Toronto Star. (2015, March 25). *Anti-Islam Group on Rise in Quebec*, p. A10.

Zickmund, S. (1997). Approaching the Radical Other: The Discursive Culture of Cyberspace. In S. Jones (Ed.), *Virtual Culture: Identity and Community in Cybersociety* (pp. 185–205). Thousand Oaks, CA: Sage.

6

Epilogue: The Trump Effect on Right-Wing Extremism in Canada

(with Dr. Tanner Mirrlees)

We could not have known when we started, or even when we finished the project, that our emphasis on the "climate of hate" would be so prescient. As we noted above, right-wing extremism (RWE) was not on the agenda in Canada. It had not been a topic of political or popular concern. All of that changed in the months leading up to and following the election of Donald Trump in the United States. The 2016 US presidential election capped off a year in which hate was mainstreamed. Republican nominee, billionaire and former reality TV star, Donald Trump ran an explicitly racist, sexist and xenophobic campaign. Fashioning himself as a right-wing populist man of white, conservative, Christian and working-class US-borne American "people", Trump's campaign constructed minorities, liberals, Muslims, professionals and immigrants as un-American "others" and blamed these "people" for a number of social problems they did not cause. Trump's campaign resonated with white supremacists. Key figures like David Duke, Andrew Anglin and Richard Spencer rallied around Trump, hoping that if

---

Portions of this chapter are reprinted by permission from Institute for Hate Studies, Gonzaga University: *Journal of Hate Studies*, The Dangers of Porous Borders: The "Trump Effect" in Canada, Barbara Perry, Tanner Mirrlees, and Ryan Scrivens, 2019.

© The Author(s) 2019
B. Perry and R. Scrivens, *Right-Wing Extremism in Canada*,
Palgrave Hate Studies, https://doi.org/10.1007/978-3-030-25169-7_6

elected, Trump would use his power to "make America great again" by making it all white. When Trump won the election to become president, white supremacists rejoiced. He helped to engender a climate "where 'difference' is being highlighted, the Other further entrenched with outsider status, and fear and loathing promoted as part of the mainstream of media and political debate" (White and Perrone 2001: 162–163). Dubbed the "Trump Effect", this resurgent white supremacy is real and violent: in the weeks following Trump's win, hate crimes in the United States surged to a level not seen since the days immediately after 9/11.

The Trump Effect has been widely discussed in the US context. But it has also garnered significant interest in Canada. Between us, we have conducted more than two hundred media interviews, including CBC News Canada, the Toronto Star, the New York Times, the LA Times and BBC News. As a favourite maxim goes, when the United States sneezes, Canada catches a cold. Thus, it has become apparent that the American politics of hate unleashed by Trump's right-wing populist posturing has also galvanized Canadian white supremacist ideologies, identities, movements and practices. Following Trump's win, posters plastered on telephone poles in Canadian cities invited "white people" to visit alt-right websites. Neo-Nazis spray-painted swastikas on a mosque, a synagogue and a church with a black pastor. Online, a reactionary white supremacist subculture violated hate speech laws with impunity while stereotyping and demonizing non-white people. Most strikingly, in January 2017, Canada witnessed its most deadly homegrown terrorist incident to that point: Alexandre Bissonnette, a RWE and Trump supporter, murdered six men at the Islamic cultural centre of Quebec City. Thus, in this chapter, we offer thoughts on what has changed—for the worst—since 2015. We explore the "Trump Effect" in Canada and argue that Trump's right-wing populist and white nationalist political campaign galvanized Canadian-based white supremacist ideologies, identities, movements and practices. We argue that Trump's election victory has reenergized white identity politics as a mainstream form of political expression in Canada. In other words, the resurgence of the RWE in Canada that followed Trump's presidential victory was not caused by the shocking election or Canadian RWE alone, but rather, are symptomatic of the continuing legacy of white supremacy that we noted in Chapter 4.

We examine the impact of the Trump Effect in Canada in four sections. The first section conceptualizes "Trumpism" as a form of right-wing populism convergent with an emboldened white supremacy. The second section gives evidential weight to the Trump Effect in Canada by documenting the recent uptick in Canadian RWE organizing, propagandizing and hate crimes, online and on-the-ground. To contextualize the antecedents of this Trump Effect, the third section highlights the ways in which mainstream forms of hate noted in Chapter 4 have taken even deeper root, thereby facilitating the uptake of Trumpism in Canada. We conclude by noting that, at present, resistance to the Trump Effect in the United States, Canada and worldwide is spreading.

Trumpism: Right-Wing Populism and White Supremacy

Trumpism is the most recent expression of right-wing populism that has enjoyed resurgence of late in many countries around the world. Political parties running on right-wing populist platforms have garnered increasing support and have successfully mobilized around politically divisive issues such as immigration, free trade and social entitlements (Mudde 2004). We conceptualize Trumpism as right-wing populism and illustrate how Trump employed populist communication strategies to win the consent of some people to his presidency.

Albertazzi and McDonnell (2008: 3) define populism as an

> Ideology which pits a virtuous and homogeneous people against a set of elites and dangerous 'others' who are together depicted as depriving (or attempting to deprive) the sovereign people of their rights, values, prosperity, identity and voice.

Populism is most suitably conceptualized as a communication strategy used by a plurality of actors—from professional politicians to activists—to construct "the people" and articulate the people to a movement against a real or imagined elite. In a helpful survey of current research on populism, Engesser et al. (2016) identify five key communication strategies that populist political actors employ in battles to win the consent of the people to their power, each of which provides a framework to understand Trumpism and the Trump Effect. Populists tend to: (1) emphasize the sovereignty of the people; (2) advocate for the people; (3) attack the elite on behalf of the people; (4) ostracize "bad others" juxtaposed against "good people", especially along racial lines; and (5) invoke the national community or heartland, typically as a vision under threat from "foreigners" or "outsiders".

Firstly, right-wing populists emphasize the power of the people's will and the sovereignty of the people. They frame their opponents as elites that have deprived "the people" of self-rule. This allows right-wing politicians to portray themselves as the only entities able to restore the sovereignty of the people by replacing the elite and all other representative and intermediary institutions (Albertazzi and McDonnell 2008; Mudde 2004; Shils 1956).

Second, they construct and advocate for the people, depicting the "people" in often partial and selective ways, but always as a unified and inherently virtuous group of good, moral and innocent people afflicted in some way by "bad others" (Albertazzi and McDonnell 2008; Jagers and Walgrave 2007; Jansen 2011; Taggart 2000). Populists also represent themselves as hailing from the people, closely related to the people or at least empathetic to the people's real needs and wants (Taggart 2000).

Third, right-wing populists construct a corrupt (i.e. abusive, guilty, unaccountable, arrogant) "elite" that rules or dominates society against the will or wishes of the "people", and at the people's moral and material expense (Albertazzi and McDonnell 2008; Mudde 2004; Rooduijn 2014). In this right-wing populist narrative, elites are represented as an alliance of educated, cosmopolitan and professionally minded individuals: in many cases, people of colour, non-Christians, feminists, liberals and intellectuals. These "coastal" elites supposedly occupy positions of power within government institutions, the mainstream news media, and the education system.

Fourth, right-wing populists construct and ostracize "dangerous" and "threatening" others (Albertazzi and McDonnell 2008; Rooduijn 2014). Like elites, these "others" are contrasted to the people and depicted as the enemy of the people. While the populist depicts the elite as internal threats to the interests of the mainstream society, these others are portrayed as external threats, or threats "from below" (Jagers and Walgrave 2007). They are framed as a group that is unfairly or unjustly favoured by the elite, or even as the elite's partner in a conspiracy against the people. The right-wing populist lumps various groups into this "other" category: immigrants, ethnic minorities, feminists, their political rivals or opponents, religious groups, criminals and communists (Abts and Rummens 2007; Betz and Johnson 2004; Rooduijn 2014). Finally, right-wing populists construct and invoke an ideal of the "national community" that plays upon nostalgia for a supposedly better time, promising to restore the nation to a time that is better than the present (Taggart 2004).

Trump's campaign, undeniably, channelled these populist themes. His political rhetoric whipped up the people's angst and resentments at the Democratic Party and elite political structures, channelling white conservative anger towards racial, religious and cultural minorities. Incredibly, Trump's campaign constructed Hillary Clinton as a symbol of a corrupt, liberal globalist power elite as part of his effort to differentiate himself as a "person of the people". Yet Trump, the inheritor of a family fortune, an Ivy League graduate, a billionaire real estate mogul, and a reality TV celebrity, is very much part of the US economic and political elite, not the common folk. That Trump differentiated himself from this "elite" in the minds of millions of Americans reflects the efficacy of his populist communications campaign. The "people" addressed by and attracted to Trump's populist campaign, however, brought together sections of the white working-class and the white petite bourgeoisie, a voting bloc that was in the past, fascism's demographic base (Myerson 2017; Rosenfeld 2017; Taylor 2017). As Shihipar (2017: 1) notes, "white people, of all ages, education statuses, and genders voted for Trump. While it is true that out-of-work coal miners from West Virginia cast ballots for Trump, so too did the affluent in cozy suburbs". Not all white people voted for Trump, but millions of white people—poor and rich, uneducated and educated, rural and suburban—did (Myerson 2017; Rosenfeld 2017; Shihipar 2017; Taylor 2017). It comes as no surprise, then, that Trump attracted an explicitly white supremacist subculture aimed at re-establishing a white nationalist State. In response to increasing diversity, political gains made by communities of colour, multicultural policies and practices, and increased immigration, white supremacist groups claimed that white American citizens were victims that had lost their place in society.

Early in the 2016 US election campaign, some white men saw Trump as someone who would champion them and their "race". Using the moniker of the "alt-right" to distinguish themselves from old-fashioned loathsome white supremacist groups like the *Ku Klux Klan (KKK)* and the *American Nazi Party*, as well as from mainstream Republicanism, these *rebranded* and digitally savvy white nationalist supremacists supported Trump's race to the White House. Keep in mind, however, that the term "alt-right" has not only been embraced by those holding overtly racist or white nationalist beliefs. The "alt-right" is a heterogeneous group of disparate people who may also hold nativist and protectionist ideologies, believe in conspiracy theories and advocate traditionally conservative values such as limited government, low taxes, patriarchal families, evangelical Christianity and strict crime control policies (Neiwert 2017). While their messaging retains a distinct nationalist fervour, the variety of personalities and groups bundled together under the moniker of the alt-right seeks to couch their ideology in more sanitized terms. For example, despite their evident ties to white nationalist causes, these mostly young white men claimed that their support for Trump was based purely on his political platform and his promise to "make America great again".

Among the myriad examples, immediately after Trump's win, white power activists in the United States such as Andrew Anglin, Richard Spencer and David Duke tweeted and shared exuberance at the prospects for their racist utopia. These and other white nationalists tend to retweet and promote Trump's tweets when they align with their ideological agenda, but ignore or criticize them when they don't. It must be noted, however, that Trump's presidential campaign and subsequent victory did not cause these RWEs to emerge. Rather, his right-wing populist campaign emboldened the haters to openly preach and practice racist hate. In the first few weeks following Trump's election win, The *Southern Poverty Law Center (SPLC)*, for example, documented more than 800 reports of hate crimes: a swastika was spray-painted on a Mexican-American family home in Washington; a Georgia-based

Muslim high school teacher's students left her a note telling her to use her headscarf to "hang herself"; and "TRUMP NATION WHITES ONLY" was painted on the wall of an African American church in Maryland (Potok 2017).

Trump's right-wing populist campaign tethered a message of economic prosperity and political freedom to white nationalist fantasies of returning to a time where the complexion of American society was different and where the supremacy of whites was unquestioned, reigniting white claims to power. To be sure, many issues gave rise to Donald Trump's appeal: socio-economic inequality, precarious and alienating employment, dissatisfaction with the political process, and anger at a rigged political system designed to work for elites rather than average citizens. Trump's right-wing populist campaign filtered these economic and political grievances through the prism of white victimhood and dreams of reclaiming white power and culture or, in simple terms, to make America great again by making America white again. A similar brand of sentiment made its way north of the United States, crossing into Canada's border.

Signs of Trumpism in Canada

In the weeks following Trump's stunning victory over Democratic presidential candidate Hillary Clinton, Canada saw evidence of increased RWE activity, wherein visible minority communities were targeted— both online and on the ground—at staggering rates. This was a stark reminder that Canadians are not immune to the "appeal" of racialized politics. We discuss this at length below.

A glimpse of Canada's daily media reports following the US election revealed that many Canadians were also attracted to the hateful political rhetoric that had emerged south of its borders, a marquee that Trump's "successful" campaign was built on—Islamophobic, anti-immigration, and anti-lesbian, gay, bisexual, transexual and queer (LGBTQ) sentiment, to name a few. To set the tempo of what was to come, disturbing graffiti was found in a Regina, Saskatchewan neighbourhood the morning following the results of the US presidential election:

"niggers go to the U.S. and let Trump deal with you" (Sharpe 2016). Similarly reported incidents and other forms of hatred emerged in Canada, immediately following the results of the US election.

In Ottawa, ON, Canada's capital city, visible minority communities were the targets of several hate-inspired incidents following Trump's victory, which began on 13 November and lasted until 19 November; two synagogues, a Jewish prayer house, a mosque, and a church with a black minister were vandalized with spray-painted racial slurs, swastikas and white supremacy symbols (Pfeffer 2017). Other Canadian cities experienced a similar up-tick in targeted hatred against visible minorities coinciding with the outcome of the US election. On 14 November, for example, Toronto, ON residents woke up to find racist posters scattered across city neighbourhoods. The hateful propaganda, titled "Hey, white person", encouraged readers to join the alt-right movement and subscribe to a list of "pro-European" websites (McGillivray 2016). That same morning, residents in a predominantly Chinese community in Richmond, BC were shocked to find racist pamphlets in their mailboxes. The flyers stated: "STEP ASIDE, WHITEY! THE CHINESE ARE TAKING OVER" (Chin 2016). Sources also reported racist graffiti in a neighbourhood in Regina, SK wherein alarming messages were scattered across an alleyway, a resident's garage and a local playground. Some of the messages included "KKK is great" and "fuck niggers" (Martin 2016). In Toronto that same week, a passer-by stopped in his tracks when he discovered a swastika spray-painted on the windshield of a car in a parking lot (Pelley 2016).

Within a single week of Trump's election victory, Canadian supporters of the ideal of a liberal, pluralistic and equitable multicultural Canada were shocked by the sheer volume of racist, xenophobic and homophobic sentiment inspired by Trump's win. However, racist attacks were not limited to the weeks immediately following the American presidential election. In November and December, for example, similar white supremacist-generated propaganda flyers were found in a neighbourhood in Hamilton, ON and Edmonton, AB as well as on university campuses in Ontario and Quebec. The flyers read: (1) "Tired of anti white propaganda? You are not alone" and (2) "It's only racist when white people do it". Flyers also directed viewers to alt-right websites for more information on what they described as a white cultural "struggle"

(Carter 2016a; Clancy 2016). Of particular interest were those posted on the McGill University campus in Montreal, QC. What was unique about this campaign was their attempt to borrow from Trump's "Make America Great Again" slogan, as the messages included: "Tired of anti-white propaganda? It's time to MAKE CANADA GREAT AGAIN!" (Shingler 2016). The time of "Canadian greatness"—the era in Canadian history which this derivative slogan points backward to—is never qualified or described by these hateful activists. Instead, they are creating a mythical golden age of "white" Anglo-Saxon and Francophone Christian dominance, a period when Canada had fewer non-white minorities and immigrants. They are perhaps harkening back to a time when multiculturalism was not Canada's official national culture.

Nonetheless, following Trump's win, Canadians also saw, first hand, levels of hatred escalate from pamphleting and vandalism, to verbal altercations and violence, to first-degree murder. For example, on 14 November a verbal altercation ensued between two men on a Toronto Transit Commission (TTC) streetcar. Caught on camera was a white man throwing racist insults at another man who allegedly punched him, a claim that was not supported by witnesses. When a pedestrian tried to intervene in the attack, calling the offender a "fucking racist", the man claimed that he was proud of it, and he simply said: "Go Trump" (Rieti 2016).

White supremacist hate and violence escalated on 26 November, as a 15-year-old youth of Muslim faith was brutally attacked by two men with a baseball bat as he was walking home from a friend's house in Hamilton, ON (Carter 2016b), resulting in serious injuries, including a cracked skull and injuries to his brain, jaw, limbs and spine. While the police found no evidence of hate, the victim's family feared that the incident was a hate crime. The family also showed concern about racial tensions and that they have felt in their community since Trump's election win (Carter 2016b).

The most alarming act of racist violence in Canada following the Trump win occurred on the evening of 29 January 2017. A 27-year-old white male entered the Centre Culturel Islamique de Québec in Ste. Foy, QC with the intention of killing Muslims. Equipped with a long gun, the lone actor murdered six Muslim men and injured 19 others while they prayed in the Centre (Perreaux and Freeze 2017). The suspect was described by his friends as a moderate conservative who, over about a year's time, became an apparent xenophobe and racist, one who overtly supported Donald Trump and far-right French politician Marine Le Pen (Dougherty 2017). In other circles, he was described as an extremist troll who frequently posted alt-right rhetoric online (McKenna 2017). While communities across Canada banded together to support the victims and communities of the tragedy, another campaign was underway: Montreal police received 29 reports of hate incidents, both online and offline, just three days following the massacre, with Muslims as the target (Perreaux and Freeze 2017).

The current uptick of the RWE movement in Canada is cause for concern. Even CSIS was finally forced to acknowledge that RWE represents a "growing threat"—something that they had heretofore ignored. Some strain of extreme-right ideology has inspired 19 murders in Canada in the past four years. In 2014, Justin Bourque shot and killed three RCMP officers. His behaviour was shaped by an anti-authority and anti-police stance derived from his extreme-right-wing views. In January of 2017, Alexandre Bissonnette killed six Muslim men at prayer. A commonly posted photo shows him in a "Make America Great Again" hat, a reflection of his admiration of Donald Trump, along with other right-leaning populists such as France's Marine Le Pen. Finally, Alek Minassian's van attack in Toronto took 10 lives. Minassian was an adherent of the misogynistic arm of the movement, "Incel" or "Involuntary Celibate". For him and his "brethren", women's increasing freedom and empowerment represent an unacceptable threat to masculinity and the right that implies to control women's bodies.

The white nationalist rallies that have peppered the country, beginning in the early part of 2017, are also tangible indicators that there is a viable and increasingly active RWE movement in Canada. However, in the lead-up and aftermath of Trump's upset presidential victory in the United States, the Canadian RWE movement appears to have shifted quantitatively and qualitatively. With their growth in numbers, the movement's adherents have also become much bolder in their online and offline activism. When we completed our three year study in 2015, we conservatively estimated that there were over 100 active groups across the country, with particular concentrations in Quebec, Ontario, Alberta and BC. In the two and a half years following Trump's election, we have seen dramatic growth in the numbers, visibility and online/offline activism associated with Canada's extreme right. We estimate at least a doubling of the number of RWE groups, including new groups and new chapters of previous groups. *PEGIDA*, for example, was struggling to gain any traction to its Islamophobic platforms in 2013 and 2014, but by 2018 had a national chapter, at least four national chapters, and a handful of city chapters (e.g. London, ON). They continue to stoke fear of terror attacks by radical Islamists, fear of the dissolution of Western values and fear of the loss of Judeo-Christian culture. *PEGIDA* has been especially active in the many rallies that continue to pepper the country, often with *Soldiers of Odin (SOO)*.

Combining "good community works" with anti-Muslim street patrols, *SOO* is appearing in cities large and small across the country. They attempt to cloak their surveillance of mosques and Muslim community centres in the guise of enhancing community safety, thereby evoking the stereotypical images of Muslims as dangerous, in physical and cultural terms. Across major Canadian cities, *SOO* could be found patrolling the streets to "protect" Canadian citizens from what they perceived as the threat: Islam, seeking to silence and marginalize Muslims through intimidation and a show of force (Makuch 2017). They have also been very active in the border patrols "guarding" the entry points of irregular migrants. This, too, is grounded in the characterization of immigrants as economic, cultural and security threats. The *SOO*, along with the *Canadian Coalition for Concerned Citizens (CCCC)* rallied against Motion 103, which was intended to limit Islamophobia and track hate crimes. On 4 March 2017, these groups protested M-103 in Toronto, ON, making the public claim that "Islam is Evil" and clashing with anti-Islamophobic protesters (Khandaker and Krishnan 2017).

Often referred to as "alt-lite", the *Proud Boys* were first seen here on Canada Day in 2016 when they disrupted an Indigenous anti-colonialism demonstration. While initially light in tone and hard to take seriously, this faction has become increasingly aggressive in stance. It is a men-only group, that professes that the only way to reclaim the superiority of the West is to return to traditional values, especially as it is feminism that has threatened the ability of men to be men, and thus their capacity to "defend" the nation. The first degree of initiation into the group is to swear the oath "I am a Western chauvinist who refuses to apologize for creating the modern world". The fourth is to beat up an adherent of the anti-racist/anti-fascist movement.

Like *PEGIDA, La Meute*—known also as the *"Wolf Pack"*—largely focuses its energies on Islam, but also extends its animosity to non-white immigrants generally. Established in 2015, they soon claimed 40,000 members online. While this is no doubt an exaggeration, *La Meute* is nonetheless generally considered the largest extreme-right group in Quebec. Founded by two ex-military men, the group follows a similarly regimented hierarchy intended to keep followers in check and on spec in terms of ideological positioning. While it is often engaged in anti-Muslim and anti-immigrant rallies, much of its activity is conducted online, and especially in closed forums.

Among the most worrying groups are the *Three Percenters*. Attracting former—and likely current—military and law enforcement personnel, they are heavily armed and actively engaged in paramilitary training, all in the interests of defending Canada's traditional heritage from enemies "both foreign and domestic". Currently that means that they too take aim at what they deem to be the inevitable invasion by Islam. Consequently, they are known for monitoring mosques for terrorist activity. So, too, do they commonly pose as "security" for rallies attended by other related extreme-right groups. The combination of hatred, heavy arms and paramilitary training is a disturbing one. So, too, is the trend towards the coalitions among these myriad groups at rallies and other events. This is contrary to what we have seen previously in terms of within and across group conflicts.

There is also a noticeable shift in the demographics of the Canadian RWE movement, with the emergence of the "alt-right". There is, it would seem, a broader audience and membership associated with the contemporary RWE movement in Canada. As noted in Chapter 3, the stereotypical image of extreme-right-wing actors is that of the black-jacketed skinhead. No doubt there remain elements of the movement that do correspond to this traditional guise. Members of *La Meute, Atalante* and *Blood & Honour*, for example, do not make any effort to soften their image. But these "shock troops" are now supplemented by those who would refer to themselves as the "alt-right"— the "intelligentsia" of the movement who sport polo shirts rather than leather jackets, and who are more "hipster" than skinhead. In truth, there is little to distinguish the so-called "alt-right" from the traditional extreme right. The messaging is the same—the west is losing its distinct Euro-culture, thanks to the misguided emphasis on multiculturalism and open immigration. It is largely only the framing of the message that is slightly different—more palatable and less extreme in rhetoric. Rather than use the coarse language of race and racism, the alt-right speaks of cultural loss, or preservation of "Canadian values". It's much harder to find fault with this coded language in isolation. It is the cumulative effect of their strident critiques of the Liberal Party (Trudeau in particular), of diversity policy, of globalization, as examples, that reveals the exclusionary core of their ideology.

Trumping Multiculturalism: Explaining the Trump Effect in Canada

A number of political factors pre-dating Trump's presidential campaign and victory established the material and ideological ground for the Trump Effect in Canada. Consider Gramsci's (1971: 181–182) assertion, noted previously, that the appeal of any political or ideological formation is dependent on pre-existing and fertile ground. Ideologies of any stripe cannot flourish in unprepared soil; rather, there must be some existing conditions, which let them bloom. And indeed, Trump's right-wing populist rhetoric found fertile ground in Canada. To understand the Trump Effect's hold in Canada, we must look outwards *and* inwards to explain the conditions conducive to the ready uptake of right-wing populism in Canada.

A global-level structural factor supporting the Trump Effect in Canada is the economic, geopolitical and technological integration of Canada and the United States. The economies of Canada and the

United States are tied together by free trade agreements, cross-border business partnerships, and two-way trade flows: 85% of Canadian exports flow to the United States and Canada is the United States' second largest trading partner. In addition, since 9/11 the Canadian security apparatus has aligned with the United States', and successive Canadian governments have supported the US-led global war on terror (Klassen and Albo 2012; McQuaig 2007). The global war on terror and the rise of Islamophobia in the United States and Canada march in lockstep: right-wing politicians, think tanks and extremist groups beat the "war on Islam" drum loudly, spew anti-Muslim rhetoric, engage in anti-Muslim practices, and satisfy anti-Muslim bigots (Kumar 2012; Kundnani 2015). Furthermore, the World Wide Web, the spread of smartphones, tablets and laptop computers, and the dominance of US-based digital giants such as *Google, YouTube, Facebook* and *Twitter* in Canada (Alexa 2017) enable cross-border virtual linkages to be formed between Trump and the Canadian public and RWE in both countries. As users of US-owned social media platforms, Canadians are fed a steady diet of Trump's hyperbole. His tweets reach us; his sound bites have made front page news in the Canadian media; the alt-right social media ecology and forums are accessible—and emulated—here. In short, the economic, geopolitical and technological integration of Canada with the United States renders Canada's border porous and enables an uninterrupted flow of American right-wing populism and Trumpism across the border.

Beneath these global-level factors and at the domestic level of politics is the fact that long before Trump burst onto the scene, Canada had already seen a shift towards the right in some contexts. Thus, a crucial backdrop to the uptake of Trumpism in Canada was provided by reactionary trends at federal, provincial and municipal levels of government, described in Chapter 4. On each of these levels, we have seen both historical and contemporary vestiges of the sort of right-wing populism onto which Trumpism could be grafted. At the federal level, the ten-year reign of Stephen Harper's Conservative government (2006–2015) ushered in a turn to the right in Canada unlike any we have seen since at least the early 1900s. Harper emerged out of the Reform party, a formation akin to the Tea Party which harnessed Western

Canadian dissatisfaction with the Federal status quo, bemoaned a central Canadian liberal elite, rejected Quebec's "distinct society" claims, rolled back the welfare state, and pushed for enhanced immigration controls—classic populist positions in Canada (Sayers and Denemark 2014). While the Reform Party gained traction in the West, it was rejected elsewhere, and ultimately merged with the right-wing Alliance Party to become the "new" Conservative Party of Canada.

During the "Harper years", the Federal government blended neo-liberalism with social neo-conservatism, mixing a pro-business agenda pushing free markets and privatization of collective public goods with regressive public policies extolling what Porter (2012: 19) described as "strong support for traditional family structures, opposition to abortion and family planning, and getting tough on crime". These years were also marked by militarism, a retreat from human rights, the elimination of hate speech protections, fear mongering and hate, anti-immigrant rhetoric, and restrictions on immigrants and refugees to Canada. Especially pronounced was Harper's vilification of Muslims. After the "terrorist" attacks in Quebec and on Parliament Hill in 2014, Harper introduced Bill C-51 with the claim that "Violent jihadism is not just a danger somewhere else. It seeks to harm us here in Canada" (Campion-Smith 2015: 1). During the 2015 election campaign, Harper ratcheted up his Islamophobia, depicting Muslim culture as contrary to Canadian values and pandering to a bigoted base. He called Islamic culture "anti-women", declared the wearing of the hijab "offensive" and said that "We do not allow people to cover their faces during citizenship ceremonies" (Chase 2015: 2).

As Prime Minister of Canada, Harper pushed for a regressive social policy regime applauded by the far-right (Mallea 2011; McDonald 2011). Some of Harper's policy initiatives included: (1) the Strengthening Canadian Citizenship Act (2015), to revoke Canadian citizenship for select Canadians for "national security" reasons; (2) Bill C51 (2015), which was a drastic expansion of police powers; (3) the Zero Tolerance for Barbaric Cultural Practices Act (2015), which tacitly targeted Muslims; (4) the Oath of Citizenship Act (2015), which intended to constrain religious observance; (5) refusal of international aid to organizations offering family planning and birth control counselling; (6) a ban on federal scientists' public discussion of research contradicting party ideologies; and (7) elimination of the long-form census, long used in planning evidence-based public policy.

Cumulatively, the rhetoric, policy proposals and strategies unleashed by the Harper years predated and paralleled some of those mobilized by Trump and supported the growth of a right-wing populist movement in Canada (Chwalisz 2015; Prince 2015). However, the move to the right did not end with Harper's electoral defeat in 2015. Significantly, "Trump-lite" figures have emerged in the context of the subsequent 2016/2017 race for leadership of the Conservative party. A key contender, Kellie Leitch, spoke of creating a tip line for reporting "barbaric cultural practices" as well as a mechanism to screen potential immigrants and refugees for "anti-Canadian values" (Tunney 2016). Channelling Trump's right-wing populism, Leitch tweeted that Trump's election win meant that "our American cousins threw out the elite" and that the win represented an "exciting message that needs to be delivered in Canada as well" (Stone 2016: 2). Observing the groundswell of support for right-wing populism to the south, Kevin O'Leary, a second "Trump-lite" contender, joined the fray in January 2017. O'Leary shared much with Trump: bombast, egotism, and reality TV fame. Like Trump, he promised to "drain the swamp" but at least refrained from capitalizing on Trump's racism and xenophobia. In 2018, Maxime Bernier fled the Conservative party, disaffected by what he saw as weak resistance to the increasing diversity of Canada as a result of "faulty" immigration policies. He created his own far-right federal political party—the People's Party of Canada—which is characterized by much the same form of right-wing populism as Trump's platform. In particular, Bernier was widely criticized for Tweeting "Why should we promote ever more diversity? More diversity will not be our strength, it will destroy what has made us a great country". If there is any doubt as to his location on the spectrum of right-wing populism, that is put to rest by his appearance on *Rebel Media's* "The Ezra Levant Show" within days of announcing his party, and by his contribution to the Rebel Live Calgary conference in November of 2018.

At the provincial level of governance, additional signs of a pre-Trump right-wing populist politics in Canada abound: Alberta and Quebec are especially relevant cases in this regard. Alberta has long been an incu-bator of right-wing populism. It was home to the anti-cultural diver-sity "Ralph Klein Revolution", headquarters of the moral conservative and religious right-embracing Reform Party and the centre for Harper's political base (Lund 2006). Alberta continues to be a bastion of right-wing populism (Rayside et al. 2012), with the Wildrose Party being a case in point. Part of the populist Wildrose-Alliance, Wildrose is a far-right party that panders to the ideology of religious conservatives and moral absolutes (Rayside et al. 2012). For example, in the run-up to the 2012 election, Wildrose's Edmonton candidate, Allan Hunsperger, wrote in a now infamous blog that homosexuals would suffer for eter-nity in a "lake of fire". Just two days later, another candidate made these racist comments:

> I think as a Caucasian I have an advantage [...] When different commu-nity leaders such as a Sikh leader or a Muslim leader speak, they really speak to their own people in many ways. As a Caucasian, I believe that I can speak to all the community. (Graveland 2012: 1)

Initially, the Wildrose Party faithful failed to challenge these divisive statements, lending credence to their characterization as a reactionary right-wing party. In spite of—or perhaps because of—the party's stance on social issues, they led the race right up to the election. While they did not win the election, they had remarkable success in southern and rural areas of the province and became the official opposition. Clearly, the party touched a resonant chord with voters—a chord very much in tune with the Trumpism that would follow just a few years later.

Arguably, Quebec provides the richest illustration of the readiness of a province in Canada to take up the sort of right-wing populist rhet-oric championed by Trump, particularly with respect to Islamophobia. We detailed this in Chapter 4. While Marois's electoral defeat in 2014 put the Charter to rest, the Islamophobic rhetoric did not disappear. The Parti Quebecois leader (Jean-François Lisée) pushed for a ban on burkas during his election campaign saying that women could hide AK-47s. Islamophobic rhetoric continues to be shored up by "Radio poubelle" (shock radio) and the conservative tabloid news, which also rants against immigrants, non-whites, Muslims, LGBTQ communities, social justice warriors and threatening "Others" in their midst. In 2017, Bill 62, which requires Quebeckers who receive or provide public services to remove their religious face coverings, was passed by the Quebec National Assembly. This has sparked considerable public and political debate, and the "religious neutrality law" has since been challenged by the *National Council of Canadian Muslims (NCCM)* and the *Canadian Civil Liberties Association (NCCLA)* in Quebec Superior Court on the basis of it targeting Muslim women (Leblanc 2018). The 2018 election of the right-leaning *Coalition Avenir Quebec (CAQ)* promises to engender yet more hostility towards immigrants. On a thinly veiled anti-Muslim platform, Party leader François Legault has vowed to reduce immigration to Quebec, require French language proficiency as well as "cultural values" testing. It is this ongoing context that RWE has swelled exponentially in Quebec, with the emergence of new and fervent groups like *La Meute, Atalante* and *SOO*. It was also in Quebec that Canada's one of Canada's worst incidents of mass homicide occurred when Alexandre Bissonette, a RWE terrorist and dutiful *Facebook* follower of Marine Le Pen and Donald Trump, shot and killed six Canadian Muslim men at prayer.

Ontario, too, has fallen under the spell of right-wing populism with the election of Rob Ford's brother Doug Ford. The one-term Toronto city counsellor won an unanticipated majority government in the 2018 spring election. Promising to lead a government "for the people", the millionaire businessman appealed to an anti-elitism in much the same way as Trump had done. Yet within the first few months of his administration, it rapidly became clear that he had in mind only some people—clearly not the most vulnerable—as he cut or weakened an array of social programs: a guaranteed income pilot project, the provincial anti-racism Directorate, a panel of experts on violence against women, the modernized and inclusive sex education curricula, and drug overdose prevention sites, to name but a few. Ford has long been friendly with the alt-right. He spoke at a *Rebel Media* event attended by *Proud Boys* founder Gavin McInness (and later posted for a photo with *Proud Boys* member Timothy Gavin Reid). "Ford Fest" 2018 included alt-right celebrities such as Jordan Peterson and the white nationalist Faith Goldy. Not surprising, given his flirtation with the alt-right, *Rebel Media*, the *Proud Boys*, the "League of the North" podcast, and Faith Goldy, endorsed Ford for premier of Ontario. Following his election, he posed for a photo with the Toronto-based white supremacist, Ronny Cameron. Cameron tweeted a modified version of the photo with the slogan, "Let's Make Ontario Great Again". Ford opened himself up to even further criticism when he was photographed at a "Ford Fest" event with Faith Goldy, one of the leading lights of the Canadian white nationalist movement.

Goldy regularly associates with known elements of the RWE movement in Canada, such as *SOO, Students for Western Civilisation*, the *NorthFront Nationalists*, and *ID Canada* (formerly *Generation Identity Canada*).[1] She has also publicly uttered the infamous "14 Words", a RWE slogan coined by the neo-Nazi group *The Order*, which murdered Jewish radio host Alan Berg in 1984.[2] Initially, Ford claimed not to have known who Goldy was or what she represented, in spite of the fact that both made regular appearances on the now-defunct *Sun TV* channel, and that they appeared together at a "Rebel Live!" event held by *Rebel Media* in 2017. It was only after three days of ongoing pressure from the public and politicians alike that Ford finally—but feebly—denounced her.

The damage had been done. Goldy exploited the photo to buoy her own run for mayor of Toronto, a campaign that signals the final level of analysis for explaining the pre-determinations of the Trump Effect in Canada: the municipal. Goldy used the image as an indication of endorsement from the provincial leader, claiming on social media that "Faith nation is Ford nation". Her team also launched a robocall branding her as the "only candidate who stands with Doug Ford". This was part of a concentrated strategy to align Goldy with the "mainstream" so

---

[1]See https://twitter.com/FaithGoldy?ref_src=twsrc%5Egoogle%7Ctwcamp%5Eserp%7Ctwgr%5Eauthor; http://anti-racistcanada.blogspot.com/2018/03/faith-goldy-and-students-for-western.html; https://anti-racistcanada.blogspot.com/2018/09/more-evidence-linking-faith-goldy-to.html; https://anti-racistcanada.blogspot.com/2018/10/faith-goldy-really-it-sic-publicity-for.html.

[2]See https://www.youtube.com/watch?v=1cpHTVvnquI; https://en.wikipedia.org/wiki/Fourteen_Words.

as to lend some legitimacy to her positioning. A far-right pundit, Mark Collett shared the intent on *Properganda TV*, a channel run by Ronny Cameron: "The aim of this campaign should be to produce provocative items of propaganda that the media will pick up on, go absolutely crazy about […] which will give Faith the chance to be featured on a TV show, on a panel discussion […]"[3] While the mainstream media refused to run ads in support of Goldy's campaign, RWE mobilized the Internet and social media platforms to propagandize on her behalf and had some success. Goldy did not win the election, but she came in third place, garnering 3.4% of the vote. The Left of centre Jennifer Keesmaat gained 23.59% of the vote, and neoliberal John Tory won a second term as mayor, taking in 63.49% of the vote. That a white nationalist who chanted the "14 Words" on a neo-Nazi YouTube channel mobilized 25,667 Torontonians to cast their ballot for her in one of the planet's most multicultural cities is shocking. That the most progressive Left candidate Saron Gebresellassi, who is a community organizer and women of colour, won 10,000 *fewer* votes than Goldy, is even more distressing.[4] While Torontonians tweeted their disgust and enthusiasm about Goldy's electoral performance, Goldy took to *Facebook* to praise her followers, and primed them for a future campaign: "SO HUMBLED by every single Torontonian who put his vote behind The People's candidate! To our volunteers: YOUR sacrifice drives me to serve in all that I do. I love you all! We had higher energy and worked harder than the others, placing on the podium. This is the beginning".[5]

Goldy's run for mayor is also a reminder that Toronto has a recent history of courting right-wing populism. In this, Canada's largest urban centre, then-mayor Rob Ford, was a masterful populist. Like his brother Doug Ford mentioned above, Rob Ford shared many of Trump's traits: egotistical, overbearing, an outsider, and someone who would help

---

[3]See https://www.youtube.com/watch?v=Zl5I_3033mM.

[4]See https://www.blogto.com/city/2018/10/toronto-election-results-2018/.

[5]See https://www.facebook.com/Faithfortoronto/?__tn__=%2Cd%2CP-R&eid=ARB1bdo0YwR 8kD8xMoMtsNAaYzP7uPL3p2Sx9DxZerMg_x4x9dzvnRV8TzqtjT_uabIayg7kTfL9xNVn.

the people take back the power from entitled elites. Kipfer and Saberi (2014: 134) capture the essence of Ford's right-wing populist strategy, noting that:

> Ford's belligerent interventions deepened existing social divides by pitting an imagined "Ford Nation"—car-driving, home-owning suburban family men, proper "taxpayers" like himself—against a range of enemy others: City workers, downtowners, cyclists, transit users, refugees, gays and lesbians, protestors, and "thugs" (gang members). Ford thus laced the antiestablishment mentality of small property and business owners with vengeful homophobic, racist, sexist, anti-labour, and anti-environmentalist elements.

The irony was that Ford, like Trump, came from a well-heeled family business and was himself a member of the economic elite. And Ford, like Trump, seemed immune to the rules of politics or society as a whole; no "indiscretion" stuck to them; consequences for them were in short supply. Yet that did not stop either one of them from presenting themselves as champions of the people against the so-called corrupt and smug liberal political insiders. Ford promised to "stop the gravy train", just as Trump promised to "drain the swamp". When caught in compromising and often illegal activities, Ford, like Trump, castigated the so-called bias of the news media and chastised his political opponents for conspiring against him (Kipfer and Saberi 2014). The endless scandals and bombastic claims and deflection of criticisms that characterized Ford's career as mayor of Toronto may be repeated by Donald Trump.

Trumping the Trump Effect in Canada

While the Trump Effect is evident in the United States and in Canada, its power to shape the hearts and minds of Americans and Canadians is being challenged. Trump is far from "hegemonic" in the United States, and his presidency does not have the consent or the approval of the majority of American citizens. According to a 2016 *Pew Research Center* poll, Trump took office as the most disliked US president in modern history (Waldman 2016). A year later, *Pew* found that a mere 16% of Americans "liked" how Trump conducts himself (Pew Research Center 2017b). Moreover, *Pew* further noted that "Trump and many of his key policies are broadly unpopular around the globe, and ratings for the U.S. have declined steeply in many nations" (Pew Research Center 2017a: 1). In Canada, the dislike of Trump is widespread. A *Forum Research* poll, for example, highlights how Canada's approval of Trump is very low, with 72% of Canadians saying they disapprove of Trump's conduct (Forum Research 2017).

Significantly, Canada mainfests some countervailing factors that may circumvent the Trump Effect and slow the worldwide spread of right-wing populism. After a decade in power, Canada's then-Prime Minister Stephan Harper was defeated in 2016 by the Liberal Party leader, Justin Trudeau, who at the time promoted Canadian multiculturalism and promised a more inclusive approach to negotiating identities and cultural differences. An additional blow to right-wing populism is reflected in the unpopularity of Kellie Leitch, as well as the defeat of both the Parti Quebecois in Quebec and the Wildrose Party in Alberta. On the whole, the Canadian public is averse to the kind of cultural chauvinism and xenophobia expressed by Trump and the alt-right (Ambrose and Mudde 2015). But this may be changing, as the fascist style of politics is not always explicit, but something that develops rhizomatically and at a subterranean level before blooming, and the seeds have been planted. Nonetheless, despite the deep integration of Canada and the United States, the countries still diverge in important ways. Numerous *Environics* polls, for example, highlight broad Canadian support for values very distinct from those conveyed by Trump: equality and equity; inclusivity; gender and sexual diversity; women's rights; immigration; and significantly, the role of the Canadian state in safeguarding these through the use of public funds (Adams 2013). Canada and the United States are still different countries. Although neo-fascists have gained some ideological ground in Canada, Canada's multicultural society and mainstream public opinion are not aligned with the extremist ideology of white nationalism that is capitalizing on and Canadianizing the Trump Effect. Some Canadian politicians, citizens and social movements have been working to counter ideologies of hate in Parliament, on *Facebook* pages, in the streets—anywhere they can.

Moreover, Canada's federal and provincial governments are actively promoting anti-hate initiatives and policies. At the federal level, Member of Parliament (MP) Iqra Khalid introduced M-103 calling for the government to "recognize the need to quell the increasing public climate of hate and fear" and "condemn Islamophobia and all forms of systemic racism and religious discrimination" (Levitz 2017). At the provincial level, governments are also condemning acts of hate. Prior to Ford's election, Ontario had passed a motion that condemns "all forms of hatred, hostility, prejudice, racism and intolerance", rebukes "the growing tide of anti-Muslim rhetoric and sentiments", "denounce[s] hate-attacks, threats of violence and hate crimes against people of the Muslim faith" and "condemn[s] all forms of Islamophobia" (CBC News 2017). That province also enacted its three-year "Anti-Racism Strategic Plan", intended to counter systemic racism across the province. Importantly, there is a resurgence of "bottom up" grassroots campaigns to counter the Trump Effect in Canada. Canadians representing diverse social movements drawing from communities of faith, peace and anti-war networks and democratic socialist groups have countered (and outnumbered) every public rally organized by the Trump-supporting *CCCC* (described above) in Canada's major cities. Anti-racist (and anti-fascist) organizing and activism is growing across Canada, and this is a direct expression of organizing "from below". Without such organizing by a plurality of local activist groups—one of the most significant being the *Coalition Against White Supremacy and Islamophobia (CAWSI)*, with over 6000 members—these anti-racist demonstrations would not exist.

At this juncture, there is a need for a progressive Left populist vision for the United States and Canada that attempts to ameliorate the real material conditions that give rise to right-wing populists like Trump. In both countries, the richest 1% have increased their share of total national income while the poorest and middle-income groups have fallen behind. The typical American CEO pockets about 340 times more than the average worker's wage; Canada's top CEOs take in 193 times the average worker's wage (Conference Board of Canada 2017;

Jackson 2015; Paddon 2016; Yalnizvan 2010). These dire economic conditions and the dispossession and grievances they entail are capitalized on by right-wing populists like Trump and by racist movements more broadly.

Trump and his supporters in the alt-right movement craftily channelled real economic grievances into attacks on racialized and demonized others, not towards "class struggles" aimed at the heavy concentration of wealth and power noted above. Of course, economic conditions do not singularly cause racism, but deteriorating economic conditions have historically shaped receptivity to racist white supremacist ideology, as promulgated by right-wing politicians. Consider the rise of fascism in Germany, or the ascendancy of Thatcher in the UK and Reagan in the United States, which were also tied to the demonization of immigrants and moral panics around racialized urban crime. In periods of capitalist downturns and rising inequality (such as the period we have been living through since the collapse of the world economy in 2008), large numbers of people are drawn to right-wing populists and thus also drawn to taking up "race war" ideology, instead of fighting for social justice, fairer redistribution of wealth and a more equal society. As Taylor (2017: n.p.) reminds us,

> Trump and the Republican Party explain the inequality experienced by workers — white workers in particular — as the fault of Mexican immigrants who steal jobs; or the fault of black criminals who make us unsafe; or the fault of Muslim terrorists who make us spend billions on defense. And meanwhile, they pursue policies intended to destroy the living standards of those same workers.

To trump the Trump Effect in the United States and in Canada, we must challenge RWE with the sorts of multi-sectoral and multidimensional response suggested in Chapter 5. We must also challenge the racist ideology that divides working people and the material conditions that foster the rise of right-wing demagogues. To this end, we conclude with a call for a two-pronged "progressive" strategy: (1) an anti-racist left internationalist populist alternative to the white nationalist populist right; and (2) participation in and support for the progressive social movements currently struggling at global, national, provincial and local levels and pushing for the development of public policies that aim to take society beyond the material conditions that have historically enabled marginal fascists to go mainstream.

References

Abts, K., & Rummens, S. (2007). Populism Versus Democracy. *Political Studies, 55*(2), 405–424.

Adams, M. (2013). *The Myth of Conservative Canada*. Policy Options. Retrieved from http://policyoptions.irpp.org/magazines/the-age-of-man/adams.

Albertazzi, D., & McDonnell, D. (Eds.). (2008). *Twenty-First Century Populism the Specter of Western European Democracy*. London, UK: Palgrave Macmillan.

Alexa. (2017). *Top Ten Websites in Canada*. Retrieved from http://ww.alexa.com/topsites/countries/CA.

Ambrose, E., & Mudde, C. (2015). Canadian Multiculturalism and the Absence of the Far Right. *Nationalism and Ethnic Politics, 21*(2), 213–236.

Betz, H. G., & Johnson, C. (2004). Against the Current—Stemming the Tide: The Nostalgic Ideology of the Contemporary Radical Populist Right. *Journal of Political Ideologies, 9*(3), 311–327.

Campion-Smith, B. (2015, January 25). Stephen Harper Says Jihadist Terrorism 'Seeks to Harm Us Here'. *Toronto Star*. Retrieved from https://www.thestar.com/news/canada/2015/01/25/stephen-harper-says-jihadist-terrorism-seeks-to-harm-us-here.html.

Carter, A. (2016a, November 21). *Flyers Decrying 'Anti-white Propaganda' Found in Hamilton*. CBC News Hamilton. Retrieved from http://www.cbc.ca/news/canada/hamilton/hamilton-fliers-1.3860327.

Carter, A. (2016b, November 30). *Muslim Teen Left with Cracked Skull After Brutal Beating*. CBC News Hamilton. Retrieved from http://www.cbc.ca/news/canada/hamilton/teen-attack-1.3874867.

CBC News. (2017, March 23). *House of Commons Passes Anti-Islamophobia Motion*. Retrieved from http://www.cbc.ca/news/politics/m-103-islamophobiamotionvote-1.4038016.

Chase, S. (2015, March 10). Niqabs 'Rooted in a Culture That Is Anti-women,' Harper Says. *The Globe and Mail*. Retrieved from https://www.

theglobeandmail.com/news/politics/niqabs-rooted-in-a-culture-that-is-anti-women-harper-says/article23395242.

Chin, J. (2016, November 21). Richmond Racist Flyers Call on 'Whitey' to Save City from Chinese People. *The Huffington Post Canada*. Retrieved from http://www.huffingtonpost.ca/2016/11/21/richmond-racist-flyers_n_13130166.html.

Chwalisz, C. (2015). The Prairie Populist: How Stephen Harper Transformed Canada. *Juncture, 22*(3), 225–229.

Clancy, C. (2016, November 21). Posters Calling Out 'Anti-white Propaganda' Put Up in Downtown Edmonton. *Edmonton Journal*. Retrieved from http://edmontonjournal.com/news/local-news/posters-calling-out-anti-white-propaganda-put-up-in-downtown-edmonton.

Conference Board of Canada. (2017). *Income Inequality*. Retrieved from http://www.conferenceboard.ca/hcp/details/society/income-inequality.aspx.

Dougherty, K. (2017, January 31). Quebec Mosque Shooting Suspect Was a Fan of Donald Trump and Marine le Pen. *Independent*. Retrieved from http://www.independent.co.uk/news/world/americas/quebec-city-mosque-shooting-latest-alexandre-bissonnette-donald-trump-marine-le-pen-face-book-social-a7554451.html.

Engesser, S., Ernst, N., Esser, F., & Büchel, F. (2016). Populism and Social Media: How Politicians Spread a Fragmented Ideology. *Information, Communication and Society, 20*(8), 1109–1126.

Forum Research. (2017, September 27). *Donald Trump Approval Down*. Retrieved from http://poll.forumresearch.com/data/64d0446a-39e6-40a7-8895-3f4476648ca1Donald%20Trump%20Sept%20.pdf.

Gramsci, A. (1971). *Selections from the Prison Notebooks*. New York: International Publishers.

Graveland, B. (2012, April 17). *Wildrose Candidate Apologizes for Suggesting He Has a White Advantage*. Global News. Retrieved from http://globalnews.ca/news/235033/wildrose-candidate-apologizes-for-suggesting-he-has-a-white-advantage-3.

Jackson, A. (2015). *The Return of the Gilded Age: Consequences, Causes and Solutions*. Ottawa, ON: The Broadbent Institute.

Jagers, J., & Walgrave, S. (2007). Populism as Political Communication Style: An Empirical Study of Political Parties' Discourse in Belgium. *European Journal of Political Research, 46*(3), 319–345.

Jansen, R. S. (2011). Populist Mobilization: A New Theoretical Approach to Populism. *Sociological Theory, 29*(2), 75–96.

Khandaker, T., & Krishnan, M. (2017, March 4). 'Islam Is Evil': Protesters Clash at Toronto Anti-M-103 Rally. Vice News. Retrieved from https://www.vice.com/en_ca/article/protestors-clash-at-pro-islamophobia-anti-m-103-rally-in-toronto.

Kipfer, S., & Saberi, P. (2014). From "Revolution" to Farce? Hard-Right Populism in the Making of Toronto. Studies in Political Economy, 93(1), 127–152.

Klassen, J., & Albo, G. (Eds.). (2012). Empire's Ally: Canada and the War in Afghanistan. Toronto, ON: University of Toronto Press.

Kumar, D. (2012). Islamophobia and the Politics of Empire. Chicago, IL: Haymarket Books.

Kundnani, A. (2015). The Muslims Are Coming! Islamophobia, Extremism and the Domestic War on Terror. New York: Verso.

Leblanc, D. (2018, January 25). Federal Government Staying Out of Court Challenge to Quebec's Face-Covering Law. The Globe and Mail. Retrieved from https://www.theglobeandmail.com/news/politics/federal-government-staying-out-of-court-challenge-to-quebecs-face-covering-law/article37741612.

Levitz, S. (2017, September 18). Iqra Khalid Urges MPs to Take Unified Approach in Islamophobia Study. The Globe and Mail. Retrieved from https://www.theglobeandmail.com/news/politics/iqra-khalid-urges-mps-to-take-unified-approach-in-islamophobia-study/article36287550/.

Lund, D. (2006). Social Justice Activism in the Heartland of Hate: Countering Extremism in Alberta. Alberta Journal of Educational Research, 52(2), 181–194.

Makuch, B. (2017, February 1). Soldiers of Odin: Inside the Extremist Vigilante Group That Claims to Be Preserving Canadian Values. Vice News. Retrieved from https://news.vice.com/story/soldiers-of-odin-inside-the-extremist-vigilante-group-that-claims-to-be-preserving-canadian-values.

Mallea, P. (2011). Fearmonger: Stephen Harper's Tough-On-Crime Agenda. Toronto, ON: James Lorimer & Company.

Martin, A. (2016, November 17). Reginans Believe Racist Graffiti Inspired by Trump's Election. Regina Leader-Post. Retrieved from http://leaderpost.com/news/local-news/reginans-believe-racist-graffiti-inspired-by-trumps-election.

McDonald, M. (2011). The Armageddon Factor: The Rise of Christian Nationalism in Canada (2nd ed.). Toronto: Vintage.

McGillivray, K. (2016, November 14). Racist Posters Promoting 'Alt-Right' Alarm Toronto Residents. CBC News Toronto. Retrieved from http://www.cbc.ca/news/canada/toronto/east-york-alt-right-racist-posters-1.3850386.

McKenna, K. (2017, January 31). *Suspect in Mosque Shooting a Moderate Conservative Turned Extremist, Say Friends, Classmates*. CBC News Montreal. Retrieved from http://www.cbc.ca/news/canada/montreal/quebec-city-mosque-alexandre-bissonnette-profile-1.3959581.

McQuaig, L. (2007). *Holding the Bully's Coat: Canada and the U.S. Empire*. Toronto, ON: Doubleday.

Mudde, C. (2004). The Populist Zeitgeist. *Government and Opposition, 39*(4), 541–563.

Myerson, J. A. (2017, May 22). Trumpism: It's Coming from the Suburbs. *The Nation*. Retrieved from https://www.thenation.com/article/trumpism-its-coming-from-the-suburbs.

Neiwert, D. (2017). *Alt-America: The Rise of the Radical Right in the Age of Trump*. New York, NY: Verso.

Paddon, D. (2016, January 3). *Canada's Top CEOs to Earn Average Worker's 2017 Salary by Lunchtime*. Huffington Post. Retrieved from http://www.huffingtonpost.ca/2017/01/03/canada-ceo-worker-pay-gap_n_13937686.html.

Pelley, L. (2016, November 23). *Toronto Man Finds 2 Swastikas Spray-Painted in His Queen Street East Neighbourhood*. CBC News Toronto. Retrieved from http://www.cbc.ca/news/canada/toronto/anti-semitic-graffiti-spotted-in-downtown-toronto-1.3864466.

Perreaux, L., & Freeze, C. (2017, February 1). Arrest Made After Hate Crimes Spike following Quebec Mosque Attack. *The Globe and Mail*. Retrieved from http://www.theglobeandmail.com/news/national/police-report-rise-in-hate-crimes-after-quebec-city-mosque-attack/article33856702.

Pew Research Center. (2017a, June 16). *U.S. Image Suffers as Publics Around World Question Trump's Leadership*. Retrieved from http://www.pewglobal.org/2017/06/26/u-s-image-suffers-as-publics-around-world-question-trumps-leadership.

Pew Research Center. (2017b, August 29). *Republicans Divided in Views of Trump's Conduct; Democrats Are Broadly Critical*. Retrieved from http://www.people-press.org/2017/08/29/republicans-divided-in-views-of-trumps-conduct-democrats-are-broadly-critical.

Pfeffer, A. (2017, February 17). *Teen Who Spray-Painted Racist Slurs, Swastikas Pleads Guilty*. CBC News Ottawa. Retrieved from http://www.cbc.ca/news/canada/ottawa/teen-swastika-racist-guilty-church-synagogue-mosque-1.3988061.

Porter, A. (2012). Neo-conservatism, Neo-liberalism and Canadian Social Policy: Challenges for Feminism. *Canadian Woman Studies, 29*(3), 19–31.

Potok, M. (2017, February 15). *The Trump Effect*. Southern Poverty Law Centre. Retrieved from https://www.splcenter.org/fighting-hate/intelligence-report/2017/trump-effect.

Prince, M. J. (2015). Prime Minister as Moral Crusader: Stephen Harper's Punitive Turn in Social Policy-Making. *Canadian Review of Social Policy, 71*(1), 53–69.

Rayside, D., Sabin, J., & Thomas, P. (2012). Faith and Party Politics in Alberta or "Danielle, This Is Alberta, Not Alabama." In *Proceedings of the Canadian Political Science Association Annual Conference*. Edmonton, AB.

Rieti, J. (2016, November 14). *Video Shows Man Hurling Racist Insults, Threats on Toronto Streetcar*. CBC News Toronto. Retrieved from http://www.cbc.ca/news/canada/toronto/toronto-streetcar-incident-1.3851108.

Rooduijn, M. (2014). The Mesmerizing Message: The Diffusion of Populism in Public Debates in Western European Media. *Political Studies, 62*(4), 726–744.

Rosenfeld, S. (2017, May 19). *12 Features of White Working Class Trump Voters Confirm Depressed and Traumatized Multitudes Voted for Him*. Salon. Retrieved from http://www.salon.com/2017/05/19/12-features-of-white-working-class-trump-voters-confirm-depressed-and-traumatized-multitudes-voted-for-him_partner.

Sayers, A. M., & Denemark, D. (2014). Radicalism, Protest Votes and Regionalism: Reform and the Rise of the New Conservative Party. *Canadian Political Science Review, 8*(1), 3–26.

Sharpe, K. (2016, November 17). *Regina Homeowners Upset After Property Tagged with Racist Graffiti*. Global News. Retrieved from http://globalnews.ca/news/3074086/regina-homeowners-upset-after-property-tagged-with-racist-graffiti.

Shihipar, A. (2017, July 4). *Why Americans Must Stop Talking About Trump's Mythical "White Working Class" Voters*. Quartz. Retrieved from https://qz.com/991072/why-americans-must-stop-talking-about-the-mythical-homogenous-white-working-class.

Shils, E. (1956). *The Torment of Secrecy*. Glencoa, IL: Free Press.

Shingler, B. (2016, December 8). *'Make Canada Great Again' Flyers with Anti-Muslim, Anti-gay Imagery Alarm McGill University Community*. CBC News Montreal. Retrieved from http://www.cbc.ca/news/canada/montreal/mcgill-canada-make-canada-great-again-1.3886871.

Stone, L. (2016, November 9). Trump Win Sends 'Exciting Message' to Canada: Conservative MP Kellie Leitch. *The Globe and Mail*. Retrieved from https://www.theglobeandmail.com/news/politics/trump-message-needs-to-come-to-canada-leitch-says-in-tory-leadership-bid/article32760294.

Taggart, P. (2000). *Populism*. Buckingham, UK: Open University Press.

Taggart, P. (2004). Populism and Representative Politics in Contemporary Europe. *Journal of Political Ideologies, 9*(3), 269–288.

Taylor, K. (2017, July 12). The Speech Racists Didn't Want You to Hear. *Jacobin*. Retrieved fromhttps://jacobinmag.com/2017/07/free-speech-fox-news-racism-trump-poor-whites.

Tunney, C. (2016, September 2). *Kellie Leitch Defends 'Anti-Canadian Values' Survey Question*. CBC News. Retrieved from http://www.cbc.ca/news/politics/leitch-responds-survey-question-1.3746470.

Waldman, P. (2016, November 21). Trump Takes Office as the Most Disliked President Ever. How Much Will That Matter? *The Washington Post*. Retrieved from https://www.washingtonpost.com/blogs/plum-line/wp/2016/11/21/trump-takes-office-as-the-most-disliked-president-ever-how-much-will-that-matter.

White, R., & Perrone, S. (2001). Racism, Ethnicity and Hate Crime. *Communal/Plural, 9*, 161–181.

Yalnizyan, A. (2010). *The Rise of Canada's Richest 1%*. Ottawa, ON: Canadian Centre for Policy Alternatives.

Appendix A:
Canadian Right-Wing Ideologues, Gurus and Lone Actors

Andrews, Don (1942–present), a Canadian white supremacist who waged war with Toronto, ON's communists in the 1970s, was the first individual to be charged in Canada with wilfully promoting hatred. He also co-founded the Edmund Burke Society with Paul Fromm and Leigh Smith in 1967, and he founded the *Nationalist Party of Canada* in 1977 (Lauder 2002), which he still leads. In 1974, Andrews ran for Toronto Mayor, coming in a distant second. Most recently, Andrews ran for the 2014 Toronto mayoral election (Hong 2014), but he was unsuccessful.

Arcand, Adrien (1899–1967) is the most notorious anti-Semitic in Quebec history, forming the *Parti National Society Chretien* in 1934 and expanding his organization to Toronto, ON under the group name *National Christian Party of Canada* in 1938, later known as the *National Unity Party* in 1949 (Barrett 1987).

Beattie, John (1942–present) founded the Toronto-based *Canadian Nazi Party* in 1965, and he later organized the *British People's League* in the late 1980s (Lauder 2002). In 1989, he hosted an outdoor

© The Editor(s) (if applicable) and The Author(s) 2019
B. Perry and R. Scrivens, *Right-Wing Extremism in Canada*,
Palgrave Hate Studies, https://doi.org/10.1007/978-3-030-25169-7

white-pride concert that attracted neo-Nazi skinheads and members of the *Canadian Airborne Regiment*, and he recently ran for municipal office in Minden Hills, ON's cottage country (Humphrey 2014).

Bourque, Justin Christian (1990–present) is accused of murdering three RCMP Mounties and injuring two other Mounties on 4 June 2014 in Moncton, NB, and he is facing three charges of first-degree murder and two counts of attempted murder (Brean 2014; Carlson 2014). Bourque was known for his anti-establishment Internet rants. His *Facebook* page portrayed him as a gun enthusiast and libertarian with an anti-authoritarian mindset, and his account was plagued by pro-gun, cop-hating and liberal-bashing propaganda (CBC News 2014; Friscolanti and Patriquin 2014). Arguably, Bourque was a self-motivated ideologue, a lone actor, and had no ties to any larger organization. Bourque used social media to educate himself on far-right libertarian preoccupations, such as the "militarization" of police, anti-authoritarianism, survivalism, "crownless kings", confiscation of guns and Canada's readiness for a Russian invasion (Brean 2014). Most interestingly, a *Globe and Mail* reporter found a large Confederate flag in Bourque's mobile home (CBC News 2014).

Burdi, George (1970–present) was the Canadian leader of the *World Church of the Creator* (Kinsella 2001), and he also organized *Church of the Creator* paramilitary training with a former member of the *Canadian Forces Airborne Regiment* (Michael 2006). In addition, Burdi's band *RaHoWa*, formed in 1989, pushing the white power music scene across the country (Kinsella 2001), and he attempted to advance white power music by launching *Resistance Records* (Michael 2006).

Christie, Douglas H. (1946–2013) founder of the *Canadian Free Speech League* in the 1970s was one of Canada's most well-known and controversial lawyers who advocated for what he called "freedom", or more specifically, encouraged individual liberty and free speech. Critics, however, regarded him as dishonourable, labelling him as the legal defence and "battling barrister" for the anti-Semites, the white supremacist, the Holocaust deniers and individuals charged with hate crimes

(Watts and Dickson 2013). For example, Christie represented some of Canada's most reviled hate mongers, including: James Keegstra in 1983 (Alberta teacher, convicted of promoting hatred against Jewish people), Ernst Zundel in 1984 (a Toronto-based publisher, Holocaust denier and Nazi sympathizer, who printed and distributed an array of anti-Semitic literature), Paul Fromm (white supremacist and self-proclaimed Nazi sympathizer), Malcolm Ross (anti-Semitic conspiracy theorist), Doug Collins, John Ross Taylor and Terry Tremain (white supremacists), Michael Seifert (Nazi prison guard, convicted of war crimes), Tony McAleer (white supremacist and founder of *Canadian Liberty Net*) and Imre Finta (Nazi war criminal).

Droege, Wolfgang (1948–2005), former *Nationalist Party of Canada* member, was an ultra-violent founding member of the *Heritage Front*, a successful neo-Nazi white supremacist organization established in 1989 (Kinsella 2001; Lauder 2002).

Farr, Joseph (1900–unknown), a sergeant major in the British Army and member of the *Orange Order*, replaced Taylor to lead the *National Christian Party of Canada* in 1938 (Barrett 1987).

Fromm, Frederick Paul (1949–present), Canada's central right-wing leader and one of Canada's most notorious white nationalist activists, is recognized for his relentless critique of and attacks on foreign aid, highlighting the effects of inflation, unemployment and government spending sprees, to name but a few. His most noteworthy group associations were with the *Edmund Burke Society* and *Campus Alternative* in 1967, and *Western Guard* in 1972, and he is currently the leader of the *Canadian Association for Free Expression (CAFE)* and *Citizens for Foreign Aid Reform (C-FAR)* (Kinsella 2001). He has spoken at a number of white power rallies, such as the 1989 Toronto Skinheads "Domination Day celebration", and many *Heritage Front* rallies, including a December 1990 rally commemorating the death of *Silent Brotherhood* leader Robert Mathews (Kinsella 2001). He has also shared the stage with Holocaust denier David Irving and has organized Canadian rallies to support Holocaust denier Ernst Zundel.

Gostick, Ron (1918–2005), an active member of the social credit movement, established an Ontario-based anti-Semitic publication, *Canadian Intelligence Publications* in the late 1940s, and later created the *Christian Action Movement* in 1967. He also founded the *Canadian League of Rights (CLR)* in 1968 (Barrett 1987).

Harcus, Bill (1970–present) was the "Grand Dragon" of the *Manitoba Knights of the Ku Klux Klan*. He noticed that the Manitoba *KKK* was inactive since the late 1920s, and rather than joining the *Church of Jesus Christ Christian Aryan Nations* as did most Christian Identity followers, he formed a modern Klan in 1989. By early 1991, the Klan became a formidable force, and the group was running a 24-hour telephone hate line out of Harcus's apartment (Kinsella 2001).

Levant, Ezra (1972–present), Calgary-raised lawyer and right-wing pundit, is Canada's best-known conservative analyst, political activist and TV host, and has been involved in several legal cases and controversies on free speech issues in Canada. Levant is the founder and former publisher of the "Western Standard" magazine in 2004, Canada's only media outlet to publish the Danish cartoons of Mohammed. The magazine was eventually charged with two counts of "hate speech" offenses, of which went before the Alberta government's human rights commission. Levant's battles against those attacking freedom of speech resulted in significant changes in how Canadian human rights commissions operate, and he later wrote a book titled, "Shakedown", on what he perceived as the illiberal nature of Canadian human rights commissions (Speakers' Spotlight 2014).

Long, Terry was a former *Progressive Conservative* member and former *Social Credit* supporter, founding president of the *Christian Defence League*, and the political organizer and candidate for the *Western Canada Concept Party*. He led the Canadian sector of *Aryan Nations* in 1986, building a training camp in Caroline, AB, and bringing together various extremists. He also staged a major rally and cross burning in Provost, AB (Barrett 1987; Kinsella 2001), and was known as "Canada's high Aryan warrior priest" (Kinsella 2001).

Lyle, Kelly Scott was Calgary's *Final Solution Skinheads* leader in the late 1980s and early 1990s, and was considered one of the most dangerous members of the racist skinhead movement in Canada (Kinsella 2001).

Mac a'Phearsoin, Tearlach (1948–present) was one of Canada's more elusive white supremacist leaders. In May 1972, he and his colleagues registered the *Confederate Klans of Alberta* as a society under the provincial Societies Act, and he was eventually named *Imperial Wizard of the Confederate Klans of Alberta* (Kinsella 2001). He also received copyright over a number of *KKK* symbols by the federal copyright office in Ottawa, ON, and he attempted to license or sell rights to the *KKK* insignia to a variety of neo-Nazi groups, including the Canadian branch of the *Aryan Nations*, one of the most virulently anti-Semitic and violent-prone groups in Canada (Kinsella 2001).

McKay, Matt, a former Master Corporal in the *Canadian Airborne Regiment*, was an extremely violent and hardcore *National Socialist* racist skinhead from Winnipeg, MB. He was also a member of the Klan in Manitoba and the *Final Solution Skinheads* in Winnipeg, and he frequently visited the *Final Solution Skinheads* in Edmonton, AB. McKay was involved in the Somalia Affair scandal in 1993, in which he was caught on tape saying, "we ain't killed enough niggers yet" (Anti-Racist Canada 2014; Kinsella 2001).

McKee, Kyle (1987–present) was the ultra-violent founder and spokesperson for Alberta, AB's *Aryan Guard* in 2006. In 2010, he replaced the *Aryan Guard* and founded two ultra-violent offshoot white supremacist groups, *Western European Bloodline (WEB)* and *Blood & Honour* (Jarvies 2012; One People's Project 2011).

Menard, Robert (1953–present) is the Director of the *World Freeman Society* and a "guru" or "poster boy" for the loosely knit *Freeman-on-the-Land* movement in Canada. The movement is as an anti-government group of "sovereign citizens" and "detaxers" who refuse to be governed by human laws, disrupt court operations and frustrate the legal rights of governments, corporations and individuals (Bell 2012). Police are concerned that this group, which preaches endlessly online, is growing in numbers as the economy worsens and may become increasingly violent (Bell 2012; Tucker 2013; Zerbisias 2013).

Nerland, Carney was a self-confessed fascist Saskatchewan leader of the *Ku Klux Klan (KKK)* and *Aryan Nations*. In 1991, he shot and killed a Cree man in a pawn shop and was charged with manslaughter and was sentenced to four years in prison (Kinsella 2001).

Noble, Keith Francis William (Bill) (1976–present), also recognized as "Exterminance" and "Leto Atreides II" on racist websites, message boards and forums, is well known to law enforcement officials for spreading messages of White Pride, becoming a fixture on *Stormfront* and the *Vanguard National News Forum*, as well as the now obsolete *Western Canada For Us (WCFU)* forums in 2004. He is also a member of the *National Socialist Party of Canada* and was the founder of the now defunct *National Progressivist Party of Canada*. It is also alleged by *Simon Wiesenthal Centre (SWC)* researchers in Toronto and Los Angeles that Noble registered the *Aryan Guard* website on 17 June 2007, and that he was behind a popular flyer campaign targeting immigrants in Calgary, AB (CNW 2007).

Raddatz, Norman Walter (1973–2015), described as anti-Semitic, anti-government and homophobic, is the alleged shooter in the death of an Edmonton police officer on 8 June 2015 in West Edmonton, AB. When members of the hate crimes unit visited Raddatz's home to serve him with an arrest warrant for criminal harassment, he unloaded a high-powered rifle on officers, killing one and wounding another (CBC News 2015; Simons 2015). He was suspected of harassing a local Jewish man and his family for a year-and-a-half, intimidating them with hateful messages (Simons 2015). Raddatz had a lengthy criminal record of hate-related offenses (Canadian Press 2015; CBC News 2015; Simons 2015), but it is unclear whether the lone offender was affiliated with a particular extreme right group.

Reitmeier, Robert is the co-founder of *Western European Bloodline (WEB)*. He is ultra-violent and was charged with second-degree murder in a deadly and brutal attack in Calgary, AB in 2011 (CBC News Calgary 2011).

Taylor, John Ross (1910–1994) was first named by Adrien Arcand to lead the *National Christian Party of Canada* in Ontario in 1938, and he later created a right-wing mail-order business called the *Natural Order* in the 1960s. He is also a founding member of the *Western Guard*, a white supremacist political party, formed in 1972 (Barrett 1987).

Waters, Christian, known online as "BOKcanada", is a Regina, SK resident and "Grand Dragon" of the *Ku Klux Klan (KKK)* in Saskatchewan since 2007. He is also a high-ranking officer with the Canadian branch of *Brotherhood of Klans (BOK)*, which is the largest Klan group in North America (The Leader-Post 2007). Waters has attracted new members in Saskatchewan over the past few years, causing unease, say anti-racist activists (CBC News 2007).

Whatcott, William (Bill) (1967–present) is a Canadian social conservative activist and religious anti-gay activist. He is also a born-again Christian who discovered religion following an early adulthood of drugs, crime and homosexuality (CBC News 2013; Gray 2013). With the goal of making both abortion and homosexuality illegal, Whatcott is known as an awkward revolutionary, a sexual purist and Christian fundamentalist who regrets his own homosexual and criminal conduct, denouncing it as filthy and corrupt (Brean 2013). In the early 2000s, Whatcott protested at various gay pride celebrations and outside of abortion clinics. Canada's anti-gay crusader was eventually charged with distributing flyers that promoted gay men as sodomites and pedophiles, one titled "Keep homosexuality out of Saskatoon's public schools" and the other "Sodomites in our public schools" (Canadian Press 2013; CBC News 2013; Gray 2013).

References

Anti-Racist Canada. (2014). *A History of Violence: 1970–2014*. Retrieved from http://anti-racistcanada.blogspot.ca/2011/10/history-of-violence-1989-2011.html.

Barrett, S. R. (1987). *Is God a Racist? The Right Wing in Canada*. Toronto, ON: University of Toronto Press.

Brean, J. (2013, February 26). How Former 'Street Kid' William Whatcott Became the 'Deliberately Provocative' Spark Behind the Supreme Court Hate-Speech Ruling. *National Post*. Retrieved from http://news.nationalpost.com/2013/02/26/how-former-street-kid-william-whatcott-became-the-deliberately-provocative-spark-behind-supreme-court-hate-speech-ruling/.

Brean, J. (2014, June 6). Justin Bourque's Alienation Nurtured in the Old Confines of Social Media. *National Post*. Retrieved from http://news.nationalpost.com/2014/06/06/justin-bourques-alienation-nurtured-in-the-cold-confines-of-social-media/.

Canadian Press. (2013, April 18). William Whatcott's Anti-Gay Flyers Case Won't Be Re-Open: Supreme Court. *Huffington Post*. Retrieved from http://www.huffingtonpost.ca/2013/04/18/william-whatcott-anti-gay-flyers-saskatchewan_n_3110097.html.

Canadian Press. (2015, June 9). Edmonton Police Release Details About Deadly Shootout. *Huffington Post*. Retrieved from http://www.huffingtonpost.ca/2015/06/09/edmonton-police-officer-k_n_7540386.html.

Carlson, K. B. (2014, June 12). Sister of Justin Bourque Speaks of His Troubled Life, Paranoia. *The Globe and Mail*. Retrieved from http://www.theglobeandmail.com/news/national/sister-of-justin-bourque-speaks-of-his-troubled-life-growing-paranoia/article19131608/.

CBC News. (2007, August 27). *Klan Plans Fall Rally in Sask., Says Leader*. Retrieved from http://www.cbc.ca/news/canada/saskatchewan/klan-plans-fall-rally-in-sask-says-leader-1.690030.

CBC News. (2012a, March 18). *1 Killed in Surrey Stabbing*. Retrieved from http://www.cbc.ca/news/canada/british-columbia/1-killed-in-surrey-stabbing-1.1165838.

CBC News. (2012b, March 19). *Surrey Stabbing Victim ID'd*. Retrieved from http://www.cbc.ca/news/canada/british-columbia/surrey-stabbing-victim-id-d-1.1155340.

CBC News. (2013, February 27). *Top Court Upholds Key Part of Sask. Anti-Hate Law*. Retrieved from http://www.cbc.ca/news/politics/top-court-upholds-key-part-of-sask-anti-hate-law-1.1068276.

CBC News. (2014, June 5). *Justin Bourque: Latest Revelations About Man Charged in Moncton Shooting*. Retrieved from http://www.cbc.ca/news/canada/new-brunswick/justin-bourque-latest-revelations-about-man-charged-in-moncton-shooting-1.2665900.

CBC News. (2015, June 9). *Norman Raddatz Had Extensive Police File for Hate Crimes*. Retrieved from http://www.huffingtonpost.ca/2015/06/09/edmonton-police-officer-k_n_7540386.html.

CBC News Calgary. (2011, June 1). *2 Men Charged in Deadly 2010 Attack*. Retrieved from http://www.cbc.ca/news/canada/calgary/2-men-charged-in-deadly-2010-attack-1.1017160.

Friscolanti, M., & Patriquin, M. (2014, June 6). The Full, Twisted Story of Justin Bourque. *Maclean's*. Retrieved from http://www.macleans.ca/news/canada/profile-of-justin-bourque/.

Gray, J. (2013, February 27). Supreme Court Ruling Upholds Limits on Free Speech in Case Involving Anti-Gay Proselytizer. *The Globe and Mail*. Retrieved from http://www.theglobeandmail.com/news/national/supreme-court-ruling-upholds-limits-on-free-speech-in-case-involving-anti-gay-proselytizer/article9104862/.

Hong, G. (2014, January 17). We Interviewed the White Supremacist Running for Mayor of Toronto. *Vice News*. Retrieved from http://www.vice.com/en_ca/read/we-interviewed-the-white-supremacist-running-for-mayor-of-toronto.

Humphrey, A. (2014, July 29). Canadian Nazi Party Founder Running for Office in Ontario Township. *National Post*. Retrieved from http://news.nationalpost.com/2014/07/29/canadian-nazi-party-founder-running-for-office-in-ontario-township/.

Jarvies, M. (2012). How Neo-Nazis Think: Photojournalist Spends Three Years Following Skinheads' Lives (with Photos). *Calgary Herald*. Retrieved from http://www.calgaryherald.com/news/Nazis+think+Calgary+photojournalist+spends+three+years/7208326/story.html.

Kinsella, W. (2001). *Web of Hate: Inside Canada's Far Right Network*. Toronto: HarperCollins.

Lauder, M. A. (2002). *The Far Rightwing Movement in Southwest Ontario: An Exploration of Issues, Themes, and Variations*. The Guelph and District Multicultural Centre.

Leader-Post. (2007, August 25). *KKK Revived, with Strong Regina Ties*. Retrieved from http://www.canada.com/reginaleaderpost/news/story.html?id=326a8ced-8c75-4c1b-acdc-7bcd8e090ffb.

Michael, G. (2006). RAHOWA! A History of the World Church of the Creator. *Terrorism and Political Violence, 18*(4), 561–583.

One People's Project. (2011). *Kyle McKee*. Retrieved from http://www.onepeoplesproject.com/index.php?option=com_content&view=article&id=663:kyle-mckee&catid=13:m&Itemid=3.

Simons, P. (2015, June 11). Police Constable Fought to Protect Edmonton from Hate. Sadly, Hate Killed Him. *Edmonton Journal*. Retrieved from http://www.edmontonjournal.com/news/edmonton/Simons+Police+constable+fought+protect+Edmonton+from/11127592/story.html#__federated=1.

Speakers' Spotlight. (2014). *Ezra Levant*. Retrieved from http://www.speakers.ca/speakers/ezra-levant/.

Watts, R., & Dickson, L. (2013, February 26). Victoria Lawyer Doug Christie, Who Defended Zundel and Keegstra, Is Dying. *Times Colonist*. Retrieved from http://www.timescolonist.com/news/local/victoria-lawyer-doug-christie-who-defended-zundel-and-keegstra-is-dying-1.80575.

Zerbisias, A. (2013, September 29). Talking with the Guru of the Freemen on the Land. *Toronto Star*. Retrieved from https://www.thestar.com/news/canada/2013/09/29/talking_with_the_guru_of_the_freemen_on_the_land.html.

Appendix B:
Incidents Related to Canadian Right-Wing Extremists, 1980–2015

1980s

Ontario

1981, Toronto, ON

James Alexander McQuirter, "Grand Wizard" of the Canadian *KKK*, had his car stopped at a routine police check, and they found two ounces of cocaine and 5000 pills. His home was later searched, and another *KKK* member threatened police officers with a loaded shotgun (Anti-Racist Canada 2014; St. Joseph News Press 1981).

1982, Toronto, ON

James Alexander McQuirter, "Grand Wizard" of the Toronto *KKK* and an outspoken Canadian racist who helped start the Toronto *KKK*, paid an undercover police officer, posing as a hit man, $2000 to murder Gary MacFarlane. It was believed that MacFarlane, a former Klansman, interfered with Klan activity (Anti-Racist Canada 2014).

© The Editor(s) (if applicable) and The Author(s) 2019
B. Perry and R. Scrivens, *Right-Wing Extremism in Canada*,
Palgrave Hate Studies, https://doi.org/10.1007/978-3-030-25169-7

1983, Toronto, ON
Famed abortion provider and pro-choice activist, Dr. Henry Morgentaler was attacked by a man with garden shears outside his clinic. The clinic was firebombed that same year (Huffington Post 2013).

1987, Ottawa, ON
Members of the *Aryan Resistance Movement (ARM)* Mark Bauer, Brian McQuaid and a 16-year-old male fired a weapon at the home of Jaajpe Ladan, hitting her in the face. Ladan survived, and the three men were later arrested. All three pled guilty to criminal negligence causing bodily harm and were given two-year suspended sentences and ordered to stay away from one another (Anti-Racist Canada 2014; Kinsella 2001: 311).

1987, Toronto, ON
White supremacist Detlev Michael Kiklas and another man were arrested and charged for extortion and death threats. The victim claimed that he was threatened with death for failure to pay a debt (Anti-Racist Canada 2014; Toronto Star 1987).

1988, Ottawa, ON
Richard Arbic, *Aryan Resistance Movement (ARM)* member and two other neo-Nazi skinheads brutally assaulted Michael Jeffries, a Carleton University student, in an unprovoked attack. Jeffries suffered serious head and chest injuries (Anti-Racist Canada 2014; Kinsella 2001: 318).

1989, Toronto, ON
Chris Newhook, a *Heritage Front* member originally from Nova Scotia, attacked a Vietnamese shopkeeper, and she was left blind in one eye (Anti-Racist Canada 2014; Canadian Press 2009).

Alberta
1988, Calgary, AB
Tearlach Mac a'Phearsoin, "Imperial Wizard" of Alberta's *Invisible Empire, Knights of the Ku Klux Klan* was charged with gross indecency after a mentally disabled teenager filed a complaint against him. Mac a'Phearsoin was fined $1000 (Anti-Racist Canada 2014; Kinsella 2001: 33).

1988, Calgary, AB
Robert Hamilton and Tim Heggen, two members of Mac a'Phearsoin's *Invisible Empire, Knights of the Ku Klux Klan* were arrested and charged with conspiracy to commit murder, conspiracy to commit property damage and serious injury by use of explosives. The men targeted a Jewish businessman and the *Calgary Jewish Centre*, and they were convicted and sentenced to five years in prison (Anti-Racist 2013; Kinsella 2001: 33).

1990s

Quebec
1994, Montreal, QC
Sacha Clouatre, *Northern Hammerskins* member, was arrested for firing blanks at employees at restaurant. When police showed up to the scene, Clouatre pointed his gun at an officer and was subsequently shot in the shoulder. Clouatre pled guilty to four counts of assault with a weapon and received a suspended sentence (Anti-Racist Canada 2014; The Gazette 1995).

1994, Montreal, QC
Northern Hammerskins Brant Smith spent 60 days in prison after pleading guilty to pointing a firearm at an individual (Anti-Racist Canada 2014; The Gazette 1995).

1997, Montreal, QC
Neo-Nazis Richard Stack and Steve Lavallee were arrested for attacking two anti-racists. Stack, Lavallee and four of their friends waited outside of a bar and ambushed the anti-racists as they left; however, the anti-racists successfully resisted their attackers (Anti-Racist Canada 2014).

1997, Montreal, QC
Eight members of the *Vinland Hammerskins* and *Berzerker Boot Boys* carried out a series of attacks, injuring approximately 30 individuals. Four planned attacks took place at three bars. Brant Smith, Claude Brunet,

Daniel Brunet, Sylvain Quiron, Mathieu Dubois, Jonathan Cote, Steve Lavallee and Alain Letart were arrested in connection with the assaults (Anti-Racist Canada 2014). When the arrests were made, police uncovered caches of knives, switchblades, mace, pepper spray, assault rifles, telescopic sights and silencers on the men, all of which resulted in 240 separate charges. Prior to the arrests, a growing number of similar attacks were taking place in the city that year (Anti-Racist Canada 2014).

Ontario
1990, Toronto, ON
Kevin Dyer Lake, 21-year-old member of *Aryan Resistance Movement (ARM)*, was found guilty of murdering Tony Le, a 15-year-old Vietnamese refugee, and was sentenced to 12 years in prison. Le was fatally stabbed in the heart after intervening in a confrontation between his friends, Lake and another neo-Nazi. Le's friend, Mukesh Narayan, 18, also tried to intervene and was stabbed five times by Lake (Anti-Racist Canada 2014; Toronto Star 1990b).

1990, Toronto, ON
Jeffrey Paul Jusczel 25-year-old *Hammerskin* member, and two men attacked a fellow Toronto *Hammerskin*. Jusczel beat and choked the man, stole his money and credit cards, and dragged him naked through the streets while beating him. Jusczel was charged with robbery, aggravated assault and endangering a life (Anti-Racist Canada 2014; Toronto Star 1990a).

1991, Scarborough, ON
Sean Maguire, *Aryan Nations* member from Idaho and *Heritage Front* affiliate, was arrested and deported from Canada on weapons violations. A 12-gauge shotgun and an assault rifle were found in a car that Maguire and Grant Bristow were occupying (Anti-Racist Canada 2014; Toronto Star 1991).

1992, Toronto, ON
A plot to seriously harm Jewish community leaders was connected to *Heritage Front* member Leslie Jasinksi. *Heritage Front* member Ken Barker told Wolfgang Droege that Jasinksi planned to walk into the Toronto offices of the *Canadian Jewish Congress* and "take out some

people". CSIS and the Toronto Police investigated the threat (Anti-Racist Canada 2014).

1992, Oshawa, ON
Heritage Front members Ken Barker, 31, and Leslie Jasinksi, 25, were charged with armed robbery and weapons offenses in connection with a robbery at a coffee shop. Jasinksi brandished a sawed-off shotgun and stole $275 from the teller. Weeks later, another *Heritage Front* member, Phil Grech, 21, robbed a bank in a clown mask and was arrested when he fled to Barker's apartment. Police then found a cache of weapons, including ammunition and a shotgun, a crossbow, a sword, batteries wired to a timer to look like a bomb, as well as a police scanner, neo-Nazi propaganda and a large sum of cash at Baker's home (Anti-Racist Canada 2014). Barker was arrested and charged with robbery, possession of a prohibited weapon, careless storage of a firearm, possession of a dangerous weapon, use of a firearm in an indictable offence, disguise with intent and possession of an explosive device. Jasinksi was also arrested when he showed up at Barker's court hearing. His intention was to confess to the coffee shop robbery, all in an effort to clear Barker (Anti-Racist Canada 2014; Toronto Star 1993b).

1992, Toronto, ON
Dr. Henry Morgentaler's clinic was firebombed. The damage was so severe that the building had to be demolished (Huffington Post 2013).

1992, Kitchener, ON
The home of anti-racist activist Monna Zentner, 55, was firebombed hours after attending a protest against British Holocaust denier David Irving. No one was hurt in the attack, but the fire caused $100,000 in damage. Police ruled it arson, and the attack was suspected to have been in retaliation by Irving supporters (Anti-Racist Canada 2014; The Global Jewish News Source 1992).

1992, Toronto, ON
A cache of weapons was found at the home of *Heritage Front* member Richard Manley. Canada Customs investigated Manley, who was a security enforcer for the *Heritage Front* and for George Burdi, on allegations that he was importing a gun part to convert semi-automatic

weapons to fully automatic weapons. Police searched his home and uncovered several weapons, including an AR-15 assault rifle and an Uzi automatic pistol (Anti-Racist Canada 2014; Peace Magazine 1995).

29 May 1993, Ottawa, ON
Hundreds of people gathered in Ottawa to protest a planned *RaHoWa* concert. Conflict soon erupted on Parliament Hill between the *Heritage Front* and anti-racist activists, and neo-Nazis attacked both anti-racist protestors and innocent bystanders (Lauder 2002). Four neo-Nazis were later charged with assault, and George Burdi, then leader of *RaHoWa* and the Canadian branch of the *World Church of the Creator*, was sentenced to one year in prison for kicking then *Anti-Racist Action(ARA)* member Alicia Reckzin in the face, breaking her nose (Anti-Racist Canada 2014; New York Times 1995).

1993, Toronto, ON
Members of the *Church of Creator*, Drew Maynard and brothers Elkar Fischer and Eric Fischer, kidnapped Tyrone Alexander Mason, a 22-year-old *Heritage Front* member, who was resigning from the organization. The men believed that Mason stole a *Church of Creator* computer that contained a membership list and names of neo-Nazis in the Canadian military (Anti-Racist Canada 2014). Mason was handcuffed, beaten and threatened with injections of window cleaner. In a police raid on the homes of six *Church of the Creator* members, a cache of guns was discovered, and the three kidnappers were arrested. The Fischer brothers were members of the infamous *Canadian Airborne Regiment*, and Eric Fischer was a former sergeant and the head of security for the *Heritage Front* (Anti-Racist Canada 2014; Toronto Star 1995).

1993, Toronto, ON
Heritage Front members Wolfgang Droege, Peter Mitrevski and Chris Newhook were charged with aggravated assault and weapons offenses in connection with an attack on anti-racists outside of a bar. The attack took place after a militant *Anti-Racist Action (ARA)* demonstration (Anti-Racist Canada 2014; Canadian Anti-Racism Education and Research Society 2013b).

1993, Toronto, ON
Following a *RaHoWa* concert, Jason Roberts Hoolans, who had ties to the *Church of Creator* but was described by Wolfgang Droege as a "hanger on" of the *Heritage Front*, attacked 45-year-old Tamil refugee Sivarajah Vinasithamby with two other accomplices. The racially motivated attack left Vinasithamby brain damaged and partially paralysed as a result of being repeatedly kicked in the head (Anti-Racist Canada 2014).

1993, Kitchener, ON
Paul McGraw, *Heritage Front* member and neo-Nazi drug dealer, was charged with assault with a weapon and uttering threats in connection with an incident in which McGraw, Gary Danicki and one other neo-Nazi were asked to leave a store by its Jewish owner, Elliot Eisen. The storeowner was shoved, had cowboy boots thrown at him, on man tried to punch him, and McGraw threatened his life and told the man that he was going to kill all the Jews. Eisen's 18-year-old son was also spat at, and two merchandise displays were overturned (Anti-Racist Canada 2014; The Global Jewish News Source 1993).

August 1993, Kitchener, ON
The home of Jewish anti-racist activist Monna Zentner was destroyed in a second arson. It was firebombed after a protest against Holocaust denier David Irving, who was speaking at the *European Sound Imports Store* (Anti-Racist Canada 2014).

1994, Toronto, ON
Darryl Wesley Sutton, a 22-year-old neo-Nazi, was sentenced to life in prison for murdering an 18-year-old street kid named David Murray Quesnel. The victim was beaten, stabbed and left in a bath to die during a party at a city rooming house (Anti-Racist Canada 2014; Toronto Star 1993a).

1995, Toronto, ON
Violence erupted between neo-Nazis and members of *Anti-Racist Action (ARA)* in a subway, ending with a 19-year-old *ARA* member being stabbed in the stomach and jugular vein. Two neo-Nazis were charged in connection with the attack. Adrian Kaddie, 22, was charged

with attempted murder, and Kristian Brandes, 19, was charged with aggravated assault, possession of dangerous weapons and assault with a weapon (Anti-Racist Canada 2014; Toronto Sun 1995).

1995, Toronto, ON
Paul McGraw was arrested in Toronto after fleeing assault charges in Kitchener-Waterloo. Here, he broke a woman's arm with a baseball bat and attacked two others. He was subsequently charged with break and enter and assault (Anti-Racist Canada 2014).

1995, Hamilton, ON
Abortion provider, Dr. Hugh Short, was shot in the elbow while at home. The sniper is thought to have been James Kopp, an anti-abortionist, who was also implicated in the shooting of Dr. Romalis and Dr. Fainman (CBC News 2009).

1996, Toronto, ON
During a confrontation over neo-Nazi symbols, Michael Aman-Ewaschuk, 17, was fatally stabbed in the subway by 22-year-old Frank Chisholm. The Metro Hate Crimes Unit and several classmates identified the youth as being a racist skinhead, and before being killed, he reportedly was planning to attend a white power concert in London later that month. During the concert, several bands dedicated songs to Aman-Ewaschuk, and George Burdi claimed that a white power compilation CD would be released in his memory. During the trial, a reporter was attacked outside of the courthouse by several of Aman-Ewaschuk's neo-Nazi friends and had his nose broken (Anti-Racist Canada 2014; Agno 1997).

1997, Sarnia, ON
Chris Newhook was sentenced to three years in prison on 10 charges, including assault, assault with a weapon and issuing death threats (Anti-Racist Canada 2014).

1997, Kitchener, ON
Paul McGraw, 24, was charged with break and enter, assault, assault with a weapon and possession of a dangerous weapon. McGraw and 28-year-old Christopher Watt broke into an apartment and assaulted a man over a drug debt. The man was kicked in the head, face and

shoulder, and he was stabbed in the stomach with a butter knife. Charges were stayed after the victim could not be found. McGraw had a history of intimidating witnesses (Anti-Racist Canada 2014).

1998, Ajax, ON
White supremacist Ennio Stirpe was charged with murdering Michael Kiklas. Kiklas was involved with Stirpe's ex-wife, Kathy Ford, who is the sister of two Toronto Councilmen, Rob and Doug Ford (Anti-Racist Canada 2013; The Globe and Mail 2013).

1999, Kitchener, ON
Paul McGraw was charged with conspiracy to commit assault, conspiracy to commit extortion and obstructing justice after trying to arrange for an inmate to be assaulted. Allegedly, the inmate identified McGraw as the owner of a sawed-off shotgun that police discovered in McGraw's car in 1997. McGraw also attempted to have the inmate falsely identified as a sex offender so he would be assaulted in prison. Charges of conspiracy to commit extortion were laid because he and his girlfriend tried to enlist a man to settle a drug debt through intimidation (Anti-Racist Canada 2014).

British Columbia
1994, Vancouver, BC
Dr. Garson Romalis, an abortion provider, was shot in his home at his breakfast table, sustaining serious injuries. The sniper is thought to be James Kopp, the anti-abortion extremist infamous for his alleged shootings and murders of several abortion providers across North America (The Globe and Mail 2014).

1997, Surrey, BC
Nirmal Singh Gill, a 65-year-old Sikh caretaker, was beaten to death in a parking lot by neo-Nazis Nathan Leblanc, 27, Radoslaw Synderek, 24, Robert Kluch, 26, Daniel Miloszewski, 22, and Lee Nikkel, 18. During the police investigation, plans to murder more Sikhs were uncovered, including what was referred to by assailants as "Plan B", which meant killing hundreds of Sikh school children (Anti-Racist Canada 2014; CBC News 1999).

Alberta

1990, R v Keegstra

James Keegstra was charged with wilful promotion of hate against an identifiable group under s. 319(2) of the *Criminal Code* for teaching anti-Semitic beliefs to his high school students. Keegstra argued that the section of the *Criminal Code* violated his right to freedom of expression under s. 2(b) of the Charter, and while the Court agreed that the section violated his expressive rights, it was nonetheless upheld by a narrow margin as a reasonable limit on free speech under section 1 of the *Charter of Rights* (Calgary Herald 2012; Gall 2012).

1990, Edmonton, AB

Daniel Sims and Mark Swanson, 19-year-old members of the *Final Solution Skinheads* and followers of Terry Long and the *Aryan Nations*, assaulted Keith Rutherford in his home. Rutherford, a retired radio journalist who 30 years prior had broadcasted an expose on an alleged Nazi war criminal, was kicked in the groin and left blind in his right eye as a result of being struck with a club (Anti-Racist Canada 2014; Canadian Anti-Racism Education and Research Society 2013a).

1992, Alberta, Kane v Church of Jesus Christ Christian-Aryan

On 9 September 1990, the *Church of Jesus Christ Christian-Aryan Nations* (the Church) held a rally in Provost, and as a sign of their solidarity with white supremacists in the United States, the group assembled and displayed a *KKK* White Power sign, a Nazi flag and swastika, and conducted a cross-burning event (Chak and Ashcroft 2012; Gall 2012). In attendance were Terry Long, leader of the *Aryan Nations* in Canada, Kelly Scott Lyle, founder of Calgary's *Final Solution Skinheads*, and Carney Milton Nerland, the Saskatchewan leader of the *Church of Jesus Christ Christian-Aryan Nations* (Kinsella 2001: 191). Several individuals complained about the gathering, and four days later, the commission released a statement condemning the event. Massive media attention focused on the hateful display and the *Aryan Nations* organization. In December 1990 and January 1991, several human rights complaints were filed against the Church as well as individuals involved in the Church and activities (Chak and Ashcroft 2012).

The hearing took nearly five months, and the *Aryan Nations* decision was significant in several respects, but most notably, the decision recognized that free speech was not without reasonable limits and that human rights protection required a complete understanding of the political and social reality of vulnerable minority groups (Chak and Ashcroft 2012).

1996, Edmonton, AB
The Edmonton Morgentaler clinic was struck by an attack with butyric acid, in a way that is reminiscent of "advice" in the extremist anti-abortion group *Army of God* manual entitled manual "When Life Hurts, We Can Help: The Army of God". The book details "99 Covert Ways to Stop Abortion", including arson, bombing, use of butyric acid and vandalism (Pro-Choice Action Network 1997/1998).

1998, Calgary, AB
Darnell Bass, a 31-year-old Sergeant in the *Canadian Airborne Regiment,* and Patrick Steven Ryan, a 30-year-old white supremacist, disguised themselves as security guards and staged an armed heist on a *Brinks* armoured car, all in an attempt to steal $400,000 (Anti-Racist Canada 2014; Calgary Herald 2006). Described as "the most violent hold up in Calgary history", the robbery involved the use of tear gas and a hail of almost 90 gunshots. The commando-style raid on the bank ultimately failed, and police raided Ryan's apartment, uncovering neo-Nazi literature and paraphernalia, including an *Aryan Nations* flag, a David Irving book and a number of white supremacist films (Anti-Racist Canada 2014).

Manitoba
1991, Winnipeg, MB
Gordon Kuhtey was walking in an area known as the "gay stroll", in which he was beaten, stoned and thrown into a river. Five years later, charges were laid when four men were implicated in his murder: Matt McKay, a member of the Klan in Manitoba and the *Final Solution Skinheads* in Winnipeg, and *Northern Hammerskins* members Robert Welsh, James Lisik and Gary Kuffner (Anti-Racist Canada 2014; Winnipeg Free Press 2013).

1997, Winnipeg, MB
Dr. Jack Fainman becomes the third Canadian abortion provider to be shot, allegedly by James Kopp. The shot to his shoulder was so damaging that he was not able to practice medicine again. Kopp never faced charges for any of the shootings in Canada (Winnipeg Free Press 2014).

Saskatchewan
1991, Prince Albert, SK
Klan member and leader of Saskatchewan's *Aryan Nations* chapter Carney Nerland shot Cree trapper Leo LaChance in the back as he was leaving Nerland's gunship. Even though Nerland told a police officer, "if I am convicted of killing that Indian, they should give me a medal and you should pin it on me", he was charged with manslaughter instead of murder (Anti-Racist Canada 2014; CBC News Saskatchewan 2011).

2000–2010

Quebec
2000, Montreal, QC
Neo-Nazis Sacha Montreuil, 26, Adam Guerbuez, 25, and Frederic Morin, 22, beat Christian Thomas, 39, to death. As Thomas was leaving a bar, he was approached by approximately 10 men and was beaten into a coma; he later died from massive head trauma. Also at the bar that night were fellow neo-Nazis Mathieu Carriere, Jonathan Cote, Isabel Forget, Steve Lavallee and Stephen LePage. Cote and Lavallee were previously convicted in a series of Montreal bar attacks in 1998 and were not supposed to be in any bar in the city (Anti-Racist Canada 2014; CBC News 2001a).

2000, Chatham, QC
Two boys murdered fifteen-year-old Aylin Otano-Garcia. The two classmates were charged with first-degree murder after they lured Otano-Garcia to a secluded sandpit and bludgeoned her to death. One of the boys responsible for planning the murder was fascinated by Adolf Hitler, claiming that he murdered the girl because he did not like immigrants (Anti-Racist Canada 2014; CBC News 2001d).

2000, Laval, QC
Fifteen-year-old Christelle Lavigne-Gagnon was stabbed to death by Richard Germain, a 20-year-old ex-boyfriend and neo-Nazi. Germain harassed and threatening Lavigne-Gagnon for months, and after the murder, he attempted to kill himself twice. Jean-Sebastien Presseault, then leader of the Laval *KKK*, came to the trial to show his support. Germain was sentenced to life in prison with the possibility of parole after 11 years (Anti-Racist Canada 2014; Radio-Canada 2002).

2001, Montreal, QC
Neo-Nazi Steve Legault pled guilty to attacking an anti-racist at a court-house during proceedings against his friend, who was facing charges for the beating death of Christian Thomas. Legault also attempted to attack an anti-racist in a separate case outside the Montreal courthouse in 1998 (Anti-Racist Canada 2014).

2002, Montreal, QC
Evens Marseille, a 26-year-old Haitian man, was beaten and stabbed by two neo-Nazis outside of a bar. Daniel Laverdiere and Remi Chabot-Brideault were responsible for the attack. Laverdiere was on probation for mischief during the time of the incident and was described in court as a "hard-core neo-Nazi extremist". He was also a member of *Vinland Front*, whose members came to the trial to support him. Laverdiere was sentenced to four years for aggravated assault and was ordered by the *Quebec Human Rights Tribunal* to pay Marseille $35,000 in moral dam-ages and $10,000 in punitive damages. Chabot-Brideault was given a one-year conditional sentence, which was served at home, and he was forbidden from associating with "skinheads" for three years (Anti-Racist Canada 2014; Vancouver Sun 2006).

2006, Montreal, QC
Jean-Sebastien Presseault, a notorious Montreal-based white suprema-cist, was arrested and charged in 2003 with wilfully promoting hatred through a racist website that he built and managed. While on bail, he threatened to kill the judge who was presiding over his case if he was given an exemplary sentence. Police searched Presseault's home and dis-covered a loaded gun, and he was charged with threatening the judge and procuring a firearm (Anti-Racist Canada 2014; CBC News 2007a).

2006, Île Perrot, QC

Eighteen-year-old Renaud Emard, known as "necro99" on *Stormfront*, was arrested on weapons charges after being investigated for making racist threats on the Internet and posting pictures of himself posing with guns. After police raided his home, 20 firearms and other weapons were uncovered. Hate literature, an ethnic cleansing manual, and a hit list featuring the names of schoolmates were also discovered. Emard pled guilty to possession of a prohibited weapon and five counts of careless storage of firearms (Anti-Racist Canada 2014; Montreal Gazette 2006).

2008, Montreal, QC

Neo-Nazi Julien-Alexandre LeClerc, 20, and a male youth attacked several people in a series of racially motivated assaults. Initially, a group of seven young Arab men were confronted by the pair, in which racial insults were directed at them. Two Arab men were then stabbed, and one required multiple blood transfusions and 50 stitches in his head (Anti-Racist Canada 2014; CTV Montreal 2011). The perpetrators fled in a cab, and hurled racist slurs at the Haitian cab driver. They also punched him and smashed his windshield. They later attacked a second cab driver who was of Arab origin. Both LeClerc and the minor were sentenced to two years in closed custody for aggravated assault, assault and possession of a weapon for the purpose of dangerous to public peace (Anti-Racist Canada 2014; CTV Montreal 2011).

Ontario

October 2001, London, ON

James Scott Richardson, 27-year-old operator of the *Canadian Ethnic Cleansing Team (CECT)* website and a member of the *Tri-City Skins*, was charged with making death threats against Muslims and Jews post-9/11. The website also contained other hateful messages about Jews and non-whites (Anti-Racist Canada 2014). Lawyer Richard Warman filed a human rights complaint against Richardson and Alexan Kulbashian, a co-operator of the website, and the *Canadian Human Rights Tribunal* found that the two websites encouraged violence against immigrants and visible minorities. Richardson and Kulbashian were fined a total of $13,000 (Anti-Racist Canada 2014; CBC News 2001f).

2001, Toronto, ON
Approximately 10 neo-Nazis gathered on the corner of Queen and Lansdowne, which resulted in a fight between them and others on the corner. The neo-Nazis later ran into the nearby bar, yelling racist slurs at patrons and shooting random people with pepper spray. They fled before being arrested by police (Anti-Racist Canada 2014).

2002, London, ON
Neo-Nazi Christopher Broughton attacked a 23-year-old gay woman who was holding hands with her female partner in public. Broughton initially hurled homophobic nicknames at them, and then, he told the woman to perform a sex act on him. He then ensued by punching the victim, grabbed her by her ponytail, throwing her on the ground and kicking her in the head. Broughton served three years for the assault (Anti-Racist Canada 2014; Ottawa Citizen 2006).

2002, Toronto, ON
David Rosenzweig, a 48-year-old Hasidic Jew, was attacked and stabbed to death by two alleged racist skinheads—20-year-old Christopher Steven McBride and Mercedes Asante, 19. Witnesses said they heard a young man shout, "He's a rabbi" before Rosenzweig was stabbing, severing his aorta (Chicago Tribune 2002).

2004, Toronto, ON
As Tomasz Winnicki and three others were driving to a rally in support of Holocaust denier Ernst Zundel, police stopped the vehicle and found throwing knives, a bow and arrows, and body armour. Winnicki was charged with carrying a concealed weapon, having weapons at a public meeting and possession of a weapon for a dangerous purpose. He pled guilty and received a conditional discharge with six months of probation (Anti-Racist Canada 2014).

2004, Kingston, ON
Chris Newhook, a violent member of the *Heritage Front*, attacked a man with a piece of plywood and threw him through a plate-glass window during a dispute over rent expenses. He served two years for assault with a weapon (Anti-Racist Canada 2014).

13 April 2005, Scarborough, ON
Wolfgang Droege, 55-year-old founding leader of the *Heritage Front,* was shot to death by Keith Deroux, a 44-year-old with mental health issues. Droege was his cocaine dealer, and Deroux stated that he believed that Droege was sending him messages through his computer. He also believed that Droege hired bikers to watch him. In 2006, Deroux pled guilty to manslaughter and was sentenced to 10 years in prison (Anti-Racist Canada 2014; CBC News 2005; National Post 2006).

2005, Kitchener, ON
Neo-Nazi Christopher Garvey, 25, and Russell McMahen, 27, were charged with assault causing bodily harm, uttering threats and forcible entry after attacking Daniel Schwass. The victim attended a party earlier in the night and narrowly escaped from getting into a fight with Garvey and McMahen. However, once Schwass returned home, the two men showed up at his apartment and forced their way inside. They then kicked him repeatedly in the head and face with combat boots, and it took three men a total of two hours to clean up the trail of blood. Ultimately, Garvey and McMahen pled not guilty, and the victim moved to BC and did not show up to court proceedings (Anti-Racist Canada 2014).

16 April 2006, Collingwood, ON
Stephen Long, a 22-year-old white supremacist who belonged to the racist *Hammer Heads* gang (which was an offshoot group of the *Vinland Hammerskins*), was murdered by Christopher Broughton, 29, of Hamilton, ON. While sleeping, Long was attacked with a baseball bat, also known as a "nigger stick", and was engraved with white power symbols. Earlier that night, Long slapped Broughton in the face and called him an embarrassment. As such, the murder may have been in retaliation to this event. Broughton had a history of violence. He had previous assault charges, including a conviction for a hate crime against a gay woman in 2003. He was sentenced to life in prison in 2008 (Anti-Racist Canada 2014; McLaughlin 2008; Ottawa Citizen 2006).

2006, Kitchener, ON
Neo-Nazi drug dealer Paul McGraw, 38, beat a 27-year-old man, who was also a drug dealer, leaving him with brain injuries. McGraw, who was described in news reports as the leader of a violent gang known

as *The Family*, was later convicted of aggravated assault and sentenced to 15 months in prison (Anti-Racist Canada 2014; Waterloo Regional Record 2011).

16 March 2007, Toronto, ON
Jason Belfiglio, 20, was charged with mischief after three windows were smashed at a Jewish daycare centre. Belfiglio denied his ties to the neo-Nazism, even though he was arrested near the crime scene wearing a neo-Nazi t-shirt (i.e. a Celtic cross intertwined with a swastika). He was given a 90-day conditional sentence, three years of probation, 100 hours of community service, and ordered to make restitution and stay away from neo-Nazis (Anti-Racist Canada 2014; National Post 2007).

2007, Guelph, ON
Neo-Nazi Paul McGraw was arrested in connection with a series of violent offenses that took place in Guelph. After a three-hour standoff with police, McGraw and two women were charged with assault, kidnapping, sexual assault and forcible confinement in relation to an incident involving seven male and female victims. McGraw was also charged in relation to a separate assault, which took place in Orillia days before his arrest. The charges in this incident included assault, assault causing bodily harm, forcible confinement, and uttering death threats. In 2009, McGraw was sentenced to 14 years in prison, which he appealed in 2011. His appeal was denied, and he was eligible for parole in 2016 (Anti-Racist Canada 2014; Waterloo Regional Record 2011).

15 February 2009, Toronto, ON
A Russian memorabilia store was targeted by various instances of arson, vandalism and graffiti. Neo-Nazis Richard Martin and Andrew Benson were believed to be the culprits. Alexander Shapurko's store was vandalized three times in two weeks. The first incident involved the burning of a Russian flag, but the owner thought it was some kids being reckless. The second incident involved a swastika, the number "88" and the letters "WP" spray-painted on the front window of the store. The third incident involved a burning Soviet Union flag hanging in a window. Neo-Nazi graffiti was again painted on a window, another window was smashed, and shop collectibles were broken. It is unclear if charges were ever laid; however, Toronto Police are still investigating (Anti-Racist Canada 2014; Aulakh 2009).

British Columbia
2006, Vancouver, BC
Nathan Richard Fry, a 19-year-old Nazi fanatic, was convicted on five counts of first-degree murder and one count of attempted murder after murdering a Congolese family and another woman. He set the family's household on fire, using 25 litres of gasoline and a blowtorch, killing Adela Etibako, 39, and her children, 12-year-old Edita, 9-year-old Benedicta and 8-year-old Stephane (Anti-Racist Canada 2014). One of the other children, 19-year-old Bolingo, escaped the fire with serious burns, but his girlfriend, 17-year-old Ashley Singh, did not survive. It is alleged that Fry set the fire because he thought that Bolingo ratted him out for a stabbing that they were both being charged for. Fry received life in prison without the possibility of parole for 25 years (Anti-Racist Canada 2014; Canwest News Service 2010).

2009, Courtenay, BC
In the parking lot of a fast-food restaurant, three men attacked Jay Philips, a 39-year-old half black man, all while shouting racial slurs at him. The attack was caught on video, and Adam Huber, 25, Robert Rogers, 25, and David White, 20, were all convicted of assault (Anti-Racist Canada 2014). The first two men were handed conditional sentences and a third man spent one day in jail as the assault went viral on *YouTube* (CBC News British Columbia 2010). Hubert spent one day in jail and was put on 12-month-probation. Rogers was fined $500 and given eight months probation. White, who uttered the racial slurs, was sentenced under hate crime provisions of the *Criminal Code*. He was fined $100, sentenced to 30 days community service, put on a curfew and ordered to undergo psychological counselling (CBC News British Columbia 2010).

2009, Fort St. John, BC
Thirty-two-year-old Peter Anthony Houston, known for his involvement in the Canadian racist movement, was convicted of building a potentially deadly pipe bomb that was planted in a highway restroom in north-eastern BC. In 1999, the bomb was left at a rest stop on Highway 29 between Fort St. John and Hudson's Hope, BC. When Houston

was charged with attempted murder and intent to cause an explosion, the case was never made public (Anti-Racist Canada 2014; CBC News British Columbia 2009).

8 February 2009, Prince George, BC
Peter Houston was found guilty of being in possession of an explosive substance without lawful excuse and possession of a weapon contrary to an order. He was sentenced to 247 days in jail, and he received a lifetime prohibition on the possession of firearms (Anti-Racist Canada 2014; CBC News British Columbia 2009).

2009, Nanaimo, BC
Jeffrey Scott Hughes, a white supremacist involved with the Canadian branch of the *Northwest Imperative*, was death shot to by RCMP officers. Police were called to his apartment in response to a noise complaint, and RCMP testified that Hughes was shot after he threatened officers. It was believed that the man came out of his apartment holding a weapon (which was later determined to be a flare gun) and pointed it at an officer. Several years earlier, the RCMP visited Hughes at his home, responding to hate propaganda he had been distributing. He also had a history of violence, including assault and bomb threats (Anti-Racist Canada 2014; McGarrigle 2011).

Alberta
2006, Calgary, AB
The *Aryan Guard* was formed in late 2006, but was never truly active until March 2007. Claiming to be around 20 members at the time, they began to schedule a number of meetings (as was listed on their website), and the website domain was registered to Bill Noble (One People's Project 2009). *Aryan Guard* members were active before 2007, putting up fliers and blaming minorities for committing multiple crimes in the city, but it was not until 14 August that the media really began paying attention to them (One People's Project 2009). The *Aryan Guard* staged a counter rally when anti-racists organized a protest concerning the activities of the gang. Up until August 2009 when they disbanded, the gang became more active and more brazen (One People's Project 2009).

September 2006, Calgary, AB
Kyle McKee and Dallas Price of the *Aryan Guard* were charged with assault with a weapon and possession of a weapon or imitation for a dangerous purpose. The charges were in connection with a physical altercation, where one victim was stabbed and another was hit with a wooden club (Anti-Racist Canada 2014; *Southern Poverty Law Center* 2009).

2006, Calgary, AB
Aryan Guard leader Kyle McKee was arrested on assault and hate crime charges after he attacked a North African cab driver. McKee claimed that he was not responsible for the attack, but instead he was taking the fall for a friend who almost took an attempted murder charge for McKee the year prior. The charges were eventually dismissed, and McKee bragged about police officers not being able to make a positive identification of him (Anti-Racist Canada 2014; Scherr 2009).

2006, Calgary, AB
Robert Reitmeier of *Western European Bloodlines (WEB)* and formerly the *Aryan Guard* was charged with attempted murder in connection with a confrontation involving a man in his 40s being beaten into a coma and suffering skull and facial fractures. Charges against Reitmeier were later stayed (Anti-Racist Canada 2014).

October 2007, Calgary, AB
Layton Bertsch, *Aryan Guard* supporter, was arrested for throwing a bottle at an activist during an anti-racist demonstration (Anti-Racist Canada 2014; CBC News Calgary 2010a).

2008, Calgary, AB
The home of *Anti-Racist Action (ARA)* members Bonny Collins and Jason Devine was firebombed while their children were asleep inside. A Molotov cocktail was thrown at their home, missing a window, but burning the fence and patio furniture (Anti-Racist Canada 2014; Calgary Herald 2008). Fortunately, no one was injured; however, no one was charged in the incident. Collins and Devine believed that they were targeted for their anti-racist activism by affiliates of the *Aryan Guard* (Anti-Racist Canada 2014; Calgary Herald

2008). *Aryan Guard* member John Marleau later taunted Collins about the firebombing, stating, "How's your house, Bonnie? Is it nice and toasty in there? How's Jason and the kids" (Anti-Racist Canada 2014)?

2008, Edmonton, AB
Haldane Jensen-Huot, 23, who showed interest in the *Aryan Brotherhood* and identified himself as a National Socialist and Satanist, stabbed 77-year-old Hans Albers to death in a random attack. One hour before the murder, he posted a video on *Facebook*, which included documentaries about the *Aryan Brotherhood* and a US white supremacist on death row. He also had a history of violence. He was convicted of assault causing bodily harm on his father, and he was charged with second-degree murder in 2006, which was later upgraded to first-degree murder (Anti-Racist Canada 2014; CBC News Edmonton 2009).

2008, Calgary, AB
Asako Okazaki, a 26-year-old Japanese woman, was attacked by a 17-year-old *Aryan Guard* member. The youth first made disparaging comments about Asians and then followed Okazaki as she left a bar, dropkicking her in the back of the head with steel-toed boots. She was also kicked repeatedly while she was on the ground. The youth was charged with assault with a weapon, assault causing bodily harm and three counts of breaching probation from previous convictions (Anti-Racist Canada 2014; Calgary Herald 2009).

2009, Edmonton, AB
Lacey Dan Snyder, 22, and Dylan Alfred Trommel, 23, were charged in a racially motivated attack on 32-year-old Congolese student Valentin Masepode. Snyder and Trommel confronted Masepode in a convenience store, calling him a "nigger" and telling him that, "this is our country nigger". The pair then called the student outside, and when he would not comply, the two walked back into the store and bear sprayed him in the face. Trommel, who had a swastika tattoo on his back, claimed that the harassment was because he was intoxicated (Anti-Racist Canada 2014; Blais 2010).

2009, Calgary, AB
A cinderblock was thrown through the living room window of *Anti-Racist Action (ARA)* Calgary members Bonnie Collins and Jason Devine. A smaller projectile was also thrown into the bedroom of their three sleeping children, and the front door of their home was spray-painted with "C-18" and a swastika (Anti-Racist Canada 2014).

2009, Calgary, AB
Tyler Sturrup, member of *Western European Bloodlines (WEB)*, and Carolyne Kwatiek, a white nationalist, were targets of two homemade pipe bombs planted by 17-year-old *Aryan Guard* founder Kyle McKee. He was later charged with attempted murder, possessing, making or controlling explosives, and possession of a weapon for a dangerous purpose. McKee pled guilty to possessing explosive devices, but attempted murder charges were dropped (Anti-Racist Canada 2014; Canoe 2010).

Nova Scotia
2000, Dartmouth, NS
Donna Marie Upson, AKA "Baby Hitler" and 22-year-old *KKK* and *Aryan Nations* member, was sentenced to two years in prison for threatening to kill Elias Mutales, a black pastor. Upson was also convicted of threatening to kill black people and threatening to destroy property at a United Baptist Church (Anti-Racist Canada 2014; CBC News 2000a).

2001, Dartmouth, NS
Donna Marie Upson failed to appear in court on charges of assaulting two prison workers at a prison in Nova Scotia, and a warrant was issued for her arrest. The assaults occurred while she was incarcerated on charges of threatening to kill a black pastor (Anti-Racist Canada 2014; CBC News 2001b).

2007, Halifax, NS
Chris Newhook was convicted of aggravated assault, as he stabbed a man in the forehead during a dispute over rent. It was not the first time that Newhook violently assaulted someone over rent concerns (Anti-Racist Canada 2014; CBC News Nova Scotia 2010a).

New Brunswick

2001, Moncton, NB
Donna Marie Upson was arrested and denied bail after attempted arson. One month after being released from a Nova Scotia prison on charges of assault and failure to appear, she refused a bed at a shelter and was seen trying to set fire to the exterior of the building (Anti-Racist Canada 2014; CBC News 2001c).

2001, Moncton, NB
James Frederick Hanley, a 19-year-old who had a history of making derogatory comments about black people and was suspended from school for possessing hate literature, and Matthew Charles Duncan, a violent individual who had racist tattoos, burned a cross on the lawn of a black family in Moncton. Both men were charged with wilful promotion of hatred (Anti-Racist Canada 2014; CBC News 2001e).

2005, Saint John, NB
Chinese students at the University of New Brunswick were targeted in a series of racially motivated attacks. Over a period of several weeks, students were screamed at and told to go back to China. They also had lit fireworks thrown at them, were pelted with eggs, and one couple was assaulted with a cup of ice (Anti-Racist Canada 2014; Canwest News Service 2007).

2007, Saint John, NB
Four Chinese university students were attacked with baseball bats and wooden sticks, and days later, two more Chinese students were attacked, and a bus stop was spray-painted with the words, "Gooks go home". The assaults and vandalism took place in the same neighbourhood where Chinese students were attacked with eggs, ice and fireworks two years prior. Neo-Nazis Jonathan Clifford Martin, 19, and two minors aged 17 and 15 were charged in connection with the 2007 assaults. Martin was charged for the bus shelter vandalism and for possession of a knife for a purpose dangerous to the public peace. The minor youths were charged with assault and possession of a dangerous weapon (Anti-Racist Canada 2014; Canwest News Service 2007).

2007, Saint John, NB
Saint John City Councillor Jay-Young Chang received death threats two weeks after the two violent attacks on Chinese students. A threatening telephone message was left for the Korean councillor, and the message included racial slurs, threats to harm Chang with a weapon and threats to kill him (Anti-Racist Canada 2014; CBC News New Brunswick 2007).

Prince Edward Island
2000, Charlottetown, PEI
Dwayne Finlayson, organizer for the *Heritage Front* in Prince Edward Island, and neo-Nazi Jonathan Petrie attacked two Asian women of Japanese decent. The men smashed pizza into the face of one of the women, shouted racist insults, and they physically attacked a bystander who tried to intervene. Charges of inciting hatred were dropped in exchange for Finlayson pleading guilty to assault and causing a disturbance. Petrie also pled guilty to assault and causing a disturbance. He was additionally charged with failing to appear for his sentencing. Notably, Finalyson is the cousin of Carl Finlayson who committed suicide in 2010 and was involved with the *Heritage Front* in PEI and the *Brotherhood of Klans (BOK)* in Regina, SK (Anti-Racist Canada 2014; CBC News 2000b).

2007, Charlottetown, PEI
Tony Laviolette, 19-year-old neo-Nazi, was sentenced to 30 months for eight charges, including: sexual assault, uttering threats, two counts of arson, and break and enters. He was also found guilty of having sex with a 13-year-old girl and threatening to kill her if she saw anyone else. Laviolette was also convicted for setting fire to a building and a vacant home, and for three breaks and enters, including one at a skating rink which he vandalized with a swastika and racial slurs (Anti-Racist Canada 2014; CBC News 2007; Mayne 2007).

2010–2015

Ontario

July 2010, Hamilton, ON

23-year-old Richard Martin and 38-year-old Shane Gill were arrested for threatening a woman and an 11-year-old girl (Anti-Racist Canada 2014; The Spec 2010). Martin, who lived near the victims, harassed them for weeks; however, the first incident occurred when the woman saw Martin standing outside making gunshot sounds and shooting gestures at her house. Days later, Martin and another man stood near her bedroom window singing racist songs and yelling, "Go back to Africa" (Anti-Racist Canada 2014). The last incident occurred on July 16 as the woman was walking with her friend's 11-year-old daughter (The Spec 2010). Confronted by Martin and Gill, Martin made gunshot sounds and the sign of a gun in her direction, and as the victims turned and began to flee back to her home, Gill and Martin chanted, "We hate niggers". They then followed her home and Gill pounded on the door (Anti-Racist Canada 2014). Martin was later sentenced to nine months in prison and three years of probation, and Gill received six months in prison and three years probation. They were also ordered to submit DNA samples and to refrain from possessing weapons, ammunition and explosives for 15 years (Anti-Racist Canada 2014).

May 2011, Kitchener, ON

White supremacist gang *True White Boys* faced assault and weapons charges. Matthew Armstrong, 19, was charged after an incident in which he elbowed, punched and kicked a man in the head because he thought the victim spread rumours about another *True White Boys* member. Police also investigating a break-in and found seven members of the gang in an apartment which contained a cache of weapons, including a machete and knives, bandanas and drugs (Anti-Racist Canada 2014; Waterloo Regional Record 2011).

August 2013, Kitchener, ON
Former *Aryan Guard* member Jessie Lajoie, 24, was arrested on charges of aggravated assault and disguise with intent and conspiracy. The victim, who was allegedly a guest of the McKee-aligned *Blood & Honour* in Calgary, AB, was attacked with an unknown edged weapon and a hard metal object, receiving a cut to his head and abdomen. Two others, Marissa Kissack, 23, and Eric Marshall, 25, were also charged in the incident. Marissa was charged with aggravated assault, public mischief and obstructing police, and Eric was charged with aggravated assault and disguise with intent and conspiracy (Anti-Racist Canada 2014; CTV News Kitchener 2013).

June 2014, St. Catharines, ON
Christian Edmunds, 18, was arrested for a month-long campaign of alleged racist harassment and intimidation of an elderly couple in St. Catharines. Edmunds, who has connections with the *Southern Ontario Skins*, was charged with criminal harassment (Niagara Falls Review 2014).

British Columbia
6 April 2010, Abbotsford, BC
Two weeks after activists held an anti-Nazi rally in BC's Lower Mainland, the home of an anti-racist organizer was bombed, causing a fire that damaged the exterior of the home. Fortunately, no one was injured (Anti-Racist Canada 2014). Activist Maitland Cassia was with *ShinHeads Against Racial Prejudice (SHARP)* and *Anti-Racist Action (ARA)*. Some speculate that neo-Nazis targeted the home because the organizer's name and photo were published in the Abbotsford Times and gained significant publicity (Anti-Racist Canada 2013; Oommen 2010).

2011, Vancouver, BC
Members of *Blood & Honour*, Shawn Macdonald, Alastair Miller and Rob de Chazal, were arrested for a series of assaults in Vancouver between 2008 and 2011. MacDonald was charged with three counts of assault for allegedly attacking two men and one woman, and Chazal was charged with aggravated assault for allegedly setting a man of Filipino descent on fire. Chazal was also charged with assault causing bodily

harm in connection with an incident in which he attacked a man who was black. Race was a factor in each attack (Anti-Racist Canada 2014; CBC News British Columbia 2012).

March 2012, Surrey, BC
Blood & Honour associate Jan Korinth, 26, was fatally stabbed during his attempt to break into a home (Bolan 2012; CBC News 2012a, b). Korinth was known to police and convicted in Vancouver, BC community court the previous November for assault causing bodily harm (Bolan 2012). Police claimed that it was not clear if or how the men knew each other, and that the motive had not yet been determined, but appeared to be gang-related and an attempted home invasion or break-in (CBC News 2012a). Korinth was a friend of Shawn Macdonald, who along with Rob de Chazal and Alastair Miller was charged in December 2011 with carrying out a series of assaults against minorities in Vancouver (Anti-Racist Canada 2012). Police were concerned that the fatal stabbing of a white supremacist in southern BC could fuel simmering tensions between gangs in the area (CTV News 2012).

November 2014, North Delta, BC
A minor league hockey coach lost his job after posting what is described as "a shrine to Adolf Hitler and Nazism" on his *Facebook* page. In an interview with the Vancouver Sun, he showed himself to be a Holocaust denier, asserting that "there is no such plan, there was no idea" (The Huffington Post 2014).

Alberta
2010, Calgary AB
John Marleau, affiliate of the *Aryan Guard/Blood & Honour*, was arrested after attacking a non-white C-train operator. After someone accidentally pressed the emergency button in the train, the driver came into the car where Marleau was, and he lunged at the operator. Police officials did not believe that the operator was lured by Marleau; however, he was arrested and charged with three counts of assault with a weapon, and one count of possession of a weapon, carrying a concealed weapon and causing a disturbance (Anti-Racist Canada 2014; Calgary Sun 2010).

2010, Edmonton, AB
Dave Burns, a 55-year-old known as "The Nazi" and white supremacist around his office, walked into his workplace and started shooting.
He eventually shot and killed his co-worker Garth Radons before killing himself, and a second co-worker was also shot and critically injured.
Burns, who reportedly had a swastika tattoo and a very hot temper, was
suspended from work for making racist remarks and posting a sexually explicit photo on a staff bulletin board (Anti-Racist Canada 2014;
CBC News Edmonton 2010). Thirty-six years earlier, Burns stabbed an
18-year-old boy to death and served four years for manslaughter (Anti-
Racist Canada 2014).

March 2010, Calgary, AB
During an anti-racist demonstration, William Kaiser Miettinen, AKA
"Willis", was charged with assaulting cameraman Jason Beers with a
skateboard. During the court proceedings, Miettinen denied any skinhead or neo-Nazi ties, even though he ripped his shirt open to display
white supremacist tattoos during the rally (Anti-Racist Canada 2014;
Martin 2011).

2010, Calgary, AB
Five masked men, armed with bats and hammers, invaded the home of
Anti-Racist Action (ARA) Calgary members Bonnie Collins and Jason
Devine. Devine was beaten on the head, back and arms, sustaining
serious back injuries, and a friend who was in the home had his arm
broken. Overall, three adults and four children were in the house at
the time of the attack (Anti-Racist Canada 2014; CBC News Calgary
2010b). No arrests were made; however, police spoke with a number of
suspects, including Kyle McKee, who was charged in connection with a
pair of homemade bombs left outside of a Calgary apartment last year
(CBC News Calgary 2010b). A few months later, McKee was charged
with uttering threats after he asked Devine if he would like another visit
to his home. Police believed the home was targeted, although they did
not confirm a motive. Devine posted a number of pictures of suspected
white supremacists on his blog, and he and his wife put up posters in
their neighbourhood "outing" people they claimed were neo-Nazis
(CBC News Calgary 2010b).

2010, Calgary, AB

Three members and affiliates of *Aryan Guard/Blood & Honour* Calgary beat an 18-year-old girl at a party, leaving her with broken teeth. Kyle McKee was later charged as one of the attackers (Anti-Racist Canada 2014; The Globe and Mail 2011).

October 2011, Calgary, AB

Leaders of the white supremacist group *Western European Bloodline (WEB)*, Robert Reitmeier, 24, and Tyler Williams Sturrup, 26, were charged with second-degree murder (CBC News Calgary 2011; Humphreys 2011; Martin 2011). Mark Mariani was found dead in an alley and was an apparent victim of a group attack while returning to his car after shopping (CBC News Calgary 2011; Humphreys 2011; Martin 2011). Staff Sergeant Doug Andrus said that it appeared to be a random act of violence (Anti-Racist Canada 2009; CBC News Calgary 2011; Humphreys 2011; Martin 2011). Tyler Sturrup pled guilty to murder charges, and on 4 March 2013, he was sentenced to life in prison with no chance of parole for 10 years. Robert Reitmeier was sentenced to life in prison with no chance of parole for 13 years (CBC News Calgary 2013).

February 2011, Calgary, AB

Four affiliates of *Blood & Honour* Calgary were charged during a sequence of racial assaults (Anti-Racist Canada 2011; CTV Edmonton 2011). Three individuals were physically assaulted, and more than 10 random people had racist or hate comments directed at them during the course of the night, all of which were unprovoked (CTV Edmonton 2011; Edmonton Sun 2011). James Andrew Brooks, 25, was charged with criminal harassment, mischief, cause disturbance, utter threats and assault. David Roger Goodman, 18, was charged with criminal harassment, mischief, cause disturbance, utter threats and assault. Jason Anthony Anderson, 32, was charged with criminal harassment, mischief, cause disturbance and assault. Lastly, Keith Virgil Decu, 32, was charged with criminal harassment, mischief, cause disturbance and assault (CTV Edmonton 2011). The charges came after the four were seen handing out flyers to strangers and posting flyers on poles about a white supremacist group (Blais 2011; CTV Edmonton 2011; Edmonton Sun 2011).

March 2011, Calgary, AB
Kyle Robert McKee, 25, of the *Aryan Guard* and *Blood & Honour* was imprisoned for 60 days for racist motivated threats and assault (Calgary Herald 2011). McKee pled guilty to uttering threats and possession of a dangerous weapon in relation to an incident involving *Anti-Racist Action (ARA)* member Jason Devine on 13 February 2011. A few months earlier, Devine had been the victim of a home invasion in which he and a friend were seriously injured (Calgary Herald 2011).

31 August 2011, Peace River, AB
Ian Michael Butz, 28, and his brother Jason Avery Butz, 26, were charged with two counts of armed robbery at a gas station (CBC News British Columbia 2013). They are alleged to be neo-Nazis (Anti-Racist Canada 2014).

December 2012, Lloydminster, AB
Four members of Alberta's drug gang, *The White Boy Posse*, were charged in a series of three murders (CBC News Edmonton 2012). Randy James Wayne O'Hagan, 22, was charged with three counts of first-degree murder and attempted murder. Nikolas Jon Nowytzkyj, 32, was charged with attempted murder. Kyle Darren Halbauer, 22, was charged with two counts of first-degree murder and attempted murder. And Joshua Petrin, 29, was charged first-degree murder (CBC News Edmonton 2012). One of the victims was decapitated, and his remains were located in various locations across Alberta (CBC News Edmonton 2012; Wittmeier 2012). Police said that all four men were members of the White Boy Posse, a drug gang based in Alberta with tentacles extending into Saskatoon and the Northwest Territories (CBC News Edmonton 2012), reaching from Yellowknife to Saskatoon to Medicine Hat (Wittmeier 2012). The gang were a suspected "puppet gang" of the *Hells Angels*, dealing drugs for the larger gang (CBC News Edmonton 2012). Edmonton police linked the Alberta-based *White Boy Posse* to Nazi symbols, street-level drug dealing and affiliations with the *Hells Angels* (Wittmeier 2012). The *White Boy Posse* is also a gang known for its racist ideology, cocaine dealing and violence (CBC News Saskatchewan 2012). Many of the members have swastika tattoos and hold white supremacist beliefs (CBC News Edmonton 2012).

March 2013, Edmonton, AB
Two members of *Blood & Honour* and an associate approached two men inside of a liquor store, making derogatory comments and racial slurs (Roth 2012b). The two males were attacked and assaulted, and one of the males was assaulted with a bottle of liquor (Roth 2012a). Consequently, Calgary's infamous neo-Nazi and *Blood & Honour* members Kyle McKee, 26, and Bernard Miller, 20, as well as associate member Philip Badrock, 44, were charged in the alleged bottle attack against two East Indian males (Gardner and Parrish 2012; Massinon 2012; Roth 2012a, b). McKee faced 15 weapon-related charges, as well as two stemming from the assault (Roth 2012a); Miller was charged with one count each of assault with a weapon and assault causing bodily harm. Badrock was charged with one count each of criminal harassment and assault causing bodily harm (Global Edmonton 2012).

October 2013, Okotoks, AB
Freeman-on-the-Land Darren Clifford (brother of Dean Clifford) was arrested on a series of charges, including assaulting a police officer. When Detective Christie attempted to arrest Clifford on other charges, Clifford allegedly resisted arrest, striking the officer in the process (Calgary Sun 2013).

2013, Calgary, AB
Andreas Perelli, a self-proclaimed *Freeman-on-the-Land*, was embroiled in a landlord-tenant dispute in which he refused to vacate the rented property that he had declared to be his "Embassy". He finally complied with his eviction order on 28 September. As he left the property, he was arrested on an outstanding warrant from Quebec, where he had been known as Mario Antonacci. He was accused in that province of pushing his landlady down a flight of stairs, resulting in a broken pelvis, arm, wrist and ankle (Huffington Post 2013).

March 2015, Calgary, AB
A suspected white supremacist, Morgan Thompson, disrupted an anti-racism rally with shouts of "white power". When police observing the event exited their vehicle, Thompson began to run and was chased

into an alley. An officer caught up to him, and Thompson allegedly fought against him, brandishing a metal pipe. Officers fired a number of shots, leaving him in critical condition. One officer sustained minor injuries (Calgary Sun 2015).

8 June 2015, Edmonton, AB
Norman Walter Raddatz, 42-year-old anti-Semite, anti-government and homophobe, is the alleged lone shooter in the death of an Edmonton police officer on 8 June 2015. When members of the hate crime unit visited Raddatz's home to serve him with an arrest warrant and court documents, the man refused to answer the door. Officers used a battering ram to gain access to the West Edmonton residence, and in turn the suspect fired a high-powered rifle at officers, killing Constable Daniel Woodall, 35, and injuring 38-year-old Sergeant Jason Harley. The house was later set ablaze, most likely by the suspect, and his body was located in the basement of his home (CBC News 2015; Simons 2015). The paranoid man was suspected of harassing a local Jewish man and his family for a year-and-a-half, intimidating them with increasingly violent hate messages (Simons 2015). He also posted hateful messages on the Internet about "sodomites" and "f-bomb Jews", and sharing crude jokes about the film "Brokeback Mountain". Prior to the police shootout, he was battling alcoholism and depression, had recently become divorced, lost his business and motor home and was in the process of losing his bungalow (Canadian Press 2015; CBC News 2015; Simons 2015).

New Brunswick
4 June 2014, Moncton, NB
24-year-old Justin Bourque shot and killed three RCMP officers and injured two others. He is often described as a "lone wolf" who used social media to educate himself on far-right libertarian preoccupations, such as the "militarization" of police, anti-authoritarianism, survivalism, "crownless kings", confiscation of guns and Canada's readiness for a Russian invasion (Brean 2014). His *Facebook* page revealed him to be a gun enthusiast and libertarian with an anti-authoritarian mindset, and his account was awash with pro-gun, cop-hating and liberal-bashing propaganda (CBC News 2014; Friscolanti and Patriquin 2014).

Nova Scotia

2010, Hants County, NS
An interracial couple experienced a cross burning on the lawn of their home. Michelle Lyon and Shayne Howe, a black man, reported hearing someone shout, "Die, nigger, die", before his daughter saw a 2-metre cross burning on the family's lawn with a noose hanging from it. Brothers Nathan Rehberg, 20, and Justin Rehber, 19, who are distant cousins of Lyon, were charged with inciting hatred and criminal harassment (Anti-Racist Canada 2014; CBC News Nova Scotia 2010a).

2010, Halifax, NS
Chris Newhook, long-time white supremacist and one of the first members of *Heritage Front*, was declared a dangerous offender and imprisoned indefinitely after spending half of his life in prison and accumulating roughly 50 criminal convictions, including several racist attacks on minorities. During his hearing, Newhook yelled at the crown prosecutor, "I hate your fucking guts. I wish I could cut your fucking head off with a rusty hacksaw blade" (Anti-Racist Canada 2014; CBC News Nova Scotia 2010b).

2011, Amherst, NS
Daren McCormick, 45, was arrested on firearm violations as well as uttering threats to police officers. McCormick is an avowed *Freeman-on-the-Land* adherent. He told an officer that he could outdraw police, and that if a police cruiser appeared on his property, he would kill the officers within. When police arrived at his home in response to the threats, they were met by McCormick, who allegedly carried a loaded revolver on his hip. He was convicted of the charges in 2012 (Times-Colonist 2012).

2015, Halifax NS
Lindsay Souvannarath, 23, and Randall Steven Shepherd, 20, were arrested on charges of conspiracy to commit murder, conspiracy to commit arson, illegal possession of weapons for a purpose dangerous to the public and making a threat through social media. They had allegedly planned to unleash a deadly assault on a Halifax shopping centre on Valentine's Day. A third youth who was alleged to have been part of

the conspiracy, James Gamble, 19, was found dead in his home. Based on the presence of Nazi materials in Gamble's home, it is presumed that the group was influenced by white supremacist ideals. Nonetheless, then-Justice Minister Peter MacKay publicly proclaimed that this was not a terrorist crime, noting: "The attack does not appear to have been culturally motivated, therefore not linked to terrorism" (Walkom 2015).

References

Agno, D. (1997, April 24). Hate Goes to High School. *Eye Weekly*. Retrieved from http://contests.eyeweekly.com/eye/issue/issue_04.24.97/news_views/hate.php.

Anti-Racist Canada. (2009). *So, What Has Robert Reitmeier Been Up to Lately?* Retrieved from http://anti-racistcanada.blogspot.ca/2009/08/so-what-has-robert-reitmeier-been-up-to.html.

Anti-Racist Canada. (2012). *Kyle McKee, Bernie Miller, and Others: Charged with Assault*. Retrieved from http://anti-racistcanada.blogspot.ca/2012/04/kyle-mckee-bernie-miller-and-others.html.

Anti-Racist Canada. (2014). *A History of Violence: 1970–2014*. Retrieved from http://anti-racistcanada.blogspot.ca/2011/10/history-of-violence-1989-2011.html.

Aulakh, R. (2009, February 15). Russian Émigré's Store Vandalized, Painted with Swastika. *Toronto Star*. Retrieved from http://www.thestar.com/news/gta/2009/02/15/russian_eacutemigreacutes_store_vandalized_painted_with_swastika.html.

Blais, T. (2010, May 13). Racist Man Bear-Sprayed Student. *Canoe*. Retrieved from http://cnews.canoe.ca/CNEWS/Crime/2010/05/13/13929911.html.

Blais, T. (2011, September 30). White Supremacist Jailed for Crime Spree. *Canoe*. Retrieved from http://cnews.canoe.ca/CNEWS/Crime/2011/09/30/pf-18764611.html.

Bolan, K. (2012, March 19). Police ID 26-Year-Old Man Stabbed to Death in Surrey Saturday. *Vancouver Sun*. Retrieved from http://www.vancouversun.com/news/Police+year+stabbed+death+Surrey+Saturday/6326607/story.html.

Brean, J. (2014, June 6). Justin Bourque's Alienation Nurtured in the Old Confines of Social Media. *National Post*. Retrieved from http://news.nationalpost.com/2014/06/06/justin-bourques-alienation-nurtured-in-the-cold-confines-of-social-media/.

Calgary Herald. (2006, September 22). *Money Wasn't Worth Killing For.* Retrieved from http://www.canada.com/calgaryherald/story.html?id=9d8432f8-830a-43c4-8e15-ec8751e1f361&k=99917.

Calgary Herald. (2008, February 23). *Couple Feels Neo-Nazis Behind Firebomb Attack.* Retrieved from http://www.canada.com/calgaryherald/news/city/story.html?id=b3148f46-1e8b-4e9e-a3af-c5fedc956124.

Calgary Herald. (2009, January 28). *Attack on Visitor Linked to Aryan Guard.* Retrieved from http://www.canada.com/calgaryherald/news/city/story.html?id=79a32d0b-7b3d-403e-8fb1-08512d8240b4.

Calgary Herald. (2012, July 20). *This Day in 1985—Former Teacher Jim Keegstra Fined for Promoting Hatred.* Retrieved from http://calgaryherald.com/news/local-news/this-day-in-1985.

Calgary Sun. (2010, January 7). *Suspect in Attack on C-Train Driver Linked to Racist Group.* Retrieved from http://www.calgarysun.com/news/alberta/2010/01/07/12375891-sun.html.

Calgary Sun. (2013, October 8). *Okotoks 'Freeman on the Land' Denied Bail for Allegedly Assaulting RCMP Officer and Other Charges.* Retrieved from http://www.calgarysun.com/2013/10/08/okotoks-freeman-on-the-land-denied-bail-for-allegedly-assaulting-rcmp-officer-and-other-charges.

Calgary Sun. (2015, March 21). *Alleged White Supremacist Shot by Cops After Disturbing Peace Rally: Witnesses.* Retrieved from http://www.calgarysun.com/2015/03/21/cops-shoot-man-at-calgary-peace-rally.

Canadian Anti-Racism Education and Research Society. (2013a). *Anti-Racist Action in Toronto.* Retrieved from http://www.stopracism.ca/content/15-anti-racist-action-toronto-ara.

Canadian Anti-Racism Education and Research Society. (2013b). *Early Racist Skinhead Movement (Part 2).* Retrieved from http://www.stopracism.ca/content/early-racist-skinhead-movement-part-2.

Canadian Press. (2009, October 20). Offender Charged After Threatening Prosecutor During Tirade in Halifax Court. *Cape Breton Post.* Retrieved from http://www.capebretonpost.com/Justice/2009-10-20/article-768875/Offender-charged-after-threatening-prosecutor-during-tirade-in-Halifax-court/1.

Canadian Press. (2015, June 9). Edmonton Police Release Details About Deadly Shootout. *Huffington Post.* Retrieved from http://www.huffington-post.ca/2015/06/09/edmonton-police-officer-k_n_7540386.html.

Canoe. (2010, May 19). *Purported Neo-Nazi Admits to Making Explosives.* Retrieved from http://cnews.canoe.ca/CNEWS/Crime/2010/05/18/13995161.html?cid=rssnewscanada.

Canwest News Service. (2007, August 10). Racial Attacks on Chinese Students Linked to Skinheads. *Ottawa Citizen*. Retrieved from http://www.canada.com/ottawacitizen/news/story.html?id=f3b7dbc5-a6d0-4553-872c-3aed9de90a11&k=80416.

Canwest News Service. (2010, January 15). Mass Murderer Nathan Fry Seeks 'Upbeat' Pen Pal. *The Province*. Retrieved from http://kelowna.com/forums/topic/mass-murderer-nathan-fry-seeks-upbeat-pen-pal.

CBC News. (1999, October 5). *Crown Seeks Life in B.C. Skinhead Sentencing Hearing*. Retrieved from http://www.cbc.ca/news/canada/crown-seeks-life-in-b-c-skinhead-sentencing-hearing-1.192848.

CBC News. (2000a, June 5). *Woman Sentenced for Hate Crimes*. Retrieved from http://www.cbc.ca/news/canada/woman-sentenced-for-hate-crimes-1.207968.

CBC News. (2000b, July 6). *Charlottetown Man in Court over Hate Crime and Assault*. Retrieved from http://www.cbc.ca/news/canada/charlottetown-man-in-court-over-hate-crime-and-assault-1.232804.

CBC News. (2001a, May 5). *Deliberations Set to Begin at Murder Trial*. Retrieved from http://www.cbc.ca/news/canada/deliberations-set-to-begin-at-murder-trial-1.294128.

CBC News. (2001b, May 29). *Arrest Warrant Issued for Klan Recruiter*. Retrieved from http://www.cbc.ca/news/canada/arrest-warrant-issued-for-klan-recruiter-1.285446.

CBC News. (2001c, June 19). *'Baby Hitler' Denied Bail*. Retrieved from http://www.cbc.ca/news/canada/baby-hitler-denied-bail-1.290237.

CBC News. (2001d, June 21). *Teen Guilty of Racially-Motivated Murder*. Retrieved from http://www.cbc.ca/news/canada/teen-guilty-of-racially-motivated-murder-1.288013.

CBC News. (2001e, August 1). *Moncton Man Charged with Hate Crime*. Retrieved from http://www.cbc.ca/news/canada/moncton-man-charged-with-hate-crime-1.291206.

CBC News. (2001f, October 3). *Racist Accused of Threatening Jews, Muslims*. Retrieved from http://www.cbc.ca/news/canada/racist-accused-of-threatening-jews-muslims-1.287370.

CBC News. (2005, April 15). *Man Charged in Shooting Death of White Supremacist Wolfgang Droege*. Retrieved from http://www.cbc.ca/news/canada/man-charged-in-shooting-death-of-white-supremacist-wolfgang-droege-1.546492.

CBC News. (2007a, January 23). *Racist Webmaster Gets 6 Months for Hate Propaganda*. Retrieved from http://www.cbc.ca/news/canada/montreal/racist-webmaster-gets-6-months-for-hate-propaganda-1.662779.

CBC News. (2007b, August 13). *Friends of Simon Wiesenthal Center Advises of Calgary-Based Neo-Nazi's Recent Activity*. Retrieved from http://www.newswire.ca/en/story/155641/friends-of-simon-wiesenthal-center-advises-of-calgary-based-neo-nazi-s-recent-activity.

CBC News. (2009, May 27). *Charge Dropped Against Suspect in Shooting of Ontario Abortion Doctor*. Retrieved from http://www.cbc.ca/news/canada/charge-dropped-against-suspect-in-shooting-of-ontario-abortion-doctor-1.780549.

CBC News. (2012a, March 18). *1 Killed in Surrey Stabbing*. Retrieved from http://www.cbc.ca/news/canada/british-columbia/1-killed-in-surrey-stabbing-1.1165838.

CBC News. (2012b, March 19). *Surrey Stabbing Victim ID'd*. Retrieved from http://www.cbc.ca/news/canada/british-columbia/surrey-stabbing-victim-id-d-1.1155340.

CBC News. (2014, June 5). *Justin Bourque: Latest Revelations About Man Charged in Moncton Shooting*. Retrieved from http://www.cbc.ca/news/canada/new-brunswick/justin-bourque-latest-revelations-about-man-charged-in-moncton-shooting-1.2665900.

CBC News. (2015, June 9). *Norman Raddatz Had Extensive Police File for Hate Crimes*. Retrieved from http://www.huffingtonpost.ca/2015/06/09/edmonton-police-officer-k_n_7540386.html.

CBC News British Columbia. (2009, June 9). *B.C. Man Convicted of Building Bomb Planted in Highway Restroom*. Retrieved from http://www.cbc.ca/news/canada/british-columbia/b-c-man-convicted-of-building-bomb-planted-in-highway-restroom-1.861498.

CBC News British Columbia. (2010, December 21). *YouTube Assault Draws Little Jail Time*. Retrieved from http://www.cbc.ca/news/canada/british-columbia/youtube-assault-draws-little-jail-time-1.900739.

CBC News British Columbia. (2012, January 23). *Man Set on Fire in Alleged Racial Attack*. Retrieved from http://www.cbc.ca/news/canada/british-columbia/man-set-on-fire-in-alleged-racial-attack-1.1157097.

CBC News Calgary. (2010a, March 21). *Protesters, Neo-Nazis Clash at Anti-Racism Rally*. Retrieved from http://www.cbc.ca/news/canada/calgary/protesters-neo-nazis-clash-at-anti-racism-rally-1.868638.

CBC News Calgary. (2010b, November 8). *Calgary Anti-Racism Activists' Home Invaded*. Retrieved from http://www.cbc.ca/news/canada/calgary/calgary-anti-racism-activists-home-invaded-1.902197.

CBC News Calgary. (2011, June 1). *2 Men Charged in Deadly 2010 Attack*. Retrieved from http://www.cbc.ca/news/canada/calgary/2-men-charged-in-deadly-2010-attack-1.1017160.

CBC News Calgary. (2013, March 4). *Calgary Man Pleads Guilty in Deadly Beating.* Retrieved from http://www.cbc.ca/news/canada/calgary/calgary-man-pleads-guilty-in-deadly-beating-1.1305833.

CBC News Edmonton. (2009, March 27). *Man Pleads Guilty in Fatal Stabbing of Senior.* Retrieved from http://www.cbc.ca/news/canada/edmonton/man-pleads-guilty-in-fatal-stabbing-of-senior-1.809703.

CBC News Edmonton. (2010, March 13). *Edmonton Shooting Suspect a Racist: Co-Worker.* Retrieved from http://www.cbc.ca/news/canada/edmonton/edmonton-shooting-suspect-a-racist-co-workers-1.940915.

CBC News Edmonton. (2012, December 4). *Murder Charges Laid in Decapitation, 2 Other Homicides: Four Members of Alberta Drug Gang Charged in Three Killings in September, October.* Retrieved from http://www.cbc.ca/news/canada/edmonton/murder-charges-laid-in-decapitation-2-other-homicides-1.1131100.

CBC News New Brunswick. (2007, August 16). *Saint John Councilor Target of Racist Death Threats.* Retrieved http://www.cbc.ca/news/canada/new-brunswick/saint-john-councillor-target-of-racist-death-threats-1.661448.

CBC News Nova Scotia. (2010a, February 22). *N.S. Couple Shaken by Cross Burning.* Retrieved from http://www.cbc.ca/news/canada/nova-scotia/n-s-couple-shaken-by-cross-burning-1.880988.

CBC News Nova Scotia. (2010b, March 1). *Newhook Declared Dangerous Offender.* Retrieved from http://www.cbc.ca/news/canada/nova-scotia/newhook-declared-dangerous-offender-1.949012.

CBC News Saskatchewan. (2011, January 28). *LaChance Shooting Remembered in Prince Albert.* Retrieved from http://www.cbc.ca/news/canada/saskatchewan/lachance-shooting-remembered-in-prince-albert-1.1089247.

CBC News Saskatchewan. (2012, December 5). *White Boy Posse 'Incredibly Violent,' Expert Says.* Retrieved from http://www.cbc.ca/news/canada/saskatchewan/white-boy-posse-incredibly-violent-expert-says-1.1252970.

Chicago Tribune. (2002, July 16). *Skinhead Arrested in Canada Slaying.* Retrieved from http://articles.chicagotribune.com/2002-07-16/news/0207160173_1_hate-related-hate-motivated-david-rosenzweig.

CTV Edmonton. (2011, March 10). *Alleged Victims of Racist Attacks on Whyte Ave. Speak Out.* Retrieved from http://edmonton.ctvnews.ca/alleged-victims-of-racist-attacks-on-whyte-ave-speak-out-1.617109.

CTV Montreal. (2011, March 22). *22-Year-Old Found Guilty of Assault.* Retrieved from http://montreal.ctvnews.ca/22-year-old-found-guilty-of-assault-1.621919.

CTV News. (2012, March 25). *Police Fear B.C. Neo-Nazi's Death Could Spark Gang War*. Retrieved from http://www.ctvnews.ca/police-fear-b-c-neo-nazi-s-death-could-spark-gang-war-1.786894.

CTV News Kitchener. (2013, March 4). *Police Arrest Three in Connection with Victoria Park Attack*. Retrieved from http://kitchener.ctvnews.ca/police-arrest-three-in-connection-with-victoria-park-attack-1.1180833.

Edmonton Sun. (2011, March 8). *Edmonton Police Lay Charges over Alleged Hate Crimes*. Retrieved from http://www.edmontonsun.com/news/edmonton/2011/03/08/17540196.html.

Gardner, C., & Parris, J. (2012, April 17). Three Arrested by EPS Hate Crimes Unit. *CTV News*. Retrieved from http://edmonton.ctvnews.ca/three-arrested-by-eps-hate-crimes-unit-1.797199.

The Gazette. (1995, May 5). *White Supremacists Visited Regiment's Mess Hall*. Retrieved from https://cases.justia.com/federal/district-courts/california/candce/5:2008cv03889/206207/14/11.pdf.

Global Edmonton. (2012, April 17). *Edmonton Police Arrest White Supremacist Members*. Retrieved from http://www.globaltvedmonton.com/eps+arrest+-blood++honour+members/6442622681/story.html.

The Global Jewish News Source. (1992, November 11). *Anti-Nazi Activists' Home Damaged by Suspicious Fire*. Retrieved from http://www.jta.org/1992/11/11/archive/anti-nazi-activists-home-damaged-by-suspicious-fire.

The Global Jewish News Source. (1993, June 6). *Neo-Nazi Attack in Ontario Store Heightens Fears of Anti-Semitism*. Retrieved from http://www.jta.org/1993/06/07/archive/neo-nazi-attack-in-ontario-store-heightens-fears-of-anti-semitism.

The Globe and Mail. (2011, March 18). *Calgary's In-Your-Face Neo-Nazis Take to the Streets*. Retrieved from http://www.theglobeandmail.com/news/national/calgarys-in-your-face-neo-nazis-take-to-the-streets/article573162/?page=all.

The Globe and Mail. (2013, May 25). *The Ford Family's History with Drug Dealing*. Retrieved from http://www.theglobeandmail.com/news/toronto/globe-investigation-the-ford-familys-history-with-drug-dealing/article12153014/?page=all.

The Globe and Mail. (2014, February 21). *Garson Romalis Risked His Life to Perform Abortions*. Retrieved from http://www.theglobeandmail.com/news/british-columbia/garson-romalis-risked-his-life-to-perform-abortions/article17052093/.

Huffington Post. (2013, September 28). *Andreas Pirelli Evicted from Freeman "Embassy"; Rebekah Caverhill Prepares to Reclaim Home.* Retrieved from http://www.huffingtonpost.ca/2013/09/28/calgary-freeman-evicted_n_4009241.html.

Huffington Post. (2014, June 11). *Christopher Maximilian Sandau, B.C. Hockey Coach, Fired Over Pro-Nazi Facebook Posts.* Retrieved from http://www.huffingtonpost.ca/2014/11/05/christopher-maximilian-sandau-coach-fired-nazi_n_6111988.html.

Kinsella, W. (2001). *Web of Hate: Inside Canada's Far Right Network.* Toronto: HarperCollins.

Lauder, M. A. (2002). *The Far Rightwing Movement in Southwest Ontario: An Exploration of Issues, Themes, and Variations.* The Guelph and District Multicultural Centre.

Martin, K. (2011, June 16). Suspected Neo-Nazi in Plea Bargain Bid. *Calgary Sun.* Retrieved from http://www.calgarysun.com/2011/06/16/suspected-neonazi-in-plea-bargain-bid.

Mayne, L. A. (2007, December 20). Laviolette Given 30 Months. *Journal Pioneer.* Retrieved from http://www.journalpioneer.com/Justice/2007-12-20/article-1389852/Laviolette-given-30-months/1.

McGarrigle, J. (2011, July 29). Corner Told Hughes Died of Blood Loss. *BC Local News.* Retrieved from http://www.bclocalnews.com/news/126403828.html.

McLaughlin, T. (2008, September 12). Trial Probes Beating Death. *The Barrie Examiner.* Retrieved from http://www.thebarrieexaminer.com/2008/09/12/trial-probes-beating-death.

Montreal Gazette. (2006, December 11). *Trial Delayed for Teen Suspected of Posting Threats.* Retrieved from http://www.canada.com/montrealgazette/news/story.html?id=2d00a6a5-7273-4ca0-aa25-c063d23bd6d9&k=36474.

National Post. (2006, June 17). *Neo-Nazi Killer Who Acted Out of Paranoia Gets 10 Years.* Retrieved from http://www.canada.com/nationalpost/news/toronto/story.html?id=cf832bac-a6bd-4a45-b159-bc97a1e82ad3.

National Post. (2007, March 16). *Police Charge Man, 20, in Jewish Daycare Attack.* Retrieved from http://www.canada.com/nationalpost/news/toronto/story.html?id=4b59fba8-1ab8-4446-98b7-bed102262545.

New York Times. (1995, March 24). *Head of Detroit White Supremacist Group Faces Trial in Canada.* Retrieved from http://www.nytimes.com/1995/03/24/us/head-of-detroit-white-supremacist-group-faces-trial-in-canada.html.

Niagara Falls Review. (2014, June 19). *Man Charged with Criminally Harassing Elderly Couple*. Retrieved from http://www.niagarafallsreview.ca/2014/06/19/man-charged-with-criminally-harassing-elderly-couple.

One People's Project. (2009). *Bill Noble*. Retrieved from http://onepeoplesproject.com/index.php/en/rogues-gallery/14-n/128-bill-noble.

Oommen, I. (2010, April 26). Mainstream Media Fumbles Abbotsford Attack. *Vancouver Media Co-Op*. Retrieved from http://vancouver.mediacoop.ca/story/3300.

Ottawa Citizen. (2006, April 18). *Murder Charges Laid in Death of Ottawa Man*. Retrieved from http://www.canada.com/ottawacitizen/news/story.html?id=a9f4eaa8-1f44-4217-b988-8ca489147158&k=38214.

Peace Magazine. (1995, July–August). *Urban Terrorism: Could It Happen Here?* Retrieved from http://peacemagazine.org/archive/v11n4p18.htm.

Pro-Choice Action Network. (1997/1998). New Lead in Doctor Shootings. *Pro-Choice Press*. Retrieved from http://www.prochoiceactionnetwork-canada.org/prochoicepress/9798win.shtml.

Radio-Canada. (2002, June 6). *Richard Germain est Condamné à la Prison*. Retrieved from http://ici.radio-canada.ca/nouvelles/Montreal/nouvelles/200206/06/006-germain-condamnation.asp.

Roth, P. (2012a, April 17). Calgary White Supremacist Arrested over Edmonton Racial Attack. *Calgary Sun*. Retrieved from http://www.calgarysun.com/2012/04/17/calgary-white-supremacist-arrested-over-edmonton-racial-attack.

Roth, P. (2012b, April 17). White Supremacists Charged in Alleged Bottle Attack. *Calgary Sun*. Retrieved from http://www.calgarysun.com/2012/04/17/white-supremacists-charged-in-alleged-bottle-attack.

Scherr, S. (2009). Aryan Guard Marches on Calgary. *Southern Poverty Law Center*. Retrieved from http://www.splcenter.org/get-informed/intelligence-report/browse-all-issues/2009/summer/northern-exposure.

The Spec. (2010, September 15). *Racists Going to Jail for Taunts*. Retrieved from http://www.thespec.com/news-story/2170372-racists-going-to-jail-for-taunts/.

St. Joseph News Press. (1981, November 27). *Canadian Klan Chief Is Charged*. Retrieved from http://news.google.com/newspapers?id=HdlbAAAAIBAJ&sjid=n1INAAAAIBAJ&pg=2910,5603839&dq=james+alexander+mcquirter&hl=en.

Times-Colonist. (2012). *'Freeman on the Land' Movement Worries CSIS*. Retrieved from http://www.timescolonist.com/news/national/freeman-on-the-land-movement-worries-csis-1.37071.

Toronto Star. (1987, July 17). *Death Threat in Extortion Case 2 Men Charged.* Retrieved from http://pqasb.pqarchiver.com/thestar/doc/435583821.html? FMT=ABS&FMTS=ABS:FT&type=current&date=Jul%2017,%20 1987&author=&pub=Toronto%20Star&edition=&startpage= &desc=Death%20threat%20in%20extortion%20case%202%20men%20 charged.

Toronto Star. (1990a, March 8). *Injured Man Found Near Railway Tracks.* Retrieved from http://pqasb.pqarchiver.com/thestar/doc/436154957.html?FMT=ABS&F-MTS=ABS:FT&type=current&date=Mar%2008,%201990&author=&-pub=Toronto%20Star&edition=&startpage=&desc=Injured%20man%20 found%20near%20railway%20tracks.

Toronto Star. (1990b, June 26). *Ex-Skinhead Gets 12 Years for Killing Teen.* Retrieved from http://pqasb.pqarchiver.com/thestar/doc/436226366.html? FMT=ABS&FMTS=ABS:FT&type=current&date=Jun%2026,%20 1990&author=Gary%20Oakes%20Toronto%20Star&pub=Toronto%20 Star&edition=&startpage=&desc=Ex-skinhead%20gets%2012%20 years%20for%20killing%20teen.

Toronto Star. (1991, September 21). *Metro Police Arrest White Supremacist.* Retrieved from http://pqasb.pqarchiver.com/thestar/doc/436472932.html?FMT=ABS&F-MTS=ABS:FT&type=current&date=Sep%2021,%201991&author=&-pub=Toronto%20Star&edition=&startpage=&desc=Metro%20police%20 arrest%20white%20supremacist.

Toronto Star. (1993a, April 29). *Second Man Charged After Teen's Body Found in Tub.* Retrieved from http://pqasb.pqarchiver.com/thestar/ doc/436817238.html?FMT=ABS&FMTS=ABS:FT&type=cur-rent&date=Apr%2029,%201993&author=&pub=Toronto%20 Star&edition=&startpage=&desc=Second%20man%20charged%20 after%20teen's%20body%20found%20in%20tub.

Toronto Star. (1993b, October 28). *Police Arrest 2 Men in Oshawa Robberies.* Retrieved http://pqasb.pqarchiver.com/thestar/doc/436918031.htm-l?FMT=ABS&FMTS=ABS:FT&type=current&date=Oct%2028,% 201993&author=Gail%20Swainson%20Toronto%20 Star&pub=Toronto%20Star&edition=&startpage=&desc=Police%20 arrest%202%20men%20in%20Oshawa%20robberies.

Toronto Star. (1995, November 9). *Judge Stayed Charges Because of Long Delay.* Retrieved from http://pqasb.pqarchiver.com/thestar/doc/437362091. html?FMT=ABS&FMTS=ABS:FT&type=current&date=Nov%20 09,%201995&author=By%20Dale%20Brazao%20Toronto%20 Star&pub=Toronto%20Star&edition=&startpage=&desc=Judge%20 stays%20charges%20because%20of%20long%20delay.

Vancouver Sun. (2006, August 6). *Hate Crime Carries High Price*. Retrieved from http://www.canada.com/story_print.html?id=fea20c32-2431-4f3c-b097-067f48bbfabc&sponsor.

Walkom, T. (2015, February 17). Halifax Murder Plot Shows Absurdity of Anti-Terror Laws. *Toronto Star*. Retrieved from https://www.thestar.com/news/canada/2015/02/17/halifax-murder-plot-shows-absurdity-of-anti-terror-laws-walkom.html.

Waterloo Regional Record. (2011, May 10). *Second Teen Gang Member Pleads Guilty to Assault, Theft*. Retrieved from http://www.therecord.com/news-story/2580579-second-teen-gang-member-pleads-guilty-to-assault-theft/.

Winnipeg Free Press. (2013, September 19). *Why Does Same-Sex Affection Draw Anger?* Retrieved from http://www.winnipegfreepress.com/local/why-does-same-sex-affection-draw-anger-224361501.html.

Winnipeg Free Press. (2014, March 8). *Brilliant Doctor, Graceful Humanist*. Retrieved from http://www.winnipegfreepress.com/local/brilliant-doctor-graceful-humanist-249104791.html.

Wittmeier, B. (2012, December 9). Money, Drugs and Violence: The Evolution of White Boy Posse—In the Wake of Recent High-Profile Killings, Experts Look at Criminal Gang Behaviour. *Edmonton Journal*. Retrieved from http://www.edmontonjournal.com/news/Money+drugs+violence+evolution+White+Posse/7673689/story.html.

Appendix C: Right-Wing Extremist Groups in Canada (1830–2015)

28 Supporters Club[1]
Alternative Forum
Aryan Brotherhood
Aryan Guard
Aryan Nations
Aryan Resistance Movement (ARM)
Asatru Folk Assembly (AFA)
Atalante
BC White Pride
Black and Red Front
Blood & Honour
British Canada Party
British Israel
British People's League (and Party)
Campus Alternative

---

[1]Groups active shortly before or during the period of the study (2010–2015) are in italics.

© The Editor(s) (if applicable) and The Author(s) 2019
B. Perry and R. Scrivens, *Right-Wing Extremism in Canada*,
Palgrave Hate Studies, https://doi.org/10.1007/978-3-030-25169-7

Canadian Action
Canadian Advocates for Charter Equality (CANACE)
Canadian Anti-Soviet Action Committee (CASAC)
Canadian Association for Free Expression (CAFE)
Canadian Ethnic Cleansing Team (CECT)
Canadian Free Speech League
Canadian Heritage Alliance
Canadian National Party
Canadian Nazi Party
Canadian Union of Fascists
Canadian White National Association
Canadian Youth Corps
Christ Is the Answer, Inc.
Christian Action Movement
Christian Defence Council
Christian Fellowship Assembly
Christian Mutual Defence Fund
Church of Creativity
Church of Jesus Christ Christian-Aryan Nations
Citizens for Foreign Aid Reform (C-FAR)
Combat 18 (C-18)
Committee for Free Speech in Canada
Concerned Parents of German Descent
Cornerstone Alliance
Creativity Movement Toronto
Crew 38
Dead Boys Crew
Deutsche Bund
Direct Action
Ezra Pound Institute of International Studies
Federation for Individual Rights and Equality
Final Solution Skinheads
Folkish Women's Front
Freeman-on-the-Land
FreeMan Society of Canada
German Freedom Fighters

German-Jewish Historical Commission
Hammer Heads
Heritage Front
House of Freedom (and Free Speech)
Human Life International
Hungarian Freedom Fighters Federation
Identity
Immigration Watch Canada (IWC)
KKK: Brotherhood of Klans (BOK)
KKK: Brotherhood of Knights
KKK: Confederate Klans of Alberta
KKK: Imperial Knights of the Ku Klux Klan
KKK: Invisible Empire, Knights of the Ku Klux Klan
KKK: Kanadian Knights of the Ku Klux Klan
KKK: National Knights of the Ku Klux Klan
Légion Nationaliste
Legionne Nationale
Longitude 74
National Advancement Party
National Alliance
National Association for the Advancement of White People (NAAWP)
National Christian Party of Canada
National Citizens Alliance
National Progressivist Party of Canada
National Social Christian Party
National Social Party
National Social Underground
National Socialist Alliance
National Socialist Liberation Front
National Socialist Movement of Canada
National Socialist (Nazi) Party
National Socialist Party
National Socialist Party of Canada (Quebec)
National Unity Party
National White American Party
Nationalist Front

Nationalist Party of Canada
Natural Order (and Faith)
North American Labor Party
North York Skins
Northern Hammerskins
Northwest Imperative
Orange Order
Parti National Society Chretien
Patriotic Europeans Against the Islamization of the West (PEGIDA)
Party for the Commonwealth of Canada
Quebec Radical
Quebec Stompers
Ragnarok
Ragnarok Vinland
Realist Party
Royal Canadian Infidels
Samisdat Publishers Ltd.
Slingers
Social Credit Association of Ontario, Inc.
Southern Ontario Skins
Sovereign Citizens
Swastika Association of Canada
Toronto Swastika Club
Tri-City Skins
Troisieme Wai
True White Boys
Union of Fascists (Canada)
United Anglo-Saxon Liberation Front
United Klans of Canada
United Skinheads of Montreal
Vinland Front
Vinland Hammerskins
Vinland Warriors
Volksfront
Waffen
Western Canada For Us (WCFU)

Western European Bloodline (WEB)
Western Guard
Western Guard Universal
White Boys Posse
White Knights
White Canada Christian/Patriot Rights Association
White Canada Council
White Canada Party
White Federation
White Legion
White Nationalist Front
White Nationalist Revolutionary Army
White People's Vigilantes
Women for Aryan Unity
World Church of the Creator
World Freeman Society

Bibliography

Abts, K., & Rummens, S. (2007). Populism Versus Democracy. *Political Studies, 55*(2), 405–424.

Adamczyk, A., Gruenewald, J., Chermak, S., & Freilich, J. (2014). The Relationship Between Hate Groups and Far-Right Ideological Violence. *Journal of Contemporary Criminal Justice, 30*(3), 310–332.

Adams, M. (2013). *The Myth of Conservative Canada.* Policy Options. Retrieved from http://policyoptions.irpp.org/magazines/the-age-of-man/adams.

Adams, J., & Roscigno, V. (2005). White Supremacists, Oppositional Culture and the World Wide Web. *Social Forces, 84*(2), 759–778.

Agno, D. (1997, April 24). Hate Goes to High School. *Eye Weekly.* Retrieved from http://contests.eyeweekly.com/eye/issue/issue_04.24.97/news_views/hate.php.

Ahmed, K. (2016). Radicalism Leading to Violent Extremism in Canada: A Multi-level Analysis of Muslim Community and University Based Student Leaders' Perceptions and Experiences. *Journal for Deradicalization, 6,* 231–271.

Ahmed, S. (2015). The 'Emotionalization of the "War on Terror"': Counter-Terrorism, Fear, Risk, Insecurity and Helplessness. *Criminology and Criminal Justice, 15*(5), 545–560.

Albertazzi, D., & McDonnell, D. (Eds.). (2008). *Twenty-First Century Populism the Specter of Western European Democracy.* London, UK: Palgrave Macmillan.

Alexa. (2017). *Top Ten Websites in Canada.* Retrieved from http://ww.alexa.com/topsites/countries/CA.

Allan, E. (2014). Minority Identities in a Minority Nation: A Critical Analysis of Quebec's Interculturalism Policy. *The UBC Journal of Political Studies, 16*(1), 13–21.

Ambrose, E., & Mudde, C. (2015). Canadian Multiculturalism and the Absence of the Far Right. *Nationalism and Ethnic Politics, 21*(2), 213–236.

Ameli, S., & Merali, A. (2014). *Only Canadian: The Experience of Hate Moderated Differential Citizenship for Muslims.* Wembley: Islamic Human Rights Commission.

Anahita, S. (2006). Blogging the Borders: Virtual Skinheads, Hypermasculinity, and Heteronormativity. *Journal of Political and Military Sociology, 32*(1), 143–164.

Anti-Defamation League. (1996). *Hate Groups in America.* New York: ADL.

Anti-Defamation League. (2011). *Bigots on Bikes: The Growing Links Between White Supremacists and Biker Gangs.* Washington, DC: Anti-Defamation League.

Anti-Defamation League. (2018). *Murder and Extremism in the United States in 2018.* Washington, DC: Anti-Defamation League.

Anti-Racist Canada. (2007). *A Neo-Nazi Group in Alberta: The Aryan Guard.* Retrieved from http://anti-racistcanada.blogspot.ca/2007/12/aryan-guard-members-and-associates.html.

Anti-Racist Canada. (2009). *So, What Has Robert Reitmeier Been Up to Lately?* Retrieved from http://anti-racistcanada.blogspot.ca/2009/08/so-what-has-robert-reitmeier-been-up-to.html.

Anti-Racist Canada. (2012). *Kyle McKee, Bernie Miller, and Others: Charged with Assault.* Retrieved from http://anti-racistcanada.blogspot.ca/2012/04/kyle-mckee-bernie-miller-and-others.html.

Anti-Racist Canada. (2014). *A History of Violence: 1970–2014.* Retrieved from http://anti-racistcanada.blogspot.ca/2011/10/history-of-violence-1989-2011.html.

Appleton, C. (2014). Lone Wolf Terrorism in Norway. *The International Journal of Human Rights, 18*(2), 127–142.

Aulakh, R. (2009, February 15). Russian Émigré's Store Vandalized, Painted with Swastika. *Toronto Star.* Retrieved from http://www.thestar.com/news/gta/2009/02/15/russian_eacutemigreacutes_store_vandalized_painted_with_swastika.html.

Back, L. (2002). Aryans Reading Adorno: Cyber-Culture and Twenty-First Century Racism. *Ethnic and Racial Studies, 25*(4), 628–651.

Back, L., Keith, M., & Solomos, J. (1996). Technology, Race and Neo-fascism in a Digital Age: The New Modalities of Racist Culture. *Patterns of Prejudice, 30*(2), 3–27.

Bahdi, R. (2003). No Exit: Racial Profiling and Canada's War Against Terrorism. *Osgoode Hall Law Journal, 41*(1–2), 293–316.

Bailey, J. (2006). Strategic Alliances: The Inter-Related Roles of Citizens, Industry and Government in Combating Internet Hate. *Canadian Issues,* 56–59.

Bakker, E., & De Graaf, B. (2011). Preventing Lone Wolf Terrorism: Some CT Approaches Addressed. *Perspectives on Terrorism, 5*(5–6), 43–50.

Baron, S. (1997). Canadian Male Street Skinheads: Street Gang or Street Terrorists? *Canadian Review of Sociology and Anthropology, 34*(2), 125–154.

Barrett, S. R. (1987). *Is God a Racist? The Right Wing in Canada.* Toronto, ON: University of Toronto Press.

Bartlett, J., & Birdwell, J. (2013). *Cumulative Radicalisation Between the Far-Right and Islamist Groups in the UK: A Review of Evidence.* London: Demos.

Basham, P., Merrifield, J., & Hepburn, C. (2007). *Home Schooling: From the Extreme to the Mainstream.* Studies in Educational Policy: Fraser Institute Occasional Paper. Vancouver: The Fraser Institute.

Bates, R. (2012). Dancing with Wolves: Today's Lone Wolf Terrorists. *Journal of Public and Professional Sociology, 4*(1), 1–14.

Becker, M. (2014). Explaining Lone Wolf Target Selection in the United States. *Studies in Conflict and Terrorism, 37*(11), 959–978.

Bell, S. (2010, October 29). Who Are Canada's 'Freemen'? *National Post.* Retrieved from http://www.activistpost.com/2010/10/who-are-canadas-freemen.html.

Bell, S. (2011, August 6). A Hater Among Us. *National Post.* Retrieved from http://news.nationalpost.com/news/canada/a-hater-among-us.

Bell, S. (2012, September 28). Judge's Scathing Ruling Against Alberta 'Freeman' Could Signal Clampdown on Anti-Government Movement. *National Post.* Retrieved from http://news.nationalpost.com/news/canada/judges-scathing-ruling-against-alberta-freeman-could-signal-clampdown-on-anti-government-movement.

Benford, R., & Snow, D. (2000). Framing Processes and Social Movements: An Overview and Assessment. *Annual Review of Sociology, 26,* 611–639.

Berger, J. M., & Strathearn, B. (2013). *Who Matters Online: Measuring Influence, Evaluating Content and Countering Violent Extremism in Online*

Social Networks. London: The International Centre for the Study of Radicalisation and Political Violence.

Berube, M., & Campana, A. (2015). Les violences motivées par la haine. Idéologies et modes d'action des extrémistes de droite au Canada. *Criminologie, 48*(1), 215–234.

Betz, H. G., & Johnson, C. (2004). Against the Current—Stemming the Tide: The Nostalgic Ideology of the Contemporary Radical Populist Right. *Journal of Political Ideologies, 9*(3), 311–327.

Bjørgo, T., & Horgan, J. (Eds.). (2009). *Leaving Terrorism Behind: Individual and Collective Disengagement.* London: Routledge.

Black, D. (2004). Terrorism as Social Control. In M. Deflem (Ed.), *Terrorism and Counter-Terrorism: Criminological Perspectives* (pp. 9–18). Boston: Elsevier.

Blais, T. (2010, May 13). Racist Man Bear-Sprayed Student. *Canoe.* Retrieved from http://cnews.canoe.ca/CNEWS/Crime/2010/05/13/13929911.html.

Blais, T. (2011, September 30). White Supremacist Jailed for Crime Spree. *Canoe.* Retrieved from http://cnews.canoe.ca/CNEWS/Crime/2011/09/30/pf-18764611.html.

Blazak, R. (2001). White Boys to Terrorist Men: Target Recruitment of Nazi Skinheads. *American Behavioral Scientist, 44*(6), 982–1000.

Blee, K. M. (2002). *Inside Organized Racism: Women in the Hate Movement.* Berkeley: University of California Press.

Blee, K. M., & Creasap, K. A. (2010). Conservative and Right-Wing Movements. *Annual Review of Sociology, 36,* 269–286.

Boeveld, S. (2013, March 12). Controversial Free Speech Defender Douglas H. Christie, Lawyer for Canada's Most Prominent Hatemongers, Dead at 66. *National Post.* Retrieved from http://news.nationalpost.com/2013/03/12/controversial-free-speech-defender-douglas-h-christie-lawyer-for-canadas-most-prominent-hatemongers-dead-at-66/.

Bolan, K. (2012, March 19). Police ID 26-Year-Old Man Stabbed to Death in Surrey Saturday. *Vancouver Sun.* Retrieved from http://www.vancouversun.com/news/Police+year+stabbed+death+Surrey+Saturday/6326607/story.html.

Borchgrevink, A. (2013). *A Norwegian Tragedy: Anders Behring Breivik and the Massacre on Utøya* (G. Puzey, Trans.). Malden, MA: Polity.

Borgeson, K., & Valeri, R. (2005). Identifying the Face of Hate. *Journal of Applied Sociology, 22*(1), 91–104.

Bostdorff, D. M. (2004). The Internet Rhetoric of the Ku Klux Klan: A Case Study in Web Site Community Building Run Amok. *Communication Studies, 55*(2), 340–361.

Boutilier, A. (2015, March 15). CSIS Highlights White Supremacist Threat Ahead of Radical Islam. *Toronto Star*. Retrieved from https://www.thestar.com/news/canada/2015/03/15/csis-highlights-white-supremacist-threat-ahead-of-radical-islam.html.

Bowling, B. (1993). Racial Harassment and the Process of Victimization. *British Journal of Criminology, 33,* 231–250.

Bowman-Grieve, L. (2009). Exploring "Stormfront:" A Virtual Community of the Radical Right. *Studies in Conflict and Terrorism, 32*(11), 989–1007.

Brean, J. (2013, February 26). How Former 'Street Kid' William Whatcott Became the 'Deliberately Provocative' Spark Behind the Supreme Court Hate-Speech Ruling. *National Post*. Retrieved from http://news.nationalpost.com/2013/02/26/how-former-street-kid-william-whatcott-became-the-deliberately-provocative-spark-behind-supreme-court-hate-speech-ruling/.

Brean, J. (2014, June 6). Justin Bourque's Alienation Nurtured in the Old Confines of Social Media. *National Post*. Retrieved from http://news.nationalpost.com/2014/06/06/justin-bourques-alienation-nurtured-in-the-cold-confines-of-social-media/.

Browne, R. (2016). *Not-Right: This Canadian Group Appreciates These Alt-Right Posters, But They Insist They're Not White Supremacists*. Vice News. Retrieved from https://news.vice.com/story/this-canadian-group-appreciates-these-alt-right-posters-just-dont-call-them-white-supremacists?utm_source=vicetwitterca.

Bryden, J. (2015). Trudeau Calls Harper's Niqab Comments 'Pandering to Fear' of Muslims: 'It's Unworthy of Someone Who Is Prime Minister'. *National Post*. Retrieved from https://nationalpost.com/news/politics/trudeau-calls-harpers-niqab-comments-pandering-to-fear-of-muslims-its-unworthy-of-someone-who-is-prime-minister.

Burnett, J. (2017). Racial Violence and the Brexit State. *Race and Class, 58,* 85–97.

Busher, J., & Macklin, G. (2015). Interpreting "Cumulative Extremism": Six Proposals for Enhancing Conceptual Clarity. *Terrorism and Political Violence, 27*(5), 884–905.

Caiani, M., & Kröll, P. (2014). The Transnationalization of the Extreme Right and the Use of the Internet. *International Journal of Comparative and Applied Criminal Justice, 39*(4), 331–351.

Calgary Herald. (2006, September 22). *Money Wasn't Worth Killing For*. Retrieved from http://www.canada.com/calgaryherald/story.html?id=9d8432f8-830a-43c4-8e15-ec8751e1f361&k=99917.

Calgary Herald. (2008, February 23). *Couple Feels Neo-Nazis Behind Firebomb Attack*. Retrieved from http://www.canada.com/calgaryherald/news/city/story.html?id=b3148f46-1e8b-4e9e-a3af-c5fedc956124.

Calgary Herald. (2009, January 28). *Attack on Visitor Linked to Aryan Guard*. Retrieved from http://www.canada.com/calgaryherald/news/city/story.html?id=79a32d0b-7b3d-403e-8fb1-08512d8240b4.

Calgary Herald. (2012, July 20). *This Day in 1985—Former Teacher Jim Keegstra Fined for Promoting Hatred*. Retrieved from http://calgaryherald.com/news/local-news/this-day-in-1985.

Calgary Sun. (2010, January 7). *Suspect in Attack on C-Train Driver Linked to Racist Group*. Retrieved from http://www.calgarysun.com/news/alberta/2010/01/07/12375891-sun.html.

Calgary Sun. (2013, October 8). *Okotoks 'Freeman on the Land' Denied Bail for Allegedly Assaulting RCMP Officer and Other Charges*. Retrieved from http://www.calgarysun.com/2013/10/08/okotoks-freeman-on-the-land-denied-bail-for-allegedly-assaulting-rcmp-officer-and-other-charges.

Calgary Sun. (2015, March 21). *Alleged White Supremacist Shot by Cops After Disturbing Peace Rally: Witnesses*. Retrieved from http://www.calgarysun.com/2015/03/21/cops-shoot-man-at-calgary-peace-rally.

Campbell, A. (2006). The Search for Authenticity: An Exploration of an Online Skinhead Newsgroup. *New Media Society, 8*(2), 269–294.

Campion-Smith, B. (2015, January 25). Stephen Harper Says Jihadist Terrorism 'Seeks to Harm Us Here'. *Toronto Star*. Retrieved from https://www.thestar.com/news/canada/2015/01/25/stephen-harper-says-jihadist-terrorism-seeks-to-harm-us-here.html.

Canadian Anti-Racism Education and Research Society. (2013a). *Anti-Racist Action in Toronto*. Retrieved from http://www.stopracism.ca/content/15-anti-racist-action-toronto-ara.

Canadian Anti-Racism Education and Research Society. (2013b). *Early Racist Skinhead Movement (Part 2)*. Retrieved from http://www.stopracism.ca/content/early-racist-skinhead-movement-part-2.

Canadian Association of Chiefs of Police. (2016). *Federal Budget*. Retrieved from https://cacp.ca/index.html.

Canadian Council on American-Islamic Relations. (2002). *Canadian Muslims One Year After 9/11*. Ottawa, ON: CAIR.

Canadian Council on American-Islamic Relations. (2004). *Today's Media: Covering Islam and Canadian Muslims*. Submission to Standing Committee on Transport and Communications. Retrieved from http://www.caircan.ca/downloads/sctc-26022004.pdf.

Canadian Council on American-Islamic Relations. (2005). *Presumption of Guilt: A National Survey on Security Visitations of Canadian Muslims.* Retrieved from http://www.caircan.ca/downloads/POG-08062005.pdf.

Canadian Islamic Congress. (2005). *Anti-Islam in the Media 2003.* Retrieved from http://canadianislamiccongress.com/rr/rr_2003.php.

Canadian Press. (2009, October 20). Offender Charged After Threatening Prosecutor During Tirade in Halifax Court. *Cape Breton Post.* Retrieved from http://www.capebretonpost.com/Justice/2009-10-20/article-768875/Offender-charged-after-threatening-prosecutor-during-tirade-in-Halifax-court/1.

Canadian Press. (2013, April 18). William Whatcott's Anti-Gay Flyers Case Won't Be Re-Open: Supreme Court. *Huffington Post.* Retrieved from http://www.huffingtonpost.ca/2013/04/18/william-whatcott-anti-gay-flyers-saskatchewan_n_3110097.html.

Canadian Press. (2015, June 9). Edmonton Police Release Details About Deadly Shootout. *Huffington Post.* Retrieved from http://www.huffingtonpost.ca/2015/06/09/edmonton-police-officer-k_n_7540386.html.

Canadian Security and Intelligence Service. (2012). *Intelligence Assessment: 2012 Domestic Threat Environment in Canada (Part I): Left-Wing/Right-Wing Extremism.* CSIS IA 2011-12/115.

Canoe. (2010, May 19). *Purported Neo-Nazi Admits to Making Explosives.* Retrieved from http://cnews.canoe.ca/CNEWS/Crime/2010/05/18/13995161.html?cid=rssnewscanada.

Canwest News Service. (2007, August 10). Racial Attacks on Chinese Students Linked to Skinheads. *Ottawa Citizen.* Retrieved from http://www.canada.com/ottawacitizen/news/story.html?id=f3b7dbc5-a6d0-4553-872c-3aed9de90a11&k=80416.

Canwest News Service. (2010, January 15). Mass Murderer Nathan Fry Seeks 'Upbeat' Pen Pal. *The Province.* Retrieved from http://kelowna.com/forums/topic/mass-murderer-nathan-fry-seeks-upbeat-pen-pal.

Capehard, J. (2015, June 19). Dylan Roof: 'White Supremacist Lone Wolf'. *The Washington Post.* Retrieved from https://www.washingtonpost.com/blogs/post-partisan/wp/2015/06/19/dylann-roof-white-supremacist-lone-wolf/?utm_term=.13d019dc9898.

Carlson, K. B. (2014, June 12). Sister of Justin Bourque Speaks of His Troubled Life, Paranoia. *The Globe and Mail.* Retrieved from http://www.theglobeandmail.com/news/national/sister-of-justin-bourque-speaks-of-his-troubled-life-growing-paranoia/article19131608/.

Carter, A. (2016a, November 21). *Flyers Decrying 'Anti-white Propaganda' Found in Hamilton*. CBC News Hamilton. Retrieved from http://www.cbc.ca/news/canada/hamilton/hamilton-fliers-1.3860327.

Carter, A. (2016b, November 30). *Muslim Teen Left with Cracked Skull After Brutal Beating*. CBC News Hamilton. Retrieved from http://www.cbc.ca/news/canada/hamilton/teen-attack-1.3874867.

Castells, M. (2001). *The Internet Galaxy: Reflections on the Internet, Business, and Society*. New York: Oxford University Press.

Catholics for Choice. (2011). *An Investigative Series on Those Who Oppose Women's Rights and Reproductive Health*. Washington, DC: Human Life International.

CBC News. (1998, December 1). *Soldiers Blame Airborne for Robbery*. Retrieved from https://www.cbc.ca/news/canada/soldier-blames-airborne-for-robbery-1.166500.

CBC News. (1999, October 5). *Crown Seeks Life in B.C. Skinhead Sentencing Hearing*. Retrieved from http://www.cbc.ca/news/canada/crown-seeks-life-in-b-c-skinhead-sentencing-hearing-1.192848.

CBC News. (2000a, June 5). *Woman Sentenced for Hate Crimes*. Retrieved from http://www.cbc.ca/news/canada/woman-sentenced-for-hate-crimes-1.207968.

CBC News. (2000b, July 6). *Charlottetown Man in Court over Hate Crime and Assault*. Retrieved from http://www.cbc.ca/news/canada/charlottetown-man-in-court-over-hate-crime-and-assault-1.232804.

CBC News. (2001a, May 5). *Deliberations Set to Begin at Murder Trial*. Retrieved from http://www.cbc.ca/news/canada/deliberations-set-to-begin-at-murder-trial-1.294128.

CBC News. (2001b, May 29). *Arrest Warrant Issued for Klan Recruiter*. Retrieved from http://www.cbc.ca/news/canada/arrest-warrant-issued-for-klan-recruiter-1.285446.

CBC News. (2001c, June 19). *'Baby Hitler' Denied Bail*. Retrieved from http://www.cbc.ca/news/canada/baby-hitler-denied-bail-1.290237.

CBC News. (2001d, June 21). *Teen Guilty of Racially-Motivated Murder*. Retrieved from http://www.cbc.ca/news/canada/teen-guilty-of-racially-motivated-murder-1.288013.

CBC News. (2001e, August 1). *Moncton Man Charged with Hate Crime*. Retrieved from http://www.cbc.ca/news/canada/moncton-man-charged-with-hate-crime-1.291206.

CBC News. (2001f, October 3). *Racist Accused of Threatening Jews, Muslims*. Retrieved from http://www.cbc.ca/news/canada/racist-accused-of-threatening-jews-muslims-1.287370.

CBC News. (2005, April 15). *Man Charged in Shooting Death of White Supremacist Wolfgang Droege*. Retrieved from http://www.cbc.ca/news/canada/man-charged-in-shooting-death-of-white-supremacist-wolfgang-droege-1.546492.

CBC News. (2007a, January 23). *Racist Webmaster Gets 6 Months for Hate Propaganda*. Retrieved from http://www.cbc.ca/news/canada/montreal/racist-webmaster-gets-6-months-for-hate-propaganda-1.662779.

CBC News. (2007b, February 15). *Ernst Zundel Sentenced to 5 Years for Holocaust Denial*. Retrieved from http://www.cbc.c/new/worl/ernst-zundel-sentenced-to-5-years-for-holocaust-denial-1.659372.

CBC News. (2007c, August 13). *Friends of Simon Wiesenthal Center Advises of Calgary-Based Neo-Nazi's Recent Activity*. Retrieved from http://www.newswire.ca/en/story/155641/friends-of-simon-wiesenthal-center-advises-of-calgary-based-neo-nazi-s-recent-activity.

CBC News. (2007d, August 27). *Klan Plans Fall Rally in Sask., Says Leader*. Retrieved from http://www.cbc.ca/news/canada/saskatchewan/klan-plans-fall-rally-in-sask-says-leader-1.690030.

CBC News. (2009, May 27). *Charge Dropped Against Suspect in Shooting of Ontario Abortion Doctor*. Retrieved from http://www.cbc.ca/news/canada/charge-dropped-against-suspect-in-shooting-of-ontario-abortion-doctor-1.780549.

CBC News. (2012a, March 18). *1 Killed in Surrey Stabbing*. Retrieved from http://www.cbc.ca/news/canada/british-columbia/1-killed-in-surrey-stabbing-1.1165838.

CBC News. (2012b, March 19). *Surrey Stabbing Victim ID'd*. Retrieved from http://www.cbc.ca/news/canada/british-columbia/surrey-stabbing-victim-id-d-1.1155340.

CBC News. (2012c, February 29). Finding the Freemen. *The National*. Retrieved from http://www.cbc.ca/news/canada/freemen-movement-captures-canadian-policeattention-1.1262159.

CBC News. (2013, February 27). *Top Court Upholds Key Part of Sask. Anti-Hate Law*. Retrieved from http://www.cbc.ca/news/politics/top-court-upholds-key-part-of-sask-anti-hate-law-1.1068276.

CBC News. (2014, June 5). *Justin Bourque: Latest Revelations About Man Charged in Moncton Shooting*. Retrieved from http://www.cbc.ca/news/canada/new-brunswick/justin-bourque-latest-revelations-about-man-charged-in-moncton-shooting-1.2665900.

CBC News. (2015, June 9). *Norman Raddatz Had Extensive Police File for Hate Crimes*. Retrieved from http://www.huffingtonpost.ca/2015/06/09/edmonton-police-officer-k_n_7540386.html.

CBC News. (2017, March 23). *House of Commons Passes Anti-Islamophobia Motion*. Retrieved from http://www.cbc.ca/news/politics/m-103-islamophobiamotionvote-1.4038016.

CBC News British Columbia. (2009, June 9). *B.C. Man Convicted of Building Bomb Planted in Highway Restroom*. Retrieved from http://www.cbc.ca/news/canada/british-columbia/b-c-man-convicted-of-building-bomb-planted-in-highway-restroom-1.861498.

CBC News British Columbia. (2010, December 21). *YouTube Assault Draws Little Jail Time*. Retrieved from http://www.cbc.ca/news/canada/british-columbia/youtube-assault-draws-little-jail-time-1.900739.

CBC News British Columbia. (2011, September 4). *Fugitive Brothers Arrested Near U.S. Border*. Retrieved from http://www.cbc.ca/news/canada/british-columbia/fugitive-brothers-arrested-near-u-s-border-1.1037138.

CBC News British Columbia. (2012, January 23). *Man Set on Fire in Alleged Racial Attack*. Retrieved from http://www.cbc.ca/news/canada/british-columbia/man-set-on-fire-in-alleged-racial-attack-1.1157097.

CBC News Calgary. (2010a, March 21). *Protesters, Neo-Nazis Clash at Anti-Racism Rally*. Retrieved from http://www.cbc.ca/news/canada/calgary/protesters-neo-nazis-clash-at-anti-racism-rally-1.868638.

CBC News Calgary. (2010b, November 8). *Calgary Anti-Racism Activists' Home Invaded*. Retrieved from http://www.cbc.ca/news/canada/calgary/calgary-anti-racism-activists-home-invaded-1.902197.

CBC News Calgary. (2011, June 1). *2 Men Charged in Deadly 2010 Attack*. Retrieved from http://www.cbc.ca/news/canada/calgary/2-men-charged-in-deadly-2010-attack-1.1017160.

CBC News Calgary. (2013, March 4). *Calgary Man Pleads Guilty in Deadly Beating*. Retrieved from http://www.cbc.ca/news/canada/calgary/calgary-man-pleads-guilty-in-deadly-beating-1.1305833.

CBC News Edmonton. (2009, March 27). *Man Pleads Guilty in Fatal Stabbing of Senior*. Retrieved from http://www.cbc.ca/news/canada/edmonton/man-pleads-guilty-in-fatal-stabbing-of-senior-1.809703.

CBC News Edmonton. (2010, March 13). *Edmonton Shooting Suspect a Racist: Co-Worker*. Retrieved from http://www.cbc.ca/news/canada/edmonton/edmonton-shooting-suspect-a-racist-co-workers-1.940915.

CBC News Edmonton. (2012, December 4). *Murder Charges Laid in Decapitation, 2 Other Homicides: Four Members of Alberta Drug Gang Charged in Three Killings in September, October*. Retrieved from http://www.cbc.ca/news/canada/edmonton/murder-charges-laid-in-decapitation-2-other-homicides-1.1131100.

CBC News New Brunswick. (2007, August 16). *Saint John Councilor Target of Racist Death Threats*. Retrieved http://www.cbc.ca/news/canada/new-brunswick/saint-john-councillor-target-of-racist-death-threats-1.661448.

CBC News Nova Scotia. (2010a, February 22). *N.S. Couple Shaken by Cross Burning*. Retrieved from http://www.cbc.ca/news/canada/nova-scotia/n-s-couple-shaken-by-cross-burning-1.880988.

CBC News Nova Scotia. (2010b, March 1). *Newhook Declared Dangerous Offender*. Retrieved from http://www.cbc.ca/news/canada/nova-scotia/newhook-declared-dangerous-offender-1.949012.

CBC News Saskatchewan. (2011, January 28). *LaChance Shooting Remembered in Prince Albert*. Retrieved from http://www.cbc.ca/news/canada/saskatchewan/lachance-shooting-remembered-in-prince-albert-1.1089247.

CBC News Saskatchewan. (2012, December 5). *White Boy Posse 'Incredibly Violent,' Expert Says*. Retrieved from http://www.cbc.ca/news/canada/saskatchewan/white-boy-posse-incredibly-violent-expert-says-1.1252970.

Chase, S. (2015, March 10). Niqabs 'Rooted in a Culture That Is Anti-women,' Harper Says. *The Globe and Mail*. Retrieved from https://www.theglobeandmail.com/news/politics/niqabs-rooted-in-a-culture-that-is-anti-women-harper-says/article23395242.

Chau, M., & Xu, J. (2007). Mining Communities and Their Relationships in Blogs: A Study of Online Hate Groups. *International Journal of Human Computer Studies, 65*(1), 57–70.

Chermak, S., Freilich, J., & Shemtob, Z. (2010). Law Enforcement Training and the Domestic Far Right. *Criminal Justice and Behavior, 36*(12), 1305–1322.

Chermak, S., Freilich, J., & Simone, J. (2010). Surveying American State Police Agencies About Lone Wolves, Far-Right Criminality, and Far-Right and Islamic Jihadist Criminal Collaboration. *Studies in Conflict and Terrorism, 33,* 1019–1041.

Chermak, S., Freilich, J., & Suttmoeller, M. (2013). The Organizational Dynamics of Far-Right Hate Groups in the United States: Comparing Violent to Nonviolent Organizations. *Studies in Conflict and Terrorism, 36,* 193–218.

Chicago Tribune. (2002, July 16). *Skinhead Arrested in Canada Slaying*. Retrieved from http://articles.chicagotribune.com/2002-07-16/news/0207160173_1_hate-related-hate-motivated-david-rosenzweig.

Chin, J. (2016, November 21). Richmond Racist Flyers Call on 'Whitey' to Save City from Chinese People. *The Huffington Post Canada*. Retrieved from http://www.huffingtonpost.ca/2016/11/21/richmond-racist-flyers_n_13130166.html.

Chwalisz, C. (2015). The Prairie Populist: How Stephen Harper Transformed Canada. *Juncture, 22*(3), 225–229.

City of Lethbridge. (2010). *Building Bridges: A Welcoming and Inclusive Lethbridge—Community Action Plan 2011–2021.* Retrieved from http://www.lethbridge.ca/living-here/Our-Community/documents/community%20action%20plan%202011-2021%20-%20building%20bridges%20-%20a%20welcoming%20and%20inclusive%20community.pdf.

Clancy, C. (2016, November 21). Posters Calling Out 'Anti-white Propaganda' Put Up in Downtown Edmonton. *Edmonton Journal.* Retrieved from http://edmontonjournal.com/news/local-news/posters-calling-out-anti-white-propaganda-put-up-in-downtown-edmonton.

Clement, D., & Vaugeois, R. (2013). *The Search for Justice and Equality: Alberta's Human Rights History.* Edmonton: John Humphrey Centre for Peace and Human Rights.

CNW. (2007, August 13). *Friends of Simon Wiesenthal Center Advises of Calgary-Based Neo-Nazi's Recent Activity.* Retrieved from http://www.newswire.ca/en/story/155641/friends-of-simon-wiesenthal-center-advises-of-calgary-based-neo-nazi-s-recent-activity.

Cohen, J. D. (2016). The Next Generation of Government CVE Strategies at Home: Expanding Opportunities for Intervention. *The ANNALS of the American Academy of Political and Social Science, 668*(1), 118–128.

Cole, J., Alison, E., Cole, B., & Alison, L. (2012). *Guidance for Identifying People Vulnerable to Recruitment into Violent Extremism.* Retrieved from https://safecampuscommunities.ac.uk/resources/guidance-for-identifying-people-vulnerable-to-recruitment-in-violent-extremism.

Comack, E. (2012). *Racialized Policing: Aboriginal People's Encounters with the Police.* Winnipeg, MB: Fernwood Publishing.

Conference Board of Canada. (2017). *Income Inequality.* Retrieved from http://www.conferenceboard.ca/hcp/details/society/income-inequality.aspx.

Conway, M. (2016). Determining the Role of the Internet in Violent Extremism and Terrorism: Six Suggestions for Progressing Research. *Studies in Conflict and Terrorism, 40*(1), 77–98.

Cotter, J. M. (1999). Sounds of Hate: White Power Rock and Roll and the Neo-Nazi Skinhead Subculture. *Terrorism and Political Violence, 11*(2), 111–140.

CTV Edmonton. (2011, March 10). *Alleged Victims of Racist Attacks on Whyte Ave. Speak Out.* Retrieved from http://edmonton.ctvnews.ca/alleged-victims-of-racist-attacks-on-whyte-ave-speak-out-1.617109.

CTV Montreal. (2011, March 22). *22-Year-Old Found Guilty of Assault*. Retrieved from http://montreal.ctvnews.ca/22-year-old-found-guilty-of-assault-1.621919.

CTV News. (2012, March 25). *Police Fear B.C. Neo-Nazi's Death Could Spark Gang War*. Retrieved from http://www.ctvnews.ca/police-fear-b-c-neo-nazi-s-death-could-spark-gang-war-1.786894.

CTV News Kitchener. (2013, March 4). *Police Arrest Three in Connection with Victoria Park Attack*. Retrieved from http://kitchener.ctvnews.ca/police-arrest-three-in-connection-with-victoria-park-attack-1.1180833.

Dalgaard-Nielsen, A. (2016). Countering Violent Extremism with Governance Networks. *Perspectives on Terrorism, 10,* 135–139.

De Koster, W., & Houtman, D. (2008). Stormfront Is Like a Second Home to Me. *Information, Communication & Society, 11*(8), 1155–1176.

Deloughery, K., King, R., & Asal, V. (2012). Close Cousins of Distant Relatives? The Relationship Between Terrorism and Hate Crime. *Crime and Delinquency, 58*(5), 663–688.

Department of Homeland Security. (2009). Rightwing Extremism: Current Economic and Political Climate Fueling Resurgence in Radicalization and Recruitment. *DHS Assessment, 1,* 1–10.

Deschene, M. (2011). Deradicalization: Not Soft, but Strategic. *Crime, Law and Social Change, 55,* 287–292.

Dobratz, B., & Waldner, L. (2012). Repertoires of Contention: White Separatist Views on the Use of Violence and Leaderless Resistance. *Mobilization: An International Quarterly, 17*(1), 49–66.

Dougherty, K. (2017, January 31). Quebec Mosque Shooting Suspect Was a Fan of Donald Trump and Marine le Pen. *Independent.* Retrieved from http://www.independent.co.uk/news/world/americas/quebec-city-mosque-shooting-latest-alexandre-bissonnette-donald-trump-marine-le-pen-facebook-social-a7554451.html.

Dyck, K. (2015). The (Un)Popularity of White-Power Music. In S. A. Wilson (Ed.), *Music at the Extremes: Essays on Sounds Outside the Mainstream* (pp. 157–177). Jefferson, NC: McFarland.

Edmonton Sun. (2011, March 8). *Edmonton Police Lay Charges over Alleged Hate Crimes*. Retrieved from http://www.edmontonsun.com/news/edmonton/2011/03/08/17540196.html.

Engesser, S., Ernst, N., Esser, F., & Büchel, F. (2016). Populism and Social Media: How Politicians Spread a Fragmented Ideology. *Information, Communication and Society, 20*(8), 1109–1126.

Environics Institute. (2015). *Focus Canada: Spring 2015, Immigration and Multiculturalism, Detailed Data Tables*. Retrieved from https://www.environicsinstitute.org/docs/default-source/project-documents/focus-canada-2015-survey-on-immigration-and-multiculturalism/focus-can-ada-spring-2015—immigration-and-multiculturalism—data-tables.pdf?sfvrsn=2b7b9c30_0.

Ezekiel, R., & Post, J. (1991). Worlds in Collision, Worlds in Collusion: The Uneasy Relationship Between the Policy Community and the Academic Community. In C. McCauley (Ed.), *Terrorism Research and Public Policy* (pp. 117–125). Portland, OR: Frank Cass.

Farnsworth, C. (1993, May 17). Canada Investigates Reported Ties of Rightist Militants and Military. *The New York Times*. Retrieved from http://www.nytimes.com/1993/05/17/world/canada-investigates-reported-ties-of-right-ist-militants-and-military.html.

Federal Bureau of Investigation. (2010). *Sovereign Citizens: An Introduction for Law Enforcement*. Washington, DC: Federal Bureau of Investigation. Retrieved from http://info.publicintelligence.net/FBI-SovereignCitizens.pdf.

Feldman, M. (2012, August 27). Viewpoint: Killer Breivik's Links with Far Right. *BBC News*. Retrieved from http://www.bbc.com/news/world-europe-19366000.

Ferber, A. L. (2016). White Supremacy and Gender. *The Wiley Blackwell Encyclopedia of Gender and Sexuality Studies*, 1–4.

Fernback, J. (1997). The Individual Within the Collective: Virtual Ideology and the Realization of Collective Principles. In S. Jones (Ed.), *Virtual Culture: Identity and Community in Cybersociety* (pp. 36–54). Thousand Oaks, CA: Sage.

Fetner, T. (2019). The Religious Right in the United States and Canada: Evangelical Communities, Critical Junctures, and Institutional Infrastructures. *Mobilization: An International Journal, 24*(1), 95–113.

Fleras, A., & Elliott, J. (2002). *Engaging Diversity: Multiculturalism in Canada*. Toronto: Nelson Thomson Learning.

Forum Research. (2017, September 27). *Donald Trump Approval Down*. Retrieved from http://poll.forumresearch.com/data/64d0446a-39e6-40a7-8895-3f4476648ca1Donald%20Trump%20Sept%20.pdf.

Freilich, J., Chermak, S., & Belli, (2014). Introducing the United States Extremist Crime Database (ECDB). *Terrorism and Political Violence, 26*, 372–384.

Freilich, J., Chermak, S., & Caspi, D. (2009). Critical Events in the Life Trajectories of Domestic Extremist White Supremacist Groups: A Case Study Analysis of Four Violent Organizations. *Criminology and Public Policy, 8*(3), 497–530.

Friscolanti, M., & Patriquin, M. (2014, June 6). The Full, Twisted Story of Justin Bourque. *Maclean's*. Retrieved from http://www.macleans.ca/news/canada/profile-of-justin-bourque/.

Futrell, R., & Simi, P. (2004). Free Spaces, Collective Identity, and the Persistence of U.S. White Power Activism. *Social Problems, 51*(1), 16–42.

Futrell, R., Simi, P., & Gottschalk, S. (2006). Understanding Music in Movements: The White Power Music Scene. *The Sociological Quarterly, 47*(2), 275–304.

Gardner, C., & Parris, J. (2012, April 17). Three Arrested by EPS Hate Crimes Unit. *CTV News*. Retrieved from http://edmonton.ctvnews.ca/three-arrested-by-eps-hate-crimes-unit-1.797199.

The Gazette. (1995, May 5). *White Supremacists Visited Regiment's Mess Hall*. Retrieved from https://cases.justia.com/federal/district-courts/california/candce/5:2008cv03889/206207/14/11.pdf.

Geddes, J. (2009, April 28). What Canadians think of Sikhs, Jews, Christians, Muslims. *Maclean's*. Retrieved from http://www.macleans.ca/news/canada/what-canadians-think-of-sikhs-jews-christians-muslims.

Giannasi, P. (2014). Policing Hate Crime. In N. Hall, A. Corb, P. Giannasi, & J. Grieve (Eds.), *The Routledge International Handbook on Hate Crime* (pp. 331–355). New York: Routledge.

Gill, P. (2015). *Lone-Actor Terrorists: A Behavioural Analysis*. London: Routledge.

Global Edmonton. (2012, April 17). *Edmonton Police Arrest White Supremacist Members*. Retrieved from http://www.globaltvedmonton.com/eps+arrest+-blood++honour+members/6442622681/story.html.

The Global Jewish News Source. (1992, November 11). *Anti-Nazi Activists' Home Damaged by Suspicious Fire*. Retrieved from http://www.jta.org/1992/11/11/archive/anti-nazi-activists-home-damaged-by-suspicious-fire.

The Global Jewish News Source. (1993, June 6). *Neo-Nazi Attack in Ontario Store Heightens Fears of Anti-Semitism*. Retrieved from http://www.jta.org/1993/06/07/archive/neo-nazi-attack-in-ontario-store-heightens-fears-of-anti-semitism.

The Globe and Mail. (2011, March 18). *Calgary's In-Your-Face Neo-Nazis Take to the Streets*. Retrieved from http://www.theglobeandmail.com/news/national/calgarys-in-your-face-neo-nazis-take-to-the-streets/article573162/?page=all.

The Globe and Mail. (2013, May 25). *The Ford Family's History with Drug Dealing*. Retrieved from http://www.theglobeandmail.com/news/toronto/globe-investigation-the-ford-familys-history-with-drug-dealing/article12153014/?page=all.

The Globe and Mail. (2014, February 21). *Garson Romalis Risked His Life to Perform Abortions*. Retrieved from http://www.theglobeandmail.com/news/british-columbia/garson-romalis-risked-his-life-to-perform-abortions/article17052093/.

Graham, R. (2016). Inter-Ideological Mingling: White Extremist Ideology Entering the Mainstream on Twitter. *Sociological Spectrum, 36*(1), 24–36.

Gramsci, A. (1971). *Selections from the Prison Notebooks*. New York: International Publishers.

Graveland, B. (2012, April 17). *Wildrose Candidate Apologizes for Suggesting He Has a White Advantage*. Global News. Retrieved from http://globalnews.ca/news/235033/wildrose-candidate-apologizes-for-suggesting-he-has-a-white-advantage-3.

Graves, F. (2015, March 12). The EKOS Poll: Are Canadians Getting More Racist? *iPolitics*. Retrieved from https://ipolitics.ca/2015/03/12/the-ekos-poll-are-canadians-getting-more-racist.

Gray, J. (2013, February 27). Supreme Court Ruling Upholds Limits on Free Speech in Case Involving Anti-Gay Proselytizer. *The Globe and Mail*. Retrieved from http://www.theglobeandmail.com/news/national/supreme-court-ruling-upholds-limits-on-free-speech-in-case-involving-anti-gay-proselytizer/article9104862/.

Government of Alberta. (2011). *Demographic Spotlight: The Visible Minority Population: Recent Trends in Alberta and Canada*. Edmonton: Government of Alberta, Demography Unit.

Gruenewald, J., Chermak, S., & Freilich, J. (2013). Far-Right Lone Wolf Homicides in the United States. *Studies in Conflict and Terrorism, 36*(12), 1005–1024.

Gruenewald, J., Freilich, J., & Chermak, S. (2009). An Overview of the Domestic Far-Right and Its Criminal Activities. In B. Perry & R. Blazak (Eds.), *Hate Crime: Issues and Perspectives, Vol. 4 Offenders* (pp. 1–22). New York: Praeger.

Grumke, T. (2013). Globalized Anti-globalists: The Ideological Basis of the Internationalization of Right-Wing Extremism. In S. Von Mering & T. W. McCarty (Eds.), *Right-Wing Radicalism Today: Perspectives from Europe and the US* (pp. 13–22). London: Routledge.

Gunlock, B. (2013, March 12). A New Look at Calgary's Neo-Nazi Movement. *Vice News*. Retrieved from https://www.vice.com/en_ca/article/exkmvz/a-new-look-at-calgarys-neo-nazi-movement.

Hall, N. (2012). Policing Hate in London and New York City: Some Reflections on the Factors Influencing Effective Law Enforcement, Service Provision and Public Trust and Confidence. *International Review of Victimology, 18*, 73–87.

Hamm, M. (1993). *American Skinheads: The Criminology and Control of Hate Crime.* Westport, CT: Praeger.

Hamm, M. (2007). *Terrorism as Crime.* New York: New York University Press.

Harris-Hogan, Shandon, Barrelle, K., & Zammit, A. (2015). What Is Countering Violent Extremism? Exploring CVE Policy and Practice in Australia. *Behavioral Sciences of Terrorism and Political Aggression, 8*(1), 6–24.

Heitmeyer, W. (2005). Right-Wing Terrorism. In T. Bjorgo (Ed.), *Root Causes of Terrorism: Myths, Reality and Ways Forward* (pp. 141–153). London: Routledge.

Hemmingby, C., & Bjørgo, T. (2015). *The Dynamics of a Terrorist Targeting Process: Anders B. Breivik and the 22 July attacks in Norway.* New York: Springer.

Hoffman, B. (2003). *Al Qaeda, Trends in Terrorism, and Future Potentialities: An Assessment.* Santa Monica: RAND Corporation.

Hoffman, B. (2006). *Inside Terrorism.* New York: Columbia University Press.

Hoffmann, D. (2013, March 13). Ultraconservative Bill Whatcott Clashes with U of S Students in Wake of Supreme Court Ruling on Hate Crime. *The Sheaf.* Retrieved from http://thesheaf.com/2013/03/13/ultraconserva-tive-bill-whatcott-clashes-with-u-of-s-students-in-wake-of-supreme-court-ruling-on-hate-speech/.

Hogan, J., & Haltinner, K. (2015). Floods, Invaders, and Parasites: Immigration Threat Narratives and Right-wing Populism in the USA, UK and Australia. *Journal of Intercultural Studies, 36*(5), 520–543.

hooks, b. (1994). *Outlaw Culture.* New York: Routledge.

hooks, b. (1995). *Killing Rage: Ending Racism.* New York: Holt and Co.

Hogan, M. (2012, August 6). Alleged Sikh Temple Shooter Was Frontman for White-Power Hardcore Band. *Spin.* Retrieved from http://www.spin.com/2012/08/alleged-sikh-temple-shooter-was-frontman-white-power-hardcore-band/.

Hong, G. (2014, January 17). We Interviewed the White Supremacist Running for Mayor of Toronto. *Vice News.* Retrieved from http://www.vice.com/en_ca/read/we-interviewed-the-white-supremacist-running-for-mayor-of-toronto.

Huber, L. P. (2016). Make America Great Again: Donald Trump, Racist Nativism and the Virulent Adherence to White Supremacy Amid US Demographic Change. *Charleston Law Review, 10*, 215.

Huffington Post. (2013, September 28). *Andreas Pirelli Evicted from Freeman "Embassy"; Rebekah Caverhill Prepares to Reclaim Home.* Retrieved from http://www.huffingtonpost.ca/2013/09/28/calgary-freeman-evicted_n_4009241.html.

Huffington Post. (2014, June 11). *Christopher Maximilian Sandau, B.C. Hockey Coach, Fired Over Pro-Nazi Facebook Posts.* Retrieved from http://www.huffingtonpost.ca/2014/11/05/christopher-maximilian-sandau-coach-fired-nazi_n_6111988.html.

Hughey, M. W. (2010). The (Dis)Similarities of White Racial Identities: The Conceptual Framework of 'Hegemonic Whiteness'. *Ethnic and Racial Studies, 33*(8), 1289–1309.

Humphrey, A. (2014, July 29). Canadian Nazi Party Founder Running for Office in Ontario Township. *National Post.* Retrieved from http://news.nationalpost.com/2014/07/29/canadian-nazi-party-founder-running-for-office-in-ontario-township/.

Inglehart, R., & Norris, P. (2016). *Trump, Brexit, and the Rise of Populism: Economic Have-Nots and Cultural Backlash* (Harvard Kennedy School Faculty Working Paper Series. RWP16-026).

Jackson, A. (2015). *The Return of the Gilded Age: Consequences, Causes and Solutions.* Ottawa, ON: The Broadbent Institute.

Jacoby, T. (2016). How the War Was 'One': Countering Violent Extremism and the Social Dimensions of Counter-Terrorism in Canada. *Journal for Deradicalization, 6,* 272–304.

Jagers, J., & Walgrave, S. (2007). Populism as Political Communication Style: An Empirical Study of Political Parties' Discourse in Belgium. *European Journal of Political Research, 46*(3), 319–345.

Jaggar, A. (2005). What Is Terrorism, Why Is It Wrong, and Could It Ever Be Morally Permissible? *Journal of Social Psychology, 36*(2), 202–217.

Jamin, J. (2013). Two Different Realities: Notes on Populism and the Extreme Right. In A. Mammone, E. Godin, & B. Jenkins (Eds.), *Varieties of RWE in Europe* (pp. 38–52). Abingdon: Routledge.

Jansen, R. S. (2011). Populist Mobilization: A New Theoretical Approach to Populism. *Sociological Theory, 29*(2), 75–96.

Jarvies, M. (2012). How Neo-Nazis Think: Photojournalist Spends Three Years Following Skinheads' Lives (with Photos). *Calgary Herald.* Retrieved from http://www.calgaryherald.com/news/Nazis+think+Calgary+photojournalist+spends+three+years/7208326/story.html.

Johnson, D. (2011). *Right Wing Resurgence: How a Domestic Terrorist Threat Is Being Ignored*. Lanham, MD: Rowman & Littlefield.

Johnson, D. (2012). *Right-Wing Resurgence: How a Domestic Terrorist Threat is Being Ignored*. Lanham, MD: Rowman & Littlefield.

Jones, A. (2014, March 7). *Ezra Levant, Sun News Host, Explains Trial 'Bombshell Moment'*. Huffington Post. Retrieved http://www.huffingtonpost.ca/2014/03/07/ezra-levant-libel-lawsuit_n_4922214.html.

Jupskås, A. (2012). Norway. In Institute for Strategic Dialogue, *Preventing and Countering Far-Right Extremism: European Cooperation, Country Reports* (pp. 51–54). London: Institute for Strategic Dialogue.

Khandaker, T., & Krishnan, M. (2017, March 4). *'Islam Is Evil': Protesters Clash at Toronto Anti-M-103 Rally*. Vice News. Retrieved from https://www.vice.com/en_ca/article/protestors-clash-at-pro-islamophobia-anti-m-103-rally-in-toronto.

Kim, T. K. (2006, April 19). A Look at White Power Music Today. *Southern Poverty Law Center*. Retrieved from https://www.splcenter.org/fighting-hate/intelligence-report/2006/look-white-power-music-today.

King, C. R. (2014). *Beyond Hate: White Power and Popular Culture*. Fanham, UK: Ashgate.

Kinsella, W. (2001). *Web of Hate: Inside Canada's Far Right Network*. Toronto: HarperCollins.

Kipfer, S., & Saberi, P. (2014). From "Revolution" to Farce? Hard-Right Populism in the Making of Toronto. *Studies in Political Economy, 93*(1), 127–152.

Klassen, J., & Albo, G. (Eds.). (2012). *Empire's Ally: Canada and the War in Afghanistan*. Toronto, ON: University of Toronto Press.

Komaromi, P., & Singh, K. (2016). *Post-referendum Racism and Xenophobia: The Role of Social Media Activism in Challenging the Normalisation of Xeno-Racist Narratives*. London: Institute of Race Relations.

Kornik, S. (2015, June 11). *Social Media Highlights Norman Raddatz's Hatred of Authority*. Global News. Retrieved from http://globalnews.ca/news/2048798/social-media-highlights-norman-raddatz-hatred-of-authority/.

Kumar, D. (2012). *Islamophobia and the Politics of Empire*. Chicago, IL: Haymarket Books.

Kundnani, A. (2012). *Blind Spot? Security Narratives and Far-Right Violence in Europe*. The Hague: International Centre for Counter-Terrorism.

Kundnani, A. (2015). *The Muslims Are Coming! Islamophobia, Extremism and the Domestic War on Terror.* New York: Verso.

Langman, L. (2005). From Virtual Public Spheres to Global Justice: A Critical Theory of Internetworked Social Movements. *Sociological Theory, 23*(1), 42–74.

Lauder, M. A. (2002). *The Far Rightwing Movement in Southwest Ontario: An Exploration of Issues, Themes, and Variations.* The Guelph and District Multicultural Centre.

Law Society of British Columbia. (2012). The Freemen on the Land Movement. *Benchers' Bulletin,* 4. Retrieved from https://www.lawsociety.bc.ca/page.cfm?cid=2627&t=Practice-Tips-The-Freeman-on-the-Land-movement.

Leader-Post. (2007, August 25). *KKK Revived, with Strong Regina Ties.* Retrieved from http://www.canada.com/reginaleaderpost/news/story.html?id=326a8ced-8c75-4c1b-acdc-7bcd8e090ffb.

Leblanc, D. (2018, January 25). Federal Government Staying Out of Court Challenge to Quebec's Face-Covering Law. *The Globe and Mail.* Retrieved from https://www.theglobeandmail.com/news/politics/federal-government-staying-out-of-court-challenge-to-quebecs-face-covering-law/article37741612.

Lehr, P. (2013). Still Blind in the Right Eye? A Comparison of German Responses to Political Violence from the Extreme Left and the Extreme Right. In M. Taylor, D. Holbrook, & P. M. Currie (Eds.), *Extreme Right Wing Political Violence and Terrorism* (pp. 187–214). London: Bloomsbury.

Levitz, S. (2017, September 18). Iqra Khalid Urges MPs to Take Unified Approach in Islamophobia Study. *The Globe and Mail.* Retrieved from https://www.theglobeandmail.com/news/politics/iqra-khalid-urges-mps-to-take-unified-approach-in-islamophobia-study/article36287550/.

Lindeman, T. (2015). *PEGIDA Quebéc Cancels March After Anti-racist Group Convene.* CBC News. Retrieved from https://www.cbc.ca/news/canada/montreal/pegida-québec-cancels-march-after-anti-racist-groups-convene-1.3013592.

Lund, D. (2006). Social Justice Activism in the Heartland of Hate: Countering Extremism in Alberta. *Alberta Journal of Educational Research, 52*(2), 181–194.

Macklin, G. (2013). 'Onward Blackshirts!' Music and the British Union of Fascists. *Patterns of Prejudice, 47*(4–5), 430–457.

Macnair, L., & Frank, R. (2017). Voices Against Extremism: A Case Study of a Community-Based CVE Counter-Narrative Campaign. *Journal for Deradicalization, 10,* 147–174.

Makuch, B. (2017, February 1). *Soldiers of Odin: Inside the Extremist Vigilante Group That Claims to Be Preserving Canadian Values*. Vice News. Retrieved from https://news.vice.com/story/soldiers-of-odin-inside-the-extremist-vigilante-group-that-claims-to-be-preserving-canadian-values.

Mallea, P. (2011). *Fearmonger: Stephen Harper's Tough-On-Crime Agenda*. Toronto, ON: James Lorimer & Company.

Mammone, A., Godin, E., & Jenkins, B. (Eds.). (2012). *Mapping the Extreme Right in Contemporary Europe: From Local to Transnational* (1st ed.). New York: Routledge.

Mammone, A., Godin, E., & Jenkins, B. (Eds.). (2013). *Varieties of Right-Wing Extremism in Europe*. London: Routledge.

Mares, M., & Stojar, R. (2016). Extreme Right Perpetrators. In M. Fredholm (Ed.), *Understanding Lone Actor Terrorism: Past Experience, Future Outlook, and Response Strategies* (pp. 66–86). London: Routledge.

Martin, A. (2016, November 17). Reginans Believe Racist Graffiti Inspired by Trump's Election. *Regina Leader-Post*. Retrieved from http://leaderpost.com/news/local-news/reginans-believe-racist-graffiti-inspired-by-trumps-election.

Martin, G. (2008). *Essentials of Terrorism*. Los Angeles: Sage.

Martin, K. (2010, May 19). Purported Neo-Nazi Admits to Making Explosives. *QMI Agency*. Retrieved from http://cnews.canoe.co/CNEW/Crim/201/0/1/13995161.html?cidDrssnewscanada.

Martin, K. (2011, June 16). Suspected Neo-Nazi in Plea Bargain Bid. *Calgary Sun*. Retrieved from http://www.calgarysun.com/2011/06/16/suspected-neonazi-in-plea-bargain-bid.

Mayne, L. A. (2007, December 20). Laviolette Given 30 Months. *Journal Pioneer*. Retrieved from http://www.journalpioneer.com/Justice/2007-12-20/article-1389852/Laviolette-given-30-months/1.

McDonald, M. (2011). *The Armageddon Factor: The Rise of Christian Nationalism in Canada* (2nd ed.). Toronto: Vintage.

McGarrigle, J. (2011, July 29). Corner Told Hughes Died of Blood Loss. *BC Local News*. Retrieved from http://www.bclocalnews.com/news/126403828.html.

McGillivray, K. (2016, November 14). *Racist Posters Promoting 'Alt-Right' Alarm Toronto Residents*. CBC News Toronto. Retrieved from http://www.cbc.ca/news/canada/toronto/east-york-alt-right-racist-posters-1.3850386.

McIntyre, M. (2008, June 10). *Children Seized over Neo-Nazi Allegations: Girl, Boy 'May Be at Risk Due to the Parents' Behaviour'*. Retrieved from http://www.culteducation.com/group/1071-neo-nazis/15107-children-seized-over-neo-nazi-allegations.html.

McKenna, K. (2017, January 31). *Suspect in Mosque Shooting a Moderate Conservative Turned Extremist, Say Friends, Classmates.* CBC News Montreal. Retrieved from http://www.cbc.ca/news/canada/montreal/quebec-city-mosque-alexandre-bissonnette-profile-1.3959581.

McLaughlin, T. (2008, September 12). Trial Probes Beating Death. *The Barrie Examiner.* Retrieved from http://www.thebarrieexaminer.com/2008/09/12/trial-probes-beating-death.

McMartin, P. (2013, March 13). Doug Christie—Defender of Free Speech, Symbol of Democracy. *Vancouver Sun.* Retrieved from http://www.vancouversun.com/news/Pete+McMartin+Doug+Christie+defender+free+speech+symbol+democracy/8093191/story.html.

McQuaig, L. (2007). *Holding the Bully's Coat: Canada and the U.S. Empire.* Toronto, ON: Doubleday.

Michael, G. (2006). RAHOWA! A History of the World Church of the Creator. *Terrorism and Political Violence, 18*(4), 561–583.

Mills, C. E., Freilich, J. D., & Chermak, S. M. (2015). Extreme Hatred: Revisiting the Hate Crime and Terrorism Relationship to Determine Whether They Are "Close Cousins" or "Distant Relatives". *Crime & Delinquency, 63*(10), 1191–1223.

Minkenberg, M. (2011). The Radical Right in Europe Today: Trends and Patterns in East and West. In N. Langenbacher & B. Schellenberg (Eds.), *Is Europe on the "Right" Path? Right Wing Extremism and Right Wing Populism in Europe* (pp. 37–56). Berlin: Friedrich-Ebert-Stiftung Forum.

Mississauga News. (2014, September 17). *Paul Fromm: Mississauga Mayoral Candidate.* Retrieved from December 28, 2015, http://www.mississauga.com/news-story/4865617-paul-fromm-mississauga-mayoral-candidate.

Montpetit, J. (2016a, September 5). *Quebec's Charter of Values, Revisited.* CBC News Montreal. Retrieved from http://www.cbc.ca/news/canada/montreal/caq-quebec-charter-of-values-identity-politics-1.3748084.

Montpetit, J. (2016b, December 14). *Inside Quebec's Far Right: Soldiers of Odin Leadership Shake-Up Signals Return to Extremist Roots.* CBC News Montreal. Retrieved February 13, 2017, from http://www.cbc.ca/news/canada/montreal/quebec-far-right-soldiers-of-odin-1.3896175.

Montreal Gazette. (2006, December 11). *Trial Delayed for Teen Suspected of Posting Threats.* Retrieved from http://www.canada.com/montrealgazette/news/story.html?id=2d00a6a5-7273-4ca0-aa25-c063d23bd6d9&k=36474.

Moore, D. (2013). *'Freeman on the Land' Movement Concerns Police, Notaries.* Huffpost British Columbia. Retrieved from http://www.huffingtonpost.ca/2013/09/02/freemen-on-the-land_n_3856845.html.

Mudde, C. (2004). The Populist Zeitgeist. *Government and Opposition, 39*(4), 541–563.

Mulholland, S. (2013). White Supremacist Groups and Hate Crime. *Public Choice, 157*(1–2), 91–113.

Myerson, J. A. (2017, May 22). Trumpism: It's Coming from the Suburbs. *The Nation*. Retrieved from https://www.thenation.com/article/trumpism-its-coming-from-the-suburbs.

National Post. (2006, June 17). *Neo-Nazi Killer Who Acted Out of Paranoia Gets 10 Years*. Retrieved from http://www.canada.com/nationalpost/news/toronto/story.html?id=cf832bac-a6bd-4a45-b159-bc97a1e82ad3.

National Post. (2007, March 16). *Police Charge Man, 20, in Jewish Daycare Attack*. Retrieved from http://www.canada.com/nationalpost/news/toronto/story.html?id=4b59fba8-1ab8-4446-98b7-bed102262545.

Navigator Research. (2013). *Summary of Findings*. Private Exchange.

Neumann, P. (2013). Options and Strategies for Countering Online Radicalization in the United States. *Studies in Conflict and Terrorism, 36,* 431–459.

New York Times. (1995, March 24). *Head of Detroit White Supremacist Group Faces Trial in Canada*. Retrieved from http://www.nytimes.com/1995/03/24/us/head-of-detroit-white-supremacist-group-faces-trial-in-canada.html.

Niagara Falls Review. (2014, June 19). *Man Charged with Criminally Harassing Elderly Couple*. Retrieved from http://www.niagarafallsreview.ca/2014/06/19/man-charged-with-criminally-harassing-elderly-couple.

Neiwert, D. (2017). *Alt-America: The Rise of the Radical Right in the Age of Trump*. New York, NY: Verso.

Noble. (n.d.). *Part V: Raid and Arrests*. Retrieved from http://www.exterminance.org/bio5.html.

Oaten, A. (2014). The Cult of the Victim: An Analysis of the Collective Identity of the English Defence League. *Patterns of Prejudice, 48*(4), 331–349.

Oberschall, A. (2004). Explaining Terrorism: The Contribution of Collective Action Theory. *Sociological Theory, 22*(1), 26–37.

One People's Project. (2009). *Bill Noble*. Retrieved from http://onepeoplesproject.com/index.php/en/rogues-gallery/14-n/128-bill-noble.

One People's Project. (2011). *Kyle McKee*. Retrieved from http://www.onepeoplesproject.com/index.php?option=com_content&view=article&id=663:kyle-mckee&catid=13:m&Itemid=3.

Ontario Hate Crime Community Working Group. (2006). *Addressing Hate Crime in Ontario.* Retrieved from https://www.attorneygeneral.jus.gov. on.ca/english/about/pubs/hatecrimes/HCCWG_full.pdf.

Oommen, I. (2010, April 26). Mainstream Media Fumbles Abbotsford Attack. *Vancouver Media Co-Op.* Retrieved from http://vancouver.mediacoop.ca/ story/3300.

Ottawa Citizen. (2006, April 18). *Murder Charges Laid in Death of Ottawa Man.* Retrieved from http://www.canada.com/ottawacitizen/news/story. html?id=a9f4eaa8-1f44-4217-b988-8ca489147158&k=38214.

Ottawa Citizen. (2012, June 17). *Canadian Forces Warned of Possible Infiltration by White Supremacist Group.* Retrieved from http:// www.ottawacitizen.com/life/Canadian+Forces+warned+possible+ infiltration+white+supremacist+group/6801966/story.html.

Paddon, D. (2016, January 3). *Canada's Top CEOs to Earn Average Worker's 2017 Salary by Lunchtime.* Huffington Post. Retrieved from http://www.huffingtonpost.ca/2017/01/03/canada-ceo-worker-pay-gap_n_13937686.html.

Pantucci, R. (2011). What Have We Learned About Lone Wolves from Anders Behring Breivik? *Perspectives on Terrorism, 5*(5–6), 27–42.

Parent, R., & Ellis, J. (2014). *Right Wing Extremism in Canada* (No. 14-03). Vancouver: Canadian Network for Research on Terrorism, Security and Society.

Parkin, W. S., & Freilich, J. D. (2015). Routine Activities and Right-Wing Extremists: An Empirical Comparison of the Victims of Ideologically-and Non-ideologically-motivated Homicides Committed by American Far-Rightists. *Terrorism and Political Violence, 27*(1), 182–203.

Parmar, A. (2011). Stop and Search in London: Counter-Terrorist or Counter-Productive? *Policing and Society, 21*(4), 369–382.

Peace Magazine. (1995, July–August). *Urban Terrorism: Could It Happen Here?* Retrieved from http://peacemagazine.org/archive/v11n4p18.htm.

Pelley, L. (2016, November 23). *Toronto Man Finds 2 Swastikas Spray-Painted in His Queen Street East Neighbourhood.* CBC News Toronto. Retrieved from http://www.cbc.ca/news/canada/toronto/anti-semitic-graffiti-spotted-in-downtown-toronto-1.3864466.

Perliger, A. (2012). *Challengers from the Sidelines: Understanding America's Far Right.* West Point, NY: Combating Terrorism Center.

Perreaux, L., & Freeze, C. (2017, February 1). Arrest Made After Hate Crimes Spike following Quebec Mosque Attack. *The Globe and Mail.* Retrieved from http://www.theglobeandmail.com/news/national/police-report-rise-in-hate-crimes-after-quebec-city-mosque-attack/article33856702.

Perry, B. (2000). "Button-Down Terror": The Metamorphosis of the Hate Movement. *Sociological Focus, 33*(2), 113–131.

Perry, B. (2001). *In the Name of Hate: Understanding Hate Crimes*. New York: Routledge.

Perry, B. (2008). *Silent Victims: Hate Crime Against Native Americans*. Tucson: University of Arizona Press.

Perry, B. (2009). *Policing Race and Place: Under- and Over-Policing in Indian Country*. Lanham, MD: Lexington Press.

Perry, B. (2015). "All of a Sudden, There Are Muslims": Identities, Visibilities, and Islamophobic Violence in Canada. *Journal for Crime, Justice and Social Democracy, 4*(3), 4–15.

Perry, B., & Alvi, S. (2011). "We Are All Vulnerable:" The *In Terrorem* Effects of Hate Crime. *International Review of Victimology, 18*(1), 57–72.

Perry, B., & Blazak, R. (2010). Places for Races: The White Supremacist Movement Imagines U.S. *Geography. Journal of Hate Studies, 8*, 29–51.

Perry, B., Hofmann, D. C., & Scrivens, R. (2017). *Broadening Our Understanding of Anti-authority Movements in Canada*. The Canadian Network for Research on Terrorism, Security and Society Working Paper Series.

Perry, B., Hofmann, D. C., & Scrivens, R. (2018). "Confrontational but Not Violent": An Assessment of the Potential for Violence by the Anti-Authority Community in Canada. *Terrorism and Political Violence*. Ahead of Print, 1–21.

Perry, B., & Olsson, P. (2009). Cyberhate: The Globalization of Hate. *Information and Communications Technology Law, 18*(2), 185–199.

Perry, B., & Scrivens, R. (2015). *Right-Wing Extremism in Canada: An Environmental Scan*. Ottawa, ON: Public Safety Canada.

Perry, B., & Scrivens, R. (2016). Uneasy Alliances: A Look at the Right-Wing Extremist Movement in Canada. *Studies in Conflict and Terrorism, 39*(9), 819–841.

Perry, B., & Scrivens, R. (2019). Who's a Terrorist? What's Terrorism? Comparative Media Representations of Lone-Actor Violence in Canada. In L. Dawson & S. Thompson (Eds.), *Canada Among Nations: Terrorism and Counterterrorism*. Toronto, ON: University of Toronto Press.

Petrou, M., & Kandylis, G. (2016). Violence and Extreme-Right Activism: The Neo-Nazi Golden Dawn in a Greek Rural Community. *Journal of Intercultural Studies, 37*(6), 589–604.

Pew Research Center. (2017a, June 16). *U.S. Image Suffers as Publics Around World Question Trump's Leadership.* Retrieved from http://www.pewglobal.org/2017/06/26/u-s-image-suffers-as-publics-around-world-question-trumps-leadership.

Pew Research Center. (2017b, August 29). *Republicans Divided in Views of Trump's Conduct; Democrats Are Broadly Critical.* Retrieved from http://www.people-press.org/2017/08/29/republicans-divided-in-views-of-trumps-conduct-democrats-are-broadly-critical.

Pfeffer, A. (2017, February 17). *Teen Who Spray-Painted Racist Slurs, Swastikas Pleads Guilty.* CBC News Ottawa. Retrieved from http://www.cbc.ca/news/canada/ottawa/teen-swastika-racist-guilty-church-synagogue-mosque-1.3988061.

Pliner, J. (2013). *Observable Indicators of Possible Radicalisation.* Paris: Fondation Pour la Recherche Stratégique. Retrieved from http://www.safire-project-results.eu/documents/focus/8.pdf.

Pollard, J. (2016). Skinhead Culture: The Ideologies, Mythologies, Religions and Conspiracy Theories of Racist Skinheads. *Patterns of Prejudice, 50*(4–5), 398–419.

Porter, A. (2012). Neo-conservatism, Neo-liberalism and Canadian Social Policy: Challenges for Feminism. *Canadian Woman Studies, 29*(3), 19–31.

Porter, T. (2015). Web of Hatred: Internet Inspires US Far-Right Extremists to Carry Out 'Lone Wolf' Terror Attacks. *International Business Times.* Retrieved from http://www.ibtimes.co.uk/web-hatred-internet-inspires-us-far-right-extremists-carry-out-lone-wolf-terror-attacks-1492925.

Potok, M. (2017, February 15). *The Trump Effect.* Southern Poverty Law Centre. Retrieved from https://www.splcenter.org/fighting-hate/intelligence-report/2017/trump-effect.

Poynting, S. (2006). What Caused the Cronulla Riots? *Race and Class, 48,* 85–92.

Poynting, S., & Perry, B. (2007). Climates of Hate: Media and State Inspired Victimisation of Muslims in Canada and Australia Since 9/11. *Current Issues in Criminal Justice, 19*(2), 150–171.

Pressman, E. (2009). *Risk Assessment Decisions for Violent Political Extremism.* Ottawa: Canadian Centre for Security and Intelligence Studies, Carleton University. Retrieved from http://www.publicsafety.gc.ca/cnt/rsrcs/pblctns/2009-02-rdv/2009-02-rdv-eng.pdf.

Prince, M. J. (2015). Prime Minister as Moral Crusader: Stephen Harper's Punitive Turn in Social Policy-Making. *Canadian Review of Social Policy, 71*(1), 53–69.

Pro-Choice Action Network. (1997/1998). New Lead in Doctor Shootings. *Pro-Choice Press.* Retrieved from http://www.prochoiceactionnetwork-canada.org/prochoicepress/9798win.shtml.

Public Safety Canada. (2013). *2013 Public Report on the Terrorist Threat to Canada*. Retrieved from http://www.securitepublique.gc.ca/cnt/rsrcs/pblctns/trrrst-thrt-cnd/trrrst-thrt-cnd-eng.pdf.

Pugliese, D. (2012, June 17). Canadian Forces Warned of Possible Infiltration by White Supremacist Group. *Ottawa Citizen*. Retrieved from http://www.ottawacitizen.com/life/Canadian+Forces+warned+possible+infiltration+white+supremacist+group/6801966/story.html.

Radio-Canada. (2002, June 6). *Richard Germain est Condamné à la Prison*. Retrieved from http://ici.radio-canada.ca/nouvelles/Montreal/nouvelles/200206/06/006-germain-condamnation.asp.

Ramalingham, V. (2014). *On the Front Line: A Guide to Countering Far-Right Extremism*. London: Institute for Strategic Dialogue.

Ramalingam, V., & Henry, T. (2014). *The Need for Exit Programmes: Why Deradicalisation and Disengagement Matters in the UK's Approach to Far-Right Violence*. London: Institute for Strategic Dialogue.

Ray, L., & Smith, D. (2002). Racist Violence as Hate Crime. *Criminal Justice Matters, 48*, 6–7.

Rayside, D., Sabin, J., & Thomas, P. (2012). Faith and Party Politics in Alberta or "Danielle, This Is Alberta, Not Alabama." In *Proceedings of the Canadian Political Science Association Annual Conference*. Edmonton, AB.

The Record. (2011, June 6). Violent Guelph Drug Dealer Appeals 14-Year Prison Term. Retrieved from http://www.therecord.com/news-story/2580772-violent-guelph-drug-dealer-appeals-14-year-prison-term-/l.

Ridgeway, J. (1995). *Blood in the Face*. New York: Thunder's Mouth Press.

Rieti, J. (2016, November 14). *Video Shows Man Hurling Racist Insults, Threats on Toronto Streetcar*. CBC News Toronto. Retrieved from http://www.cbc.ca/news/canada/toronto/toronto-streetcar-incident-1.3851108.

Rooduijn, M. (2014). The Mesmerizing Message: The Diffusion of Populism in Public Debates in Western European Media. *Political Studies, 62*(4), 726–744.

Rosenfeld, R. (2004). Terrorism and Criminology. In M. Deflem (Ed.), *Terrorism and Counter-Terrorism: Criminological Perspectives* (pp. 19–32). Boston: Elsevier.

Rosenfeld, S. (2017, May 19). *12 Features of White Working Class Trump Voters Confirm Depressed and Traumatized Multitudes Voted for Him*. Salon. Retrieved from http://www.salon.com/2017/05/19/12-features-of-white-working-class-trump-voters-confirm-depressed-and-traumatized-multitudes-voted-for-him_partner.

Ross, J. I. (1992). Contemporary Radical Right Wing Violence in Canada: A Quantitative Analysis. *Terrorism and Political Violence, 4*(3), 72–101.

Roth, P. (2012a, April 17). Calgary White Supremacist Arrested over Edmonton Racial Attack. *Calgary Sun*. Retrieved from http://www.calgarysun.com/2012/04/17/calgary-white-supremacist-arrested-over-edmonton-racial-attack.

Roth, P. (2012b, April 17). White Supremacists Charged in Alleged Bottle Attack. *Calgary Sun*. Retrieved from http://www.calgarysun.com/2012/04/17/white-supremacists-charged-in-alleged-bottle-attack.

Sapp, A., Holden, R., & Wiggins, M. (1991). Value and Belief Systems of Right-Wing Extremists: Rationale and Motivation for Bias-Motivated Crime. In R. Kelly (Ed.), *Bias Crime: American Law Enforcement and Legal Responses* (pp. 105–131). Chicago IL: Office of International Criminal Justice.

Sayers, A. M., & Denemark, D. (2014). Radicalism, Protest Votes and Regionalism: Reform and the Rise of the New Conservative Party. *Canadian Political Science Review, 8*(1), 3–26.

Schafer, J., Mullins, C., & Box, S. (2014). Awakenings: The Emergence of White Supremacist Ideologies. *Deviant Behavior, 35*(3), 173–196.

Scherr, S. (2009). Aryan Guard Marches on Calgary. *Southern Poverty Law Center*. Retrieved from http://www.splcenter.org/get-informed/intelligence-report/browse-all-issues/2009/summer/northern-exposure.

Schmid, A. (2013). *Radicalisation, De-radicalisation, Counter-Radicalisation: A Conceptual Discussion and Literature Review*. The Hague: International Centre for Counter-Terrorism.

Scrivens, R., Davies, G., & Frank, R. (2018). Measuring the Evolution of Radical Right-Wing Posting Behaviors Online. *Deviant Behavior*. Ahead of Print, pp. 1–17.

Scrivens, R., & Perry, B. (2017). Resisting the Right: Countering Right-Wing Extremism in Canada. *Canadian Journal of Criminology and Criminal Justice, 59*(4), 534–558.

Selim, G. (2016). Approaches for Countering Violent Extremism at Home and Abroad. *The ANNALS of the American Academy of Political and Social Science, 668*(1), 94–101.

Seth, A. (2014, February 13). *Brampton Hit with Another String of Anti-immigration Flyers*. Global News. Retrieved from http://globalnews.ca/news/1498130/brampton-hit-with-another-string-of-anti-immigration-flyers.

Shaffer, R. (2013). The Sound of Neo-fascism: Youth and Music in the National Front. *Patterns of Prejudice, 17*(4–5), 458–482.

Sharpe, K. (2016, November 17). *Regina Homeowners Upset After Property Tagged with Racist Graffiti*. Global News. Retrieved from http://globalnews.ca/news/3074086/regina-homeowners-upset-after-property-tagged-with-racist-graffiti.

Sheffield, C. (1995). Hate Violence. In P. Rothenberg (Ed.), *Race, Class and Gender in the United States* (pp. 432–441). New York: St. Martin's Press.

Shihipar, A. (2017, July 4). *Why Americans Must Stop Talking About Trump's Mythical "White Working Class" Voters.* Quartz. Retrieved from https://qz.com/991072/why-americans-must-stop-talking-about-the-mythical-homogenous-white-working-class.

Shils, E. (1956). *The Torment of Secrecy.* Glencoa, IL: Free Press.

Shingler, B. (2016, December 8). *'Make Canada Great Again' Flyers with Anti-Muslim, Anti-gay Imagery Alarm McGill University Community.* CBC News Montreal. Retrieved from http://www.cbc.ca/news/canada/montreal/mcgill-canada-make-canada-great-again-1.3886871.

Simi, P. (2010). Why Study White Supremacist Terror? A Research Note. *Deviant Behavior, 31,* 251–273.

Simi, P., Bubolz, B., & Hardman, A. (2013). Military Experience, Identity Discrepancies and Right Terrorism: An Exploratory Analysis. *Studies in Conflict and Terrorism, 36,* 654–671.

Simi, P., & Futrell, R. (2015). *American Swastika: Inside the White Power Movement's Hidden Spaces of Hate* (2nd ed.). Lanham, MD: Rowman and Littlefield Publishers.

Simi, P., Futrell, R., & Bubolz, B. F. (2016). Parenting as Activism: Identity Alignment and Activist Persistence in the White Power Movement. *The Sociological Quarterly, 57*(3), 491–519.

Simon, J. D. (2013). *Lone Wolf Terrorism: Understanding the Growing Threat.* New York: Prometheus Books.

Simons, P. (2015, June 11). Police Constable Fought to Protect Edmonton from Hate. Sadly, Hate Killed Him. *Edmonton Journal.* Retrieved from http://www.edmontonjournal.com/news/edmonton/Simons+Police+constable+fought+protect+Edmonton+from/11127592/story.html#__federated=1.

Solyom, C. (2016a, November 14). The Trump Effect and the Normalization of Hate in Quebec. *Montreal Gazette.* Retrieved from http://montrealgazette.com/news/national/the-trump-effect-and-the-normalization-of-hate.

Solyom, C. (2016b, November 22). Confessions of a Former Neo-Nazi: 'I Would Have Killed People'. *Montreal Gazette.* Retrieved from https://montrealgazette.com/news/local-news/confessions-of-a-former-neo-nazi-i-would-have-killed-people.

Southern Poverty Law Center. (2009). *Aryan Guard Marches on Calgary.* Retrieved from http://www.splcenter.org/get-informed/intelligence-report/browse-all-issues/2009/summer/northern-exposure.

Southern Poverty Law Center. (n.d.). *Paul Fromm.* Retrieved from https://www.splcenter.org/fighting-hate/extremist-files/individual/paul-fromm.

Speakers' Spotlight. (2014). *Ezra Levant*. Retrieved from http://www.speakers.ca/speakers/ezra-levant/.

The Spec. (2010, September 15). *Racists Going to Jail for Taunts*. Retrieved from http://www.thespec.com/news-story/2170372-racists-going-to-jail-for-taunts/.

Statistics Canada. (2011). *NHS Profile, London, CMA, Ontario, 2011*. Retrieved from http://www12.statcan.gc.ca/nhs-enm/2011/dp-pd/prof/details/page.cfm?Lang=E&Geo1=CMA&Code1=555&Data=Count&-SearchText=London&SearchType=Begins&SearchPR=35&A1=All&B1=All&Custom=&TABID=1.

St. Joseph News Press. (1981, November 27). *Canadian Klan Chief Is Charged*. Retrieved from http://news.google.com/newspapers?id=HdlbAAAAIBA-J&sjid=n1INAAAAIBAJ&pg=2910,5603839&dq=james+alexander+mc-quirter&hl=en.

Sterman, D. (2013, April 24). The Greater Danger: Military-Trained Right-Wing Extremists. *The Atlantic*. Retrieved from https://www.theatlantic.com/national/archive/2013/04/the-greater-danger-military-trained-right-wing-extremists/275277/.

Stern, K. (1992). *Politics and Bigotry*. New York, NY: American Jewish Committee.

Stone, L. (2016, November 9). Trump Win Sends 'Exciting Message' to Canada: Conservative MP Kellie Leitch. *The Globe and Mail*. Retrieved from https://www.theglobeandmail.com/news/politics/trump-message-needs-to-come-to-canada-leitch-says-in-tory-leadership-bid/article32760294.

Stop Racism and Hate Collective. (2015). *One People's Project: Aryan Guard Knew About Kyle McKee's Involvement in Pipebomb Attack*. Retrieved from http://www.stopracism.ca/content/one-peoples-project-aryan-guard-knew-about-kyle-mckees-involvement-pipebomb-attack.

Talty, S. (1996, February 25). The Method of a Neo-Nazi Mogul. *The New York Times*. Retrieved from http://www.nytimes.com/1996/02/25/magazine/the-method-of-a-neo-nazi-mogul.html?pagewanted=all.

Taggart, P. (2000). *Populism*. Buckingham, UK: Open University Press.

Taggart, P. (2004). Populism and Representative Politics in Contemporary Europe. *Journal of Political Ideologies, 9*(3), 269–288.

Tanner, S., & Campana, A. (2014). *The Process of Radicalization: Right Wing Skinheads in Quebec* (No. 14-07). Vancouver: Canadian Network for Research on Terrorism, Security and Society.

Taylor, K. (2017, July 12). The Speech Racists Didn't Want You to Hear. *Jacobin*. Retrieved fromhttps://jacobinmag.com/2017/07/free-speech-fox-news-racism-trump-poor-whites.

Terry, D. (2014). *Canadians Hunt Gun Control-Hater in Cop-Killing Rampage. Southern Poverty Law Center*. Retrieved from http://www.splcenter.org/blog/2014/06/05/canadians-hunt-gun-control-hater-in-cop-killing-rampage/.

Thompson, K. (2016). *The Internet Has Facilitated Alt-Right Recruiting*. Metro News Canada. Retrieved from http://www.metronews.ca/news/canada/2016/12/05/alt-right-and-the-internet.html.

Thompson, K., Hiebert, D., & Brooks, L. (2016). *Policy Brief: On the Creation of the Office of the Community Outreach and Counter-Radicalization Coordinator*. Canadian Network for Research on Terrorism, Security and Society.

Times-Colonist. (2012). *'Freeman on the Land' Movement Worries CSIS*. Retrieved from http://www.timescolonist.com/news/national/freeman-on-the-land-movement-worries-csis-1.37071.

Toronto Star. (1987, July 17). *Death Threat in Extortion Case 2 Men Charged*. Retrieved from http://pqasb.pqarchiver.com/thestar/doc/435583821.html?FMT=ABS&FMTS=ABS:FT&type=current&date=Jul%2017,%201987&author=&pub=Toronto%20Star&edition=&startpage=&desc=Death%20threat%20in%20extortion%20case%202%20men%20charged.

Toronto Star. (1990a, March 8). *Injured Man Found Near Railway Tracks*. Retrieved from http://pqasb.pqarchiver.com/thestar/doc/436154957.html?FMT=ABS&FMTS=ABS:FT&type=current&date=Mar%2008,%201990&author=&pub=Toronto%20Star&edition=&startpage=&desc=Injured%20man%20found%20near%20railway%20tracks.

Toronto Star. (1990b, June 26). *Ex-Skinhead Gets 12 Years for Killing Teen*. Retrieved from http://pqasb.pqarchiver.com/thestar/doc/436226366.html?FMT=ABS&FMTS=ABS:FT&type=current&date=Jun%2026,%201990&author=Gary%20Oakes%20Toronto%20Star&pub=Toronto%20Star&edition=&startpage=&desc=Ex-skinhead%20gets%2012%20years%20for%20killing%20teen.

Toronto Star. (1991, September 21). *Metro Police Arrest White Supremacist*. Retrieved from http://pqasb.pqarchiver.com/thestar/doc/436472932.html?FMT=ABS&FMTS=ABS:FT&type=current&date=Sep%2021,%201991&author=&pub=Toronto%20Star&edition=&startpage=&desc=Metro%20police%20arrest%20white%20supremacist.

Toronto Star. (1993a, April 29). *Second Man Charged After Teen's Body Found in Tub.* Retrieved from http://pqasb.pqarchiver.com/thestar/doc/436817238.html?FMT=ABS&FMTS=ABS:FT&type=current&date=Apr%2029,%201993&author=&pub=Toronto%20Star&edition=&startpage=&desc=Second%20man%20charged%20after%20teen's%20body%20found%20in%20tub.

Toronto Star. (1993b, October 28). *Police Arrest 2 Men in Oshawa Robberies.* Retrieved http://pqasb.pqarchiver.com/thestar/doc/436918031.html?FMT=ABS&FMTS=ABS:FT&type=current&date=Oct%2028,%201993&author=Gail%20Swainson%20Toronto%20Star&pub=Toronto%20Star&edition=&startpage=&desc=Police%20arrest%202%20men%20in%20Oshawa%20robberies.

Toronto Star. (1995, November 9). *Judge Stayed Charges Because of Long Delay.* Retrieved from http://pqasb.pqarchiver.com/thestar/doc/437362091.html?FMT=ABS&FMTS=ABS:FT&type=current&date=Nov%2009,%201995&author=By%20Dale%20Brazao%20Toronto%20Star&pub=Toronto%20Star&edition=&startpage=&desc=Judge%20stays%20charges%20because%20of%20long%20delay.

Toronto Star. (2011, July 26). *Gunman Saw Canada as Potential Junior Partner.* Retrieved from http://www.thestar.com/news/world/2011/07/26/gunman_saw_canada_as_potential_junior_partner.html.

Toronto Star. (2015a, March 15). *Terrorism Threat Runs Broad 'Gamut',* p. 1.

Toronto Star. (2015b, March 25). *Anti-Islam Group on Rise in Quebec,* p. A10.

Toronto Sun. (1995, February). *Stabbing in Subway Melee.* Retrieved from http://www.freedomsite.org/ara/articles/stabbing_in_subway.html.

Totten, M. (2014). *Gang Life: 10 of the Toughest Tell Their Stories.* Toronto: James Lorimer & Company Ltd.

Treadwell, J., & Garland, J. (2011). Masculinity, Marginalization and Violence: A Case Study of the English Defence League. *The British Journal of Criminology, 51*(4), 621–634.

Tunney, C. (2016, September 2). *Kellie Leitch Defends 'Anti-Canadian Values' Survey Question.* CBC News. Retrieved from http://www.cbc.ca/news/politics/leitch-responds-survey-question-1.3746470.

UK Home Office. (2010). *Channel: Supporting Individuals Vulnerable to Recruitment by Violent Extremists. A Guide for Local Partnerships.* London: Her Majesty's Government. Retrieved from http://tna.europarchive.org/20100419081706/http:/security.homeoffice.gov.uk/news-publications/publication-search/prevent/channel-guidance?view=Binary.

UNC School of Government. (2012). *A Quick Guide to Sovereign Citizens*. Retrieved from http://www.sog.unc.edu/sites/www.sog.unc.edu/files/R09.1% 20Sovereign%20citizens%20briefing%20paper%20Sept%2012%20 %28Crowell%29.pdf.

U.S. Department of Homeland Security. (2009). *Rightwing Extremism: Current Economic and Political Climate Fueling Resurgence in Radicalization and Recruitment*. Washington, DC: U.S. Department of Homeland Security and the Federal Bureau of Investigation.

Vancouver Sun. (2006, August 6). *Hate Crime Carries High Price*. Retrieved from http://www.canada.com/story_print.html?id=fea20c32-2431-4f3c-b097-067f48bbfabc&sponsor.

Vancouver Sun. (2014, November 6). *Minor Hockey Coach Fired for Posting Nazi Propaganda on Facebook*, p. A10.

Waldman, P. (2016, November 21). Trump Takes Office as the Most Disliked President Ever. How Much Will That Matter? *The Washington Post*. Retrieved from https://www.washingtonpost.com/blogs/plum-line/wp/2016/11/21/trump-takes-office-as-the-most-disliked-president-ever-how-much-will-that-matter.

Walkom, T. (2015, February 17). Halifax Murder Plot Shows Absurdity of Anti-Terror Laws. *Toronto Star*. Retrieved from https://www.thestar.com/news/canada/2015/02/17/halifax-murder-plot-shows-absurdity-of-anti-terror-laws-walkom.html.

Waterloo Regional Record. (2011, May 10). *Second Teen Gang Member Pleads Guilty to Assault, Theft*. Retrieved from http://www.therecord.com/news-story/2580579-second-teen-gang-member-pleads-guilty-to-assault-theft/.

Watts, R., & Dickson, L. (2013, February 26). Victoria Lawyer Doug Christie, Who Defended Zundel and Keegstra, Is Dying. *Times Colonist*. Retrieved from http://www.timescolonist.com/news/local/victoria-lawyer-doug-christie-who-defended-zundel-and-keegstra-is-dying-1.80575.

Webb, J., & Cutter, S. (2009). The Geography of U.S. Terrorist Incidents, 1970–2004. *Terrorism and Political Violence, 21*, 428–449.

Weinberg, L. (1998). An Overview of Right Wing Extremism in the Western World: A Study of Convergence, Linkage and Identity. In J. Kaplan & T. Bjørgo (Eds.), *Nation and Race* (pp. 3–33). Boston, MA: Northeastern University Press.

Welliver, D. M. (2004). Afterword: Finding and Fighting Hate Where It Lives: Reflections of a Pennsylvania Practitioner. In C. Flint (Ed.), *Spaces of Hate:*

Geographies of Discrimination and Intolerance in the U.S.A. (pp. 245–254). New York: Routledge.

White, R., & Perrone, S. (2001). Racism, Ethnicity and Hate Crime. *Communal/Plural, 9,* 161–181.

Whitworth, S. (2004). *Men, Militarism and UN Peacekeeping: A Gendered Analysis.* Boulder, CO: Lynne Rienner.

Wigerfelt, A., & Wigerfelt, B. (2014). *A Challenge to Multiculturalism: Everyday Racism and Hate Crime in a Small Swedish Town.* Retrieved from http://muep.mau.se/handle/2043/17654.

Williams, C. (2015). *Campus Campaigns Against Reproductive Autonomy: The Canadian Centre for Bioethical Reform Campus Genocide Awareness Project as Propaganda for Fetal Rights.* Retrieved from https://www.uleth.ca/dspace/bitstream/handle/10133/3645/WilliamsCampusCampaignsAgainstReproductiveAutonomyDec2014.pdf?sequence=1.

Winnipeg Free Press. (2013, September 19). *Why Does Same-Sex Affection Draw Anger?* Retrieved from http://www.winnipegfreepress.com/local/why-does-same-sex-affection-draw-anger-224361501.html.

Winnipeg Free Press. (2014, March 8). *Brilliant Doctor, Graceful Humanist.* Retrieved from http://www.winnipegfreepress.com/local/brilliant-doctor-graceful-humanist-249104791.html.

Wittmeier, B. (2012, December 9). Money, Drugs and Violence: The Evolution of White Boy Posse—In the Wake of Recent High-Profile Killings, Experts Look at Criminal Gang Behaviour. *Edmonton Journal.* Retrieved from http://www.edmontonjournal.com/news/Money+drugs+violence+evolution+White+Posse/7673689/story.html.

Wojcieszak, M. (2010). 'Don't Talk to Me': Effects of Ideological Homogenous Online Groups and Politically Dissimilar Offline Ties on Extremism. *New Media & Society, 12*(4), 637–655.

Wooden, W. S., & Blazak, R. (1995). *Renegade Kids, Suburban Outlaws: From Youth Culture to Delinquency.* Belmont, CA: Wadsworth.

Woods, A. (2015, March 24). Islam Needs to Reform or Leave, Says Canadian Leader of PEGIDA Movement. *Toronto Star.* Retrieved from https://www.thestar.com/news/canada/2015/03/24/islam-needs-to-reform-or-leave-says-canadian-leader-of-pegida-movement.html.

Yalnizyan, A. (2010). *The Rise of Canada's Richest 1%.* Ottawa, ON: Canadian Centre for Policy Alternatives.

Young, I. M. (1990). *Justice and the Politics of Difference*. Princeton, NJ: Princeton University Press.

Young, K., & Craig, L. (1997). Beyond White Pride: Identity, Meaning and Contradiction in the Canadian Skinhead Subculture. *The Canadian Review of Sociology and Anthropology, 34*(2), 175–206.

Zerbisias, A. (2013, September 29). Talking with the Guru of the Freemen on the Land. *Toronto Star*. Retrieved from https://www.thestar.com/news/canada/2013/09/29/talking_with_the_guru_of_the_freemen_on_the_land.html.

Zickmund, S. (1997). Approaching the Radical Other: The Discursive Culture of Cyberspace. In S. Jones (Ed.), *Virtual Culture: Identity and Community in Cybersociety* (pp. 185–205). Thousand Oaks, CA: Sage.

Index

© The Editor(s) (if applicable) and The Author(s) 2019
B. Perry and R. Scrivens, *Right-Wing Extremism in Canada*,
Palgrave Hate Studies, https://doi.org/10.1007/978-3-030-25169-7

white power 5, 15, 25, 39, 65, 67, 69, 71, 149, 175, 190, 192, 198, 213

white power compilation CD 190

white power movement 5, 36, 67, 68

white power music 7, 26, 66–69, 71, 75, 125, 174

white power music scene 26, 68, 174

white pride 40, 41, 65, 69, 104, 178

white supremacist 1, 10, 25, 28–30, 36, 48, 50, 62, 63, 66, 67, 73–75, 80, 96, 104, 125, 143, 144, 151, 166, 173–175, 177, 178, 184, 191–193, 195, 198, 201, 203, 207, 209, 210, 212, 213, 215, 216

white supremacist activity 2, 16

white supremacist group 25, 27, 32, 148, 177, 211

white supremacist political party 178

white supremacist subculture 144, 147

white supremacy 30–32, 71, 74, 144, 145, 150, 165

Wildrose Party 159, 164

World Church of the Creator 25, 30, 67, 174, 188

X

xenophobia 4, 5, 12, 89, 95, 134, 158, 164

xenophobic 5, 62, 68, 97, 143, 150

Y

youth 8, 49, 50, 60, 78, 92, 121, 125–128, 151, 190, 196, 203, 205, 215

YouTube 62, 63, 67–69, 80, 125, 135, 156, 162, 200

Z

Zundel, Ernst 26, 36, 39, 78, 175, 197